Chicano Workers and the Politics of Fairness

Chicano Workers and the Politics of Fairness

The FEPC in the Southwest, 1941–1945

by Clete Daniel

University of Texas Press, Austin

Printed in the United States of America

First Edition, 1991

Requests for permission to reproduce material from this work should be sent to Permissions, University of Texas Press, Box 7819, Austin, Texas 78713-7819.

(∞) The paper used in this publication meets the minimum requirements of American National Standard for Information Sciences—Permanence of Paper for Printed Library Materials, ANSI Z39.48-1984.

Library of Congress Cataloging-in-Publication Data

Daniel, Cletus E., 1943–
Chicano workers and the politics of fairness : the FEPC in the Southwest, 1941–1945 / by Clete Daniel. — 1st ed.
p. cm.
Includes bibliographical references (p.) and index.
ISBN 0-292-76521-5 (cloth)
1. Mexican Americans—Employment—Southwest, New. 2. Discrimination in employment—Southwest, New. 3. World War, 1939–1945—Manpower—United States. 4. United States. Committee on Fair Employment Practice. 5. United States—Politics and government—1933–1945. I. Title.
HD8081.M6D36 1991
331.6'36872079—dc20 90-12707
CIP

For Paul and Jake, brother and son

Contents

Preface

IF AMERICA HAS been for the better part of four centuries a land of opportunity for most of those who confronted its alluring possibilities, it has also been a place of denied opportunity for those whose race, color, creed, gender, or national origin rendered them ineligible to participate fully and equally in the singular competition for material gain and social advantage that this country fostered. For those ineligible Americans, whose dispiriting common fate it was to covet an equality of opportunity that tradition and custom routinely conspired to deny them, reconciling the America of their dreams with the America of their experience was an undertaking as daunting in its challenges as it was tantalizing in its possibilities.

Yet despite the sometimes heroic, usually unheralded, but always persistent exertions of those who endeavored to close the historic gap between promise and practice, denying economic opportunity on the grounds of race, color, creed, gender, or national origin has proven to be a habit of American life not easily broken. In a pragmatic political culture that has tended historically to deflect and evade moral imperatives rather than to confront and address them, elected leaders captive to the prejudices of majorities could seldom be counted upon to champion the cause of equal opportunity merely because it was the right thing to do. In the absence of compelling reasons to abandon or moderate those customs and traditions that shunted particular groups to the distant edges of opportunity, public and private authority alike remained steadfastly deployed in defense of majority privilege.

While sporadic agitation by blacks and women for equal employment opportunity produced few lasting gains prior to World War II, the issue of economic discrimination against each group was nevertheless forced upon the public consciousness as a result of recurring protests. Even though such unwelcome reminders of national hypocrisy typically engendered more annoyance than sympathy among the majorities toward whom they were directed, each new attempt by women and blacks to advance the cause of equal opportunity replenished the reservoir of common purpose that nurtured the hopes and emboldened the spirits of those contemplating similar efforts yet to come. These successive challenges to the status quo, though they usually fell far short of realizing the goals that inspired them, achieved a cumulative force that helped both to counter the centrifugal influence of individual preoccupations and to give otherwise discrete episodes of collective protest the ever more clearly discernible contours of a movement.

Though neither women nor blacks had succeeded by 1941 in fashioning a movement that was sufficiently united and resourceful to translate their separate but analogous demands for equal opportunity into significant advances, both groups were, because of the leadership and cohesion resulting from their previous activism, better positioned than would otherwise have been the case to exploit the opportunity for real gains that the war was destined to create. As a further consequence of their activist past, both women and blacks were also better able to avail themselves of the increasing support proffered by a newly emergent industrial union movement compelled by the logic of its inclusive organizational structure to embrace the principle of equal opportunity for all workers without regard to those considerations of race and gender that had debilitated its craft-based rival.

That is not to say, however, that either women or blacks achieved the substantial gains they sought between 1941 and 1945 or that they were able to sustain the generally modest advances they did make during the war once peace was restored. It is to say only that both groups were in a better position to try to exploit wartime conditions in the cause of equal opportunity than they would have been without the more seasoned leadership and greater organizational sophistication that resulted from their prior activism.

The relative advantage that women and blacks enjoyed in this regard is perhaps most fully appreciated when it is viewed in contrast to the distinctly less favorable prospects that other groups of historically disadvantaged workers faced when they endeavored to capitalize on wartime conditions without benefit of the internal resources that a tradition of even fitful solidarity afforded. This book is about such a group: the approximately three million Chicanos (Mexicans and Mexican Americans) who were confronted by the same apparent opportunity created by wartime conditions to gain the equal job rights that decades of pervasive and relentless Anglo bigotry had denied them.

In seeking to take advantage of those special economic and political circumstances on the homefront that appeared to increase the vulnerability of long-standing discriminatory practices in the workplace to reform, Chicano workers were generally at a loss to summon the reinforcements that a mature tradition of ethnic consciousness might have supplied. Although those processes of political cohesion and social amalgamation that would give rise to an increasingly formidable Chicano civil rights movement in the postwar era were well underway by 1941, they had not progressed to the point of effective utility. As many recent community studies collectively attest, Chicanos in the United States were not the hopelessly divided and disorganized population prior to the war that the often superficial impressions of some outside observers tended to suggest.[1] Indeed, as the most illuminating of these recent studies make plain, social, political, and cultural organizations of various types flourished in Chicano communities throughout the Southwest. What remained absent from these communities, however, were broadly based, inclusive organizations that linked them in ways that might have fostered the ethnic solidarity required to establish a political presence equal to the demands of effective action in the national arena. Chicanos had frequently organized separately as workers, intellectuals, radicals, or middle-class professionals and businesspeople, but not on the basis of a common ethnic identity that swept away or mitigated the internal divisions within their communities.

As historian Mario García has noted, Chicanos were, "despite shared experiences, still too segmented by class, region, and level of acculturation to comprise a unified, much less monolithic, movement."[2] As long as the leadership in Chicano communities was dominated by an "Immigrant Generation" that tended to regard life in the United States as a "transitory" experience, García argues, effective organization in opposition to Anglo malefactions was impeded. "They hoped to return to *la patria* and a better life," he writes: "They possessed a Mexican dream, not an American dream. They adjusted to life in the United States by attempting to reproduce a Mexican world for themselves. Having just enough time and energy to make a living, unwilling to give up their Mexican citizenship, living adjacent to their homeland, and seeing themselves as temporary sojourners, Mexican immigrants were not ripe candidates for a protracted civil rights struggle."[3]

Although Chicanos were still without the kinds of broadly inclusive organizations necessary to their effective participation in national political affairs as America went to war, the war did give further impetus to a process of change from which such organizations would later emerge.

Combining with the Great Depression to form what García calls "the twin central historical experiences for a political generation committed to actively struggling for civil rights and first-class citizenship for Mexican Americans," the war disclosed to native-born Chicanos who had risen to positions of leadership the indispensability of ethnic solidarity in realizing the promise of American life. "Coming of political age during the reform period of the New Deal and experiencing the patriotic idealism generated by World War II," García observes, "Mexican Americans expected more from American life than immigrants. For Mexican Americans, there was no going back to Mexico. The United States was their home. They hungrily pursued the American dream."[4]

Yet if preexisting tendencies toward more purposeful forms of activism among Chicanos were reinforced by their wartime experiences, they were seldom the masters of their own fate in advancing the cause of equal opportunity on the job during the war. To the limited extent that discrimination against Chicano workers was addressed within the context of special wartime policies intended to eliminate race, color, creed, and national origin as barriers to equal employment opportunity in defense industries and the federal government, it was the President's Committee on Fair Employment Practice (FEPC)—the chronically beleaguered agency responsible for their enforcement—that timidly led the way.

While the FEPC's brief but turbulent history has been the subject of various scholarly inquiries over the past forty years, the exclusive focus of previous scholarship has been on the black workers who were the committee's largest and most conspicuously wronged constituency. It was, after all, blacks who instigated and sustained the courageous protests that resulted in the creation of the FEPC in the summer of 1941. It was also blacks who fought most passionately and tirelessly throughout the war to defend the FEPC against the relentless opposition that its mere existence provoked from some quarters.

Still, even if these earlier scholars were justified in treating the Roosevelt administration's reluctant wartime experiment in fair employment practices as an episode in the larger struggle of black Americans for equal rights, the separate, but previously neglected, story of the FEPC's efforts in behalf of Chicano workers during the war is equally revealing of the extraordinary complexity attendant to the task of eradicating those forms of discrimination rooted in seemingly immutable patterns of life and work. It is the purpose of this book to tell that story.

Chicano Workers and the Politics of Fairness

1. *A People in the Distance*

IT IS ONE of the enduring paradoxes of America's never uniformly democratic experience that employment discrimination on the basis of race, color, creed, gender, and national origin has generally moderated during the periods of major wars even as those same times of national alarm and anxiety were breeding new and equally pernicious kinds of intolerance and abuse. The years of America's involvement in World War II are especially illustrative of this tendency, even if the fairer employment practices they witnessed too often failed to survive the peace. Yet the period from 1941 to 1945 is important in the larger history of the equal rights struggle in America not only because the war created social and economic exigencies that tended to afford greater opportunities to the historic victims of discrimination in the workplace, but also because it marked the first formal effort by the federal government to establish equal employment opportunity as the official public policy of the United States.[1]

That policy, proclaimed by President Franklin Roosevelt on June 25, 1941, through the issuance of Executive Order 8802, declared that "there shall be no discrimination in the employment of workers in defense industries or government because of race, creed, color, or national origin, and . . . that it is the duty of employers and labor organizations . . . to provide for the full and equitable participation of all workers in defense industries, without discrimination because of race, creed, color or national origin." Roosevelt entrusted responsibility for effectuating the policy to a Committee on Fair Employment Practice (FEPC) consisting of a chairman and four (soon to become six) members.

Yet almost at once the president's seemingly bold action was the focus of intense suspicion. And careful scrutiny of the text and context of Executive Order 8802 tended to vindicate those seasoned observers of race relations whose cynical instincts led them to question the sincerity of Roosevelt's action. The president had acted with extreme reluctance in issuing his order, only after being persuaded that the less forthright gestures his advisers had first proposed were unlikely to induce A. Philip Randolph and other black activists to rescind their threat of a potentially embarrassing and divisive "March on Washington" by perhaps 100,000 protesters against the discriminatory employment policies prevalent in America's rapidly expanding defense industries.[2] The impression of faintheartedness imparted by the administration's grudging adoption of a fair employment policy was reinforced by the flimsy enforcement authority granted to the FEPC under the terms of the president's order. The committee was authorized to "receive and investigate complaints of discrimination in violation of the . . . order," but empowered to do nothing more than "recommend . . . measures which may be deemed by it necessary or proper to effectuate the . . . order." The fact that the FEPC was directed to rectify one of the most intractable and incendiary problems in the nation's history with no more than a mere innuendo of real enforcement authority tended to confirm suspicions that Executive Order 8802 was an expedient gesture rather than an honest commitment to equal opportunity by the Roosevelt administration. Even Malcolm Ross, the FEPC's fourth, and last, chairman and a staunch believer in the sincerity of Roosevelt's devotion to racial justice, acknowledged that members of the president's "official family," when they were not openly hostile to the FEPC's mission, tended to regard the committee as little more than a "necessary nuisance." "Nearly everyone," Ross observed, "hoped that its activities could be kept harmlessly discreet."[3]

Notwithstanding the conspicuous reluctance with which Roosevelt had acted—and despite the wariness that experience dictated any time that a white man, even a president, proclaimed an end to racial inequality—most black Americans responded hopefully to the announcement of the FEPC's creation. For even if the new committee should fall short of fully establishing the principle of nondiscrimination that inspired it, blacks were assured of the residual satisfaction that derived from the knowledge that leaders of their race had forced an otherwise unwilling American president to issue a formal public acknowledgment that the racial discrimination that blocked their path to economic opportunity and civil equality affronted both the letter and the spirit of the nation's professed ideals. Indeed, whether they, or the country's white majority, realized it or not, blacks were witnessing the inauguration of the modern civil rights movement in the United States, even though the Supreme Court's decision in *Brown* v. *Board of Education* in 1954 and the launching of the Montgomery bus boycott two years later have tended to obscure the pioneering achievement of those black activists who compelled the Roosevelt administration to establish the FEPC.

Yet if the federal government's wartime experiment in equal employment opportunity is most plausibly considered as a phase of the continuing struggle by black Americans to gain equal rights—fully 80 percent of the FEPC's work was in behalf of black complainants[4]—discrimination in the workplace was practiced on so many bases in addition to race that those who undertook the enforcement of Executive Order 8802 were obliged to pursue complaints from several categories of alleged victims other than blacks. As the FEPC's campaign to publicize the federal government's new antidiscrimination policy gained momentum, those availing themselves of the guardianship the committee proffered included workers from many of these less visible categories. Jews, Catholics, Seventh-Day Adventists, and Jehovah's Witnesses claimed economic mistreatment because of creed. Germans and Italians attributed denials of equal opportunity to their national origin, while Chinese and Japanese workers alleged that considerations of both race and national origin combined to deny them fair treatment in the workplace.[5]

Had the FEPC been pressed, however, to recognize a single minority group as facing the greatest potential for mistreatment on each of the four bases proscribed by Executive Order 8802, that group would surely have been workers of Mexican ancestry. Overwhelmingly Catholic in their religious affiliation, with skin colorings reflecting the rich spectrum produced by white Spanish *peninsulares* and copper-brown Mexican *indios* after nearly four centuries of intimate proximity, and bearing a national identity that generations of Anglo denigration had made burdensome, the approximately three million Chicanos (Mexicans and Mexican Americans) living in the United States in the early 1940s had long been prime candidates for discrimination. Their vulnerability was further heightened by an ambiguous racial status fastened on them by an acutely race-conscious Anglo majority that could not decide whether Chicanos were fellow "whites" or a race apart. The U.S. Census Bureau, reflecting that confusion, classified Chicanos as a separate racial group in 1930 but as "white" in 1940. In the end, however, what mattered was not the abstract racial status conferred by diffident Anglos but the practical inequality that a preoccupation with race among the racially dominant element of American society inevitably visited upon those who comprised its racial minorities.[6]

Yet as prominent as Chicanos were to become in the statistical records of the FEPC during the war years, their congregation in the Southwest, which one study described as "one of the most conspicuous examples of geographic concentration among national minorities in the United States," served to reduce their visibility in the population at large.[7] With 90 percent of the Chicano population in the United States in 1940 living in the states of Texas, California, Arizona, New Mexico, and Colorado, those of Mexican descent constituted a minority that rarely, if ever, intruded upon the consciousness of most Americans.[8]

Even in the Southwest, social, cultural, and economic forces combined to promote the isolation of Chicanos from the main thoroughfares of Anglo life. The labor of Chicanos had long been indispensable to the profitable operation of agriculture and industry alike in the border regions of the Southwest, but with only rare exceptions their exertions earned them neither equal standing in the society they helped to sustain nor a fair share of the material prosperity they helped to create. For the most part, Chicanos in the Southwest, whether native-born citizens or recent immigrants, shared at the beginning of World War II a collective status that had remained essentially unchanged in the nearly one hundred years since the end of the Mexican-American War: servants of an Anglo community that could not do without them but refused to assimilate them.[9]

To the extent that Chicanos continued to harbor the belief, as one of their spokesmen expressed it in the fall of 1941, that America might yet become a "real melting pot where equal opportunities are not only promised but actually given," it was a hope necessarily sustained more by faith than by experience.[10]

The issuance of Executive Order 8802, however, and the announced determination of the FEPC to invest it with practical meaning, rekindled the hope that the barriers to equal opportunity that had long confronted Chicano workers in the Southwest might finally be breached. Ernesto Galarza, a young economist with the Pan American Union (and later a leading expert on Chicano workers in the United States), was sufficiently encouraged by the president's order to contact FEPC chairman Mark Ethridge shortly after the committee began operation with an offer to assist any investigations it might conduct among Chicano workers in the Southwest.

"The statement of the President regarding fair practices in employment during the national emergency and the creation of your Commission for the purpose of carrying out the President's statement of policy," Galarza wrote, "suggested to me the possibility that the problems of the Mexicans with regard to fair and equal treatment might receive more consideration now than they have in the past." With the country moving rapidly toward a war footing, Galarza reasoned, the patterns of abuse that Chicano workers in the Southwest had long endured could not be maintained without jeopardizing the success of government efforts in the region to bolster the morale of labor. The number of Chicano workers was, Galarza observed, "so large and their importance in the economy of the Southwest so obvious that the establishment of fair and just practices in employment for this large national minority might well be regarded as an important part of the national defense program."[11]

But if Galarza was encouraged by the prospect of a federal offensive against discriminatory employment practices, he was also concerned that the absence of a strong tradition of protest among the diffuse Chicano population of the Southwest might cause the FEPC to neglect its grievances in favor of those advanced by more cohesive and vocal minorities. "My rather long experience with the problems of Mexicans in this country," Galarza explained, "has led me to the conclusion that it is extremely difficult to induce them to complain of adverse conditions, improper treatment or attitudes on the part of their employers prejudicial to their interests as workers and citizens. The conditions in which Mexican workers generally find themselves in this country are such that it is easy to understand why they are loath to lodge complaints with the authorities."[12]

Galarza was not alone in fearing that the FEPC might neglect Chicano victims of job discrimination. Manuel Gonzales, executive secretary of the League of United Latin American Citizens, a Texas-based civic organization, warned in the fall of 1941 that unless the FEPC overcame its initial tendency to view employment discrimination solely in the context of black-white relations Chicano workers were not likely to receive the attention their circumstances merited. "We appreciate the patriotic attitude assumed by our President in his executive order 8802," Gonzales wrote, "but we note with regret that a great deal of effort is being exerted to create jobs for the colored people and not enough to see that a representative number of positions are given to the Latin Americans, especially in the State of Texas." If Chicanos failed to receive equal consideration from the FEPC even in those southwestern states where they were the dominant minority group, and where the evidence of discrimination against them was "abundant," they could not reasonably expect, Gonzales argued, to receive the help they deserved anywhere. The potential cost of such neglect, he warned, could be very high. For beyond reinforcing the impression "that Mexicans, regardless of culture, social, economic or intellectual standing, are not wanted," it was also likely that the government's promotion of the "Good Neighbor Policy and . . . Western Hemisphere solidarity" would be seriously undermined. In light of these considerations, Gonzales concluded, discrimination against Chicanos in the Southwest warranted "immediate investigation."[13]

If an anxiety fueled both by generations of bitter experience and an acutely self-conscious sense of cultural insularity caused some Chicano leaders to fear that the government's campaign against job discrimination might bypass those whose Mexican heritage had counted against them in the workplace, the FEPC did nothing to alleviate their concerns when it held its first public hearings. Convened during the middle of October 1941 in Los Angeles, the center of southern California's burgeoning industrial defense complex, the hearings were designed to focus public attention on the discriminatory hiring policies allegedly pursued by the region's leading military contractors, especially those in the aircraft and shipbuilding industries.

Given that they constituted the largest minority group in Los Angeles County, Chicanos might reasonably have expected that the discriminatory employment practices to which they had long been subjected would become the focus of the FEPC's investigation in southern California. Yet Chicanos, though they outnumbered blacks in the region by at least four to one, received so little attention during the course of the hearings that their unenviable status as California's leading victims of job discrimination remained largely unexplored by the committee. From beginning to end, the committee focused its attention on the complaints of discrimination lodged by spokesmen representing black workers, even though blacks constituted less than three percent of the population of Los Angeles County and less than two percent of California's total population.[14] When it did digress to consider allegations of discrimination against Jewish, Japanese, Chicano, and other minority workers, the committee was distinctly less ardent and inquisitive than it was when considering the grievances of black workers. Of the dozens of witnesses who appeared before the committee as spokesmen for minority constituencies, only two represented the interests and concerns of Chicano workers. The committee, moreover, allotted the two Chicano spokesmen only six minutes of its time to divide between themselves and immediately moved on to other considerations once their statements were entered into the official record of the hearings.[15]

Although appearances might have justified a less charitable interpretation, the relative neglect of Chicano workers during its Los Angeles hearings was less a function of the FEPC's indifference to their plight than of an understandable tendency among the committee's membership and staff to define discrimination in the first instance in terms of the historically disadvantaged status of blacks. The FEPC was, after all, the product not of a general agitation whose weight was borne proportionately by each of the minority groups it was ultimately authorized to assist but of an audacious campaign of protest that blacks alone had nurtured and propelled. Executive Order 8802 plainly owed its existence to the exertions of blacks. If they exhibited a strong proprietary outlook that prompted the FEPC, which included two black activists among its membership, to pursue its mandate in a fashion that tended to subordinate the grievances of other minority groups to those of black workers, there was an element of justice in their manifest expectation of preferential consideration.

Still, if the FEPC was predisposed during its Los Angeles hearings to regard employment discrimination as a greater problem for blacks than for other minorities, Chicanos did almost nothing to correct the committee's impression. Black victims of job bias in southern California could rely upon advocates from such well-established national organizations as the National Association for the Advancement of Colored People, the National Negro Congress, and the Urban League, as well as from several other locally based church and civic groups, to detail their complaints before the committee. But Chicano workers with no less compelling and disquieting stories of discrimination to tell were further victimized by the absence in their own comparatively less cohesive communities of equivalent social and political organizations that promoted ethnic solidarity on a sufficiently broad basis either to defend their constituents against mistreatment by Anglos or to exploit an opportunity like that afforded by the FEPC's Los Angeles hearings. Mutual aid societies (*mutualistas*) and cultural associations (*juntas patrióticas*) existed in most of the larger Chicano barrios of southern California, as well as throughout the Southwest generally. But they typically failed to bridge the numerous internal divisions based on class, civic and residency status, lifestyle, language, and depth of cultural identity that caused Carey McWilliams, a leading student of the subject, to conclude that there was "no more heterogeneous ethnic group in the United States." Impressed by the force of these internal divisions and distinctions, one federal investigator wrote in 1942:

> The Spanish-speaking people of the Southwest cannot be treated as a single population group. . . . On the basis of language, they are Spanish-

> speaking in varying degrees. By and large, the poorest people speak only Spanish; Spanish loses ground to English as one moves up in economic scale, as one moves from rural labor to urban work, or as the length of residence increases. There are, of course, many who speak only English and many bilingual families where Spanish is the subordinate language.
>
> A fundamental distinction exists between the old Spanish settlers of the Southwest and the Mexicans. Mexicans born in Mexico must be distinguished from those born in the United States. Distinctions must also be made between the Spanish-speaking "subsistence farmers," migratory farm laborers, and the urban slum dwellers.[16]

To the extent that the Los Angeles hearings afforded a basis for judging the degree of cohesiveness that existed within each of the minority communities that responded to the FEPC's invitation to testify, Chicanos seemingly lacked a collective voice. Oddly, even El Congreso del Pueblo de Habla Española (the Spanish-speaking People's Congress), whose earlier activism in behalf of equal rights for Chicano workers in the Los Angeles area ought to have made it an eager participant, was unrepresented at the hearings. Founded in 1938, El Congreso was typical of the popular front organizations created by Communists in the late 1930s as the party sought to forge alliances with liberals that might forestall the growing influence of resurgent right-wing forces in the United States. In southern California, the only area of the country in which it attracted a following, El Congreso augmented the undeniable force of its appeal in Los Angeles barrios with support from CIO unions and a handful of sympathetic Hollywood celebrities to establish an organizational presence that belied its otherwise unimpressive resources. The fact that it ultimately failed to take advantage of the opportunity that the FEPC's Los Angeles hearings afforded to expose the widespread discrimination against Chicano workers in the region was probably due, at least in part, to the alacrity with which American Communists, following Hitler's sudden invasion of the Soviet Union in June 1941, abandoned many of their earlier concerns in favor of a single-minded campaign to promote national unity and unimpeded defense production. In light of the American party's new priorities, representatives of El Congreso may well have concluded that the public attention that would have resulted from efforts to press Chicano grievances before the FEPC was likely to foster a divisiveness that might discourage national unity.[17]

Whatever the reasons for its absence, El Congreso unwittingly reinforced the impression that Chicanos in Los Angeles were a community in name only. Certainly the vague and unfocused testimony of the two spokesmen who did appear in behalf of Chicano victims of employment discrimination suggested little in the way of coherent and inclusive ethnic organization. Manuel Ruiz, a Los Angeles attorney who appeared before the committee, acknowledged the relatively unorganized character of the Chicano community in southern California when he testified that only shortly before the hearings began had steps finally been taken to "coordinate the activities of various clubs, groups, societies, and organizations among our people." There were, Ruiz observed, "approximately 250,000 persons of Latin American extraction in this community, the largest concentrated minority group by far," yet Chicanos had never established an organized presence commensurate with their number. "Unlike some other racial groups," he noted, "the American of Mexican extraction has never been a pressure group."

Reflecting an attitude not uncommon among the small middle-class element that enjoyed special prominence within a minority population that was overwhelmingly working-class in composition, Ruiz rather facilely attributed the lack of ethnic solidarity among Chicanos to "the fact that assimilation . . . into our body politic is occurring at a greater speed than can be checked by consciousness of national and racial origin." Unlike those minority groups whose distinctive racial characteristics threatened to consign them permanently to the fringes of a "white"-dominated society, Chicanos were, Ruiz suggested, "a little more fortunate . . . in that many of our people are not stamped physically, . . . and some of us get lost in the general social setup." He was quick to point out, however, that there was a "backwash" in the Chicano community "of those who are caught in the throes of discriminatory practices"—those in the barrios, especially the "dark Mexicans," who were endlessly defrauded by "false promises of equality" because a "thoughtless" Anglo majority insisted that they were "distinct and inferior."[18]

The potential effectiveness of Ruiz's testimony was undermined by his inability to proceed from vague allegations of job discrimination against Chicanos to specific examples. When John Brophy, who served on the committee as a permanent surrogate for CIO president Philip Murray, asked him to provide a more detailed accounting of the discrimination faced by Chicanos in the leading defense industries of southern California, Ruiz confessed that such information had not yet been gathered. Based on his own "summary investigation," Ruiz tentatively reported that he was not "personally" aware of any "local Mexicans" employed in the region's defense industries. He did suggest, however, that the FEPC could readily avail itself of the details it wanted by appointing a permanent representative "of Latin American extraction" for the region.[19]

Dr. Victor Egas, the only other witness to appear before the committee in behalf of Chicanos, was equally vague in his allegations of job discrimination against Chicanos in the Southwest. His brief testimony indicated, however, that the paucity of detailed information relating to employment discrimination against Chicanos was as much a function of a well-conditioned distrust of Anglo sincerity in matters of economic justice as of inadequate organization within the barrios of southern California. The true extent of job discrimination against Chicanos, Egas argued, had to be "ferreted out by an investigation of patience and perseverance . . . because the discriminatory practices are insidious and under-cover, and the victims are usually persons in those walks of life who cannot, and do not, know how to protect themselves."[20]

In most circumstances, Egas observed, the committee might reasonably expect that victims of such discrimination "should be outspoken and eager" when afforded so singular an opportunity to protest their mistreatment. "But a long and sad experience demonstrates," he insisted, "that the complaints of a victim have frequently been punished with additional cruel pressure or indirect ostracism by the powers that be. . . . The large Spanish American colony of Los Angeles is viewing this investigation expectantly. The fact that it emanates from a Federal source indicates a condition favorable for the fostering of a feeling of confidence. Some members of the colony, based on prior experience, are dubious but they are hopeful for the best; nevertheless they are not desirous of speaking up." The prevailing view among Chicanos, Egas declared, was that "there have been too many martyrs for the cause in the past without avail." As Manuel Ruiz had before him, Egas suggested that the appointment of a permanent FEPC representative in the region would help to persuade Chicanos that the federal government's newly expressed commitment to end employment discrimination in defense industries was not just another hollow promise.[21]

Had the testimony of Ruiz and Egas been of a more substantive nature, the FEPC might have exhibited more than the cursory interest that the problem of job discrimination against Chicanos in southern California evoked during the Los Angeles hearings. It is also likely, however, that greater value would have been attached to the evidence the FEPC did adduce in regard to Chicanos if in arranging the Los Angeles hearings the committee had been as keenly attuned to their plight as to that of black victims of job discrimination in the region. Earl Dickerson, a Chicago attorney and city alderman who was one of two black members of the FEPC, was assigned responsibility for planning the Los Angeles hearings;[22] he used his authority in ways that assured that the committee's first public exercise of its presidential mandate resulted in an investigation emphasizing the racist employment practices faced by black workers in California's defense industries. Consequently, the Los Angeles hearings accentuated the problem of antiblack discrimination to the point of virtually ignoring the unfair employment practices affecting other minorities, including Chicanos.

Both Ruiz and Egas complained in particular that FEPC representatives had given them so little time to prepare for the hearings that they were denied an adequate opportunity to overcome the initial reluctance among Chicano victims of job discrimination to lodge formal protests before the committee.[23] Phillip Connelly, secretary of the Los Angeles Industrial Union Council of the CIO, was equally critical of the committee's planning for the hearings. Complaining that the CIO had been given only ten days in which to collect information and prepare affidavits detailing specific allegations of employment discrimination, Connelly declared, "This is not enough time for us. We found that intimidation had reached such a point that individuals who are the object of discrimination are afraid to speak up before a Committee appointed by the President of the United States for fear of being eternally blacklisted. Especially is this true of the Spanish-speaking people."[24]

Without effective representation, and lacking the visibility and collective presence that might have caused an otherwise uninterested committee membership and staff to explore their plight with a degree of vigor equal to that commanded by the predicament of black workers, Chicanos gained little from the FEPC's Los Angeles hearings. Yet even if Chicanos never became the focus of the committee's inquiry, their status as victims of pervasive discrimination in the defense industries of southern California was nevertheless confirmed. In the course of determining the character and extent of job discrimination against blacks, the FEPC amassed evidence that was equally revealing of the unfair employment practices confronted by Chicano workers in the region. Indeed, what the hearings made clear, though as much by inadvertence as by design, was that job discrimination was as common and debilitating a problem for Chicano workers as for black workers.[25] Major defense contractors in southern California discriminated against Chicano workers in hiring, promotion, upgrading, and work assignments to the same degree that they discriminated against black workers. Likewise, when government-funded job training programs denied admission to black youths, they also barred entry to Chicano youths. Finally, when "white" workers allegedly threatened to strike if employers sought to integrate their workplaces or job classifications, their threats were as readily prompted by the prospect of working alongside Chicanos as alongside blacks.

In the aftermath of the Los Angeles hearings Chicanos had little reason to expect that the FEPC would significantly improve the treatment accorded them by employers in California's leading defense industries. The hearings had disclosed incontrovertible evidence of employment discrimination against blacks and Chicanos in particular, but the committee had appeared content to accept assurances by the major defense contractors that they would adhere to the letter and spirit of Executive Order 8802 in the future even as they ardently, if disingenuously, denied any past discrimination. The committee did issue several "recommendations" designed to encourage less ambiguous adherence to the president's nondiscrimination order by both employers and unions, but it stopped short of criticizing the policies and practices of specific companies or unions. The committee was similarly negligent in failing to require any of the employers or unions against which complaints of discrimination had been lodged during the hearings to document their subsequent efforts to achieve full compliance with the president's order.[26]

Beyond the reflexive caution that derived from the inescapable fact that it had no real power, the FEPC's apparent willingness during the Los Angeles hearings to overlook past discrimination in return for nebulous promises of future compliance with Executive Order 8802 reflected, at least in part, a desire to ensure that in the first public exercise of its controversial mandate the committee imparted an image of temperateness and good will. In an obvious attempt to allay the fears of those, especially in the southern congressional block, who instinctively construed the president's order as a thinly veiled effort to promote racial equality, the committee unfailingly emphasized that it functioned as a necessary adjunct of the nation's overall defense manpower program rather than as the instrument of an independent initiative to redress the "race problem" in America. "Every action taken by the government," the committee soothingly observed in regard to its activities, "has been taken in the light of the prevailing and expected manpower needs of the nation."[27]

To an important degree, however, the FEPC's circumspect style also reflected the belief of its chairman, if not of its full membership, that the Roosevelt administration intended Executive Order 8802 as a gesture toward equal employment opportunity rather than as the embodiment of a policy requiring vigorous implementation. Mark Ethridge, a Louisville newspaper executive whose credentials as a southern liberal had commended his appointment to the chairmanship of the FEPC, undertook his duties with a keen sensitivity not only to the inherent volatility of the task before him but also to the Roosevelt administration's undisguised concern that the political costs of the committee's operation not exceed the benefits. If the White House's conspicuous reluctance to act in the first place was not enough to persuade him that his was a job requiring a larger talent for discretion than for bold leadership, Ethridge got the message clearly enough when Stephen Early, one of Roosevelt's closest aides, combined the offer of the FEPC chairmanship with an instructive assurance that the post was one requiring only a very modest commitment of time. "As a matter of fact," Early advised, ". . . it will be possible for you to carry out the duties of the office of Chairman by spending about two days every two weeks in Washington."[28]

From the earliest days of his chairmanship Ethridge endeavored to assure Roosevelt and his White House staff that he could be counted upon to steer the FEPC along the path of least political resistance, as well as to serve as a buffer between the president and those members of the committee who insisted on interpreting Executive Order 8802 as a purposeful statement of policy requiring forthright and vigorous enforcement. Certainly in his confidential dealings with the White House Ethridge revealed a less than ardent devotion to the spirit of the president's order. In particular, he proposed that a strict construction of the language it employed in setting forth a fair employment policy and establishing a committee to implement it would be useful in restraining what he regarded as the overly zealous attitude of certain of his FEPC colleagues and the extravagant expectations of blacks who had been induced by the "agitators" behind the March on Washington movement to view "the executive order as a sort of second Emancipation Proclamation." "It is obvious," Ethridge confided to Stephen Early, a fellow southerner who did little to conceal his personal contempt for the FEPC, "that Negroes have been led to believe a good deal more than the truth by their own leaders."[29]

In acceding to the White House's view that the FEPC ought to tread softly, Ethridge was at odds with several of his fellow committee members, especially David Sarnoff, president of the Radio Corporation of America, and the two black appointees, Chicago alderman Earl Dickerson and Milton Webster, a vice-president of A. Philip Randolph's Brotherhood of Sleeping Car Porters, the country's largest and most influential union of black workers. Sarnoff and "the Negroes," as Ethridge referred to Dickerson and Webster, argued that the FEPC should not permit its administrative subordination within the Office of Production Management to impede its independence in dealing with employment discrimination. Ethridge informed the White House that an accommodation was finally reached providing that the FEPC would be "independent as far as policy-making is concerned," but free to take action in response to allegations of discrimination only after those OPM staff members responsible for minority employment matters had endeavored to resolve such grievances. "The committee," Ethridge sanguinely reported, "is to have a very small staff of not more than an Executive Secretary and Assistant and four or five trouble-shooters. It is not to act in any situation until OPM has exhausted its efforts to adjudicate."

In the hope of reinforcing the relatively unobtrusive approach that he believed the administration wanted, Ethridge advised Early that it would be helpful if Roosevelt personally suggested to FEPC members during their first meeting with the president that the problem of employment discrimination could be more profitably redressed through a policy of quiet diplomacy and patient education than one based on a strategy of direct frontal assault. "I think it would be most helpful if the President . . . would point out," Ethridge told Early, "that discrimination is as old as the world and its eradication cannot be brought about except by persistence and patience over a long time."[30]

That Ethridge regarded his essential function as one of insulating Roosevelt from the political pressures exerted by aroused blacks rather than wielding the energy of their expansive activism in the cause of equal employment opportunity was starkly revealed in December 1941. Feeling that he could no longer neglect his duties in Louisville, Ethridge wrote to Early two days before Christmas asking to be relieved of his responsibilities as chairman of the FEPC. In further justification of his departure from the committee, however, Ethridge emphasized that the job he had been recruited to do was largely accomplished. On the job for only four months, and with little more than the committee's Los Angeles hearings and a fainthearted public relations campaign to show for the "world's of time" he said the job had demanded, Ethridge nevertheless claimed that the FEPC, despite having "the lowest budget in the government," had "done a great deal." "Certainly," he insisted, "we have accomplished what the President wanted: we paralyzed any idea of a march on Washington and we have worked honestly for a better measure of justice for Negroes. They have more jobs in government and industry than they ever had; they have less cause for complaint than they ever had, and they know it."

The "flood" of complaints received by the committee in the early days of its operation had given way to only "occasional" complaints, he reported, and the focus of its attention in the future was likely to be "on the Army and Navy, rather than on industry." This record of accomplishment, he noted, was compiled even as the committee loyally refrained from using the only weapon in its otherwise nonexistent enforcement arsenal: public disclosure of discriminatory employment practices. "We have deliberately tried to keep publicity to a minimum," Ethridge acknowledged, "because we were working with dynamite."

By his own account, Ethridge had "done a job"; he had been a good soldier, one whose devotion to duty was revealed in an unwavering determination to do the impossible: implement an inherently controversial fair employment practices policy without exciting controversy. "I personally feel that I have never done a better job or a more distasteful one," he cryptically confessed to Early. "This has been [as] big [a] test of my loyalty and conviction as I have ever had."[31]

If Ethridge was justified in asserting that he had done well by the president during his brief chairmanship of the FEPC, there was very little in the way of credible evidence to support his parallel contention that the intended beneficiaries of Executive Order 8802 had been equally well served by the committee during the early months of its operation. Already severely limited in its capabilities by a niggardly budget that, according to one critic, "the President dug . . . out of his contingent fund to finance the FEPC's whole national show" during its first year,[32] the committee's effectiveness was hardly enhanced by Ethridge's apparent preoccupation with White House concerns that the president's order not become a source of undue political discomfort.

Even under the best of circumstances the FEPC's passage from ambiguous intention to functioning instrument of policy could hardly have been other than difficult given the administration's and the country's understandable absorption with the multiplying emergencies of late 1941. Fair employment practices, while sufficiently important as a civil rights issue and wartime manpower expedient to warrant the inauguration of an extraordinary federal antidiscrimination policy, probably never had the potential to be more than a secondary concern to Roosevelt or most of the American people. While the high enthusiasm and hopeful expectations of those who celebrated the birth of Executive Order 8802 were bound to erode as the FEPC struggled against both entrenched opposition and popular ambivalence to do its job, the committee made just enough headway following its Los Angeles hearings, as well as subsequent public hearings in Chicago and New York during the early months of 1942, to persuade all but the most extreme critics within its black constituency that some progress was being made in the fight for fair employment practices.[33]

In contrast, Chicanos in the Southwest, whose activism in behalf of a vigorous antidiscrimination policy remained sporadic and distinctly lethargic alongside that of blacks, found nothing in the record of the FEPC's first six months of operation to excite their hopes or heighten their expectations. The suspicion harbored by some Chicano leaders, and reinforced during the Los Angeles hearings, that the committee was predisposed to favor blacks over other minorities persisted despite a pointed declaration by Lawrence Cramer, its executive secretary, that the FEPC had "shown no favoritism toward any racial group" in the past and would "investigate every substantial complaint of discrimination made to it" in the future. To avail themselves of the committee's assistance, Cramer advised, Chicanos had only to submit complaints setting forth "specific charges" that they had suffered employment discrimination "because of their national origin."[34]

Yet if Chicanos were less willing to entrust their hopes for equal employment opportunity to the committee than were black workers, their reservations derived as much from a tendency to favor a strategic approach unique to the historical mentality of Mexican immigrants and their descendants in the Southwest as from perceptions of a problack bias within the FEPC. Those active in behalf of fair treatment for Chicanos during the latter half of 1941 were no less impressed than their black counterparts with the coming war's potential to create new forms of leverage that minorities might employ in the service of equal opportunity. But because of the proximity of Mexico and the patterns of separateness, both geographical and cultural, that had long characterized the relations between Anglos and Chicanos in the border regions of the Southwest, the latter tended to define their collective status in nationalistic terms rather than ethnic terms—to see themselves as crucial agents in the continuing processes of U.S./Mexican (and U.S./Latin American) relations rather than as an isolated ethnic minority distantly situated from the source of its cultural identity. As a consequence, Chicano activists sought to persuade the federal government during the fall of 1941 to eliminate job discrimination in the Southwest not so much because of the need to maximize the use of available manpower but because the success of the Good Neighbor Policy, which had assumed an increasing military importance, depended in part on the ability of the Roosevelt administration to convince Latin Americans that their kin in the United States would be afforded equal rights.

Consistent with their collective sense of where pressure might be most profitably applied in dealing with the problem of discrimination in the Southwest, Chicano leaders generally ignored the FEPC in favor of appeals to the Office of the Coordinator of Inter-American Affairs, a newly created agency within the Department of Commerce headed by Nelson Rockefeller. "While the Office of the Coordinator of Inter-American Affairs was apparently established without any thought of using it to improve Anglo-Hispano relations in the Southwest," noted Carey McWilliams, "Nelson Rockefeller was soon deluged with suggestions that it be used in this manner." The fact that the FEPC, rather than Rockefeller's office, had formal jurisdiction in matters of alleged job discrimination because of national origin appeared not to matter. "To many people living in the Southwest," McWilliams observed, "it seemed obvious that here [Rockefeller's office] was the logical place to invest the Good Neighbor Policy with real meaning and content."[35]

In addition to McWilliams, who acted in his capacity as California's commissioner of immigration and housing, several Chicano spokesmen, including Dr. Joaquín Ortega of the University of New Mexico, Dr. George Sanchez of the University of Texas, and Arizona state senator C.J. Carreon, also sought to convince Rockefeller during the fall of 1941 that his success in promoting hemispheric solidarity would be significantly enhanced by the kind of energetic antidiscrimination campaign in the Southwest that otherwise skeptical Latin Americans might accept as proof of America's commitment to practice at home the same democratic values that it presumed to defend abroad.[36]

Rockefeller was personally confronted by proponents of a strategy linking equal employment opportunity to the Good Neighbor Policy only a few days after the Pearl Harbor attack when a delegation of Chicano leaders traveled to Washington to lobby for a wide-ranging federal assault on discrimination in the Southwest. Led by Manuel Gonzales of the League of United Latin American Citizens, the delegation arrived in Washington convinced that a tendency among federal officials to "overemphasize the 'Negro problem' and underestimate the 'Latin-American problem,'" as well as the Roosevelt administration's apparent determination to limit the scope of its antidiscrimination policy to employment practices in the defense industries only, threatened to deny equal consideration to Chicano victims of the pervasive discrimination that existed throughout the Southwest.[37]

As ardently as they might have hoped that their pilgrimage to the seat of federal power would arouse enough concern to increase Washington's sensitivity to the collective plight of Chicanos in the Southwest, the members of the Gonzales delegation reduced their prospects for success by failing to arm themselves in advance with specific proposals for remedial action. Determined to acquaint a distant and historically uninterested federal government with the problem of discrimination in the Southwest in all of its aspects—employment, housing, education, access to public accommodations—Gonzales and his colleagues were confronted by federal officials whose ingrained sense of compartmentalized function, jurisdictional propriety, and circumscribed authority rendered them incapable of responding to a generic complaint that ranged across the fixed boundaries that segmented the federal bureaucracy.

Will Alexander, who headed the Minority Groups Branch of the Office of Production Management, complained to a subordinate after meeting with the Gonzales delegation that its members did not "understand our machinery" well enough to know "how to cooperate with us." "I talked with them for more than an hour," Alexander noted, "and it seemed to me that their greatest difficulty was that they had not thought out their ideas in specific terms." Apparently willing to concede the potential linkage between the delegation's concerns and the prospects for the Good Neighbor Policy in Latin America, Alexander was nevertheless at a loss to know how he could help beyond urging his representative in the Southwest to give equal consideration to Chicano grievances. "There is increased interest here in the Spanish-American situation, particularly because of its bearing on the relations of the nations south of us," Alexander informed his field agent in Texas. "I hope you will push this part of your work as vigorously as you have been pushing Negro employment."[38]

Officials in the Office of the Coordinator of Inter-American Affairs, though their jurisdiction in the matter of the delegation's overture was even less well defined than that of the OPM, were slightly more forthcoming. After some hesitation, Rockefeller finally created a Spanish-speaking People's Division within his office to promote better relations between Anglos and Chicanos in the Southwest. Yet because, as Carey McWilliams observed, Rockefeller "had great difficulty in making up his mind about the real function of the new division," it proved to be a largely ineffectual gesture. "Limited funds were wasted in trifling ballyhoo campaigns of one kind or another," McWilliams caustically wrote, "and too often the division functioned as though its prime objective was to induce Anglo-American clubwomen to sponsor Latin-American 'fiestas.'" Indeed, if McWilliams was correct in his assessment, the Spanish-speaking People's Division may have done more harm than good. "In many ways," he argued, "the division acted as though it wanted to frustrate any real efforts on the part of the Spanish-speaking people to improve their lot. Some of the field representatives seemed to be actually afraid of Mexican-Americans, for they insisted on working with the least representative elements in the various Spanish-speaking communities."[39]

In the end, Gonzales and his colleagues returned to the Southwest with little to show for their efforts. Hoping to persuade federal officials that a vigorous assault against discrimination in the border states would serve to validate the Roosevelt administration's increasingly ardent professions of comradeship with America's southern neighbors, the Gonzales delegation had to settle instead for vague assurances that Chicanos would be among the ultimate beneficiaries of Washington's wartime commitment to equal employment opportunity in the country's defense industries. Despite its failure to achieve its essential purpose, however, the mission to Washington produced an important residual benefit. If it was true, as Will Alexander asserted, that Gonzales and his fellow emissaries were handicapped by their ignorance of the federal bureaucracy's inner workings, their otherwise unavailing entreaties revealed what Washington officials were bound to acknowledge was an equally profound ignorance of Chicano history and culture on their own part. With the war heightening the government's desire to enlist every element of American society in support of its policies, federal officials did resolve to acquaint themselves with the manifold sources of potential disaffection among Chicanos in the Southwest even as they failed to display a sense of urgency in ameliorating them.

After decades of neglect by the federal government, Chicanos became the subjects of at least three significant studies during the early spring of 1942. Acting independently, but out of a shared concern that the discontent alleged to exist among Chicanos in the Southwest might constitute a fertile ground for the Axis propagandists and protofascist *nacionalistas* inciting anti-American sentiments throughout northern Mexico, the federal investigators dispatched to the border states encountered what one described as probably the "most submerged and destitute group in the United States—economically, intellectually and socially."[40] A study conducted by the intelligence bureau of the Office of War Information produced an equally emphatic observation on the general circumstances of Chicanos in the Southwest. "They are," the study concluded, "economically destitute, educationally deprived, socially disorganized, and are beset by severe housing, health, sanitation, and nutritional deficiencies."[41] Still another federal study in the spring of 1942 found that "most" Chicanos in the Southwest were mired "in abject poverty whether in city slums or in the country."[42]

These studies also confirmed the charges lodged by the Gonzales delegation, and other activists, that discrimination, in every conceivable form, was the essential dynamic of Anglo-Chicano relations throughout Texas, New Mexico, Arizona, California, and Colorado. David Saposs, a labor economist who surveyed conditions in the region on behalf of Rockefeller's office, reported that Chicanos, due to considerations of race, ethnicity, and national origin, were consigned by the dominant Anglo population of the Southwest to the lowest rungs of the social, civic, educational, and economic hierarchy. In addition to being denied equal access to employment opportunity, Chicanos were also, Saposs observed, generally relegated to the lowest-paid and least desirable jobs and routinely barred from vocational training programs that would have qualified them for better jobs. He further noted that Chicanos were disproportionately represented on relief, unemployment, and Works Progress Administration rolls throughout the Southwest.[43]

The study conducted by the Office of War Information confirmed Saposs's findings. The "institutionalized discrimination" confronting Chicanos in the Southwest was, the OWI concluded, not unlike that faced by blacks throughout the South. The dominant racial attitude among Anglos was "the Southern one, a circumstance profoundly affecting Mexicans, to whom . . . has been transferred the Southern attitude toward Negroes." "The result," the OWI observed, "is that the discrimination against Mexicans follows much the same pattern as Jim Crowism." In its most destructive form, the OWI study suggested, the "intensive employment, political and social discrimination" inflicted upon Chicanos in the Southwest fostered an impoverishment of the spirit as pronounced and debilitating as the material deprivation it bred. Of Chicano youth, in particular, the study noted, "The American Dream does not enter their fantasies any more than the American way of life enters their reality."[44] A third federal study of the extent of discrimination against Chicanos in the Southwest reached essentially the same conclusions. "It is notorious," this study asserted, "that in some portions of the Southwest the discrimination against the Spanish-speaking peoples is greater than that practiced against Negroes."[45]

Central to each of the studies that the federal government undertook in the Southwest during the spring of 1942 was an increasingly acute fear that the rising tide of indignation and impatience among the Chicano victims of discrimination in the border region would manifest itself in ways that threatened to undermine both the domestic and foreign policies of the Roosevelt administration. Reflecting the concern shared by each of the agencies that investigated the plight of Chicanos in the region, the Office of War Information concluded, "The existence of institutionalized discrimination against several million Latin-Americans in the American Southwest is a constant irritant in hemispheric relations, a mockery of the Good Neighbor Policy, an open invitation to Axis propagandists to depict us as hypocrites to South and Central America and, above all, a serious waste of potential manpower."[46]

In the end, however, each agency was less forthcoming in prescribing adequate solutions than it had been in delineating the potential dangers to the war effort that attended continued neglect of the Chicano "problem" in the Southwest. In his report to Rockefeller, David Saposs had warned that "the enemies of a better understanding and closer cooperation are capitalizing on the disadvantages and disabilities of resident Latin Americans in order to block a satisfactory implementation of the good neighbor policy." As a result, he reported, "it is the general opinion that our office must interest itself in this situation, and aid in any attempt to improve conditions so as to counteract enemy propaganda." Saposs was quick to point out, however, that federal officials should "guard against elements, irrespective of their motives, who are mistakenly of the opinion that it is necessary to dramatize and 'sensationalize' the miseries of this group in order to get results." Chicanos lacked the means to help themselves, he argued, and "since no large or influential group" in the country was likely to embrace their cause, it was apparent that "the responsibility devolves upon the government, particularly in the initial stages."

Saposs nevertheless emphasized that in providing this assistance federal officials should not unduly excite Chicano expectations or offend Anglo sensibilities. "Because of the delicate nature of the problem, the fact that our enemies are seeking to capitalize upon it, and in view of the general war emergency," he reasoned, "a cautious, tactful, and diplomatic procedure would be the most desirable, and would undoubtedly bring the best results." In light of what Carey McWilliams later described as the dilatory and largely ineffectual public relations campaign that the Spanish-speaking People's Division of Rockefeller's office initiated in response to the Saposs report, its determination to be cautious in addressing the admittedly legitimate grievances of Chicanos apparently outweighed its determination to be effective.[47]

While the Office of War Information was persuaded following its investigation that a merely "informational program," or any other type of "rhetorical effort to win Mexican good-will," was "bound to boomerang" when Chicanos measured its utility "against the meter of reality," it was neither equipped nor empowered to do anything more than lament the pervasive discrimination its inquiry documented.[48] Studying the causes and effects of the several varieties of injustice inflicted upon Chicanos in the Southwest was a necessary prerequisite of corrective action, but knowing the truth of the situation in the region, even when it disclosed the dangers inherent in continued neglect, did not guarantee that action would follow. When Anglos in the Southwest exploited their hegemony in ways that reinforced and perpetuated the disadvantaged status of Chicanos, they were upholding a tradition of discrimination with which the federal government had never presumed to interfere. To the extent that Executive Order 8802 authorized an intrusion upon that tradition, it was an intrusion limited both by the narrow focus of the president's order on employment practices in the nation's defense industries and by the exhausted ability and will of an understaffed, underfunded, and administratively unsettled Fair Employment Practice Committee so overwhelmed by the daunting challenge of combating discrimination against black workers that redressing the equivalent tribulations of Chicano workers was little more than a vaguely expressed intention.

Notwithstanding its inadequacies, however, the FEPC was the only federal agency authorized to respond to allegations of employment discrimination against Chicanos. Other federal agencies might decry and regret the debilitating influences of discrimination in the Southwest on various foreign and domestic policies important to the success of the nation's war effort, but if anything was to be done to remedy the situation it had become evident to all concerned by the late spring of 1942 that the FEPC, whatever its limitations, would have to do it. Those Chicano leaders who attempted to promote federal action against discrimination in the Southwest by claiming that it subverted the Good Neighbor Policy could congratulate themselves on having excited considerable apprehension in Washington, but in hoping that such concerns would be translated into ameliorative action they underestimated the inherent discretion of even an aroused bureaucracy when jurisdictional considerations come into play.

Given the FEPC's continuing neglect of their situation during the winter and spring of 1942, Chicanos in the Southwest were hardly unjustified in looking to other federal agencies for help in relieving the oppressive discrimination confronting them. In light of the vastness of the job before it and the paucity of its resources, however, the FEPC can perhaps be forgiven for its apparent delinquency in attending to the relatively obscure predicament of Chicanos. Under its new chairman, Malcolm MacLean, who succeeded Mark Ethridge in February 1942,[49] the committee had its hands full sustaining even the modest momentum created by its public hearings in Los Angeles, Chicago, and New York. MacLean, a white liberal who had gained the confidence of many influential blacks while serving as president of Hampton Institute, assumed the FEPC chairmanship without the personal reservations toward his mission that had complicated Ethridge's tenure. While he initially acquiesced in the view urged on him by White House aides that the committee's job was "to keep the heat off the 'Boss' and at the same time to make as steady progress in practical ways as we can,"[50] MacLean, whether on his own initiative or because of the pressures exerted by his increasingly frustrated and impatient colleagues, established himself in time as a reasonably strong advocate of vigorous implementation of the president's order.

MacLean began his chairmanship of the FEPC at a time of mounting restiveness within the committee, as well as among its minority constituencies, over the depth and sincerity of the Roosevelt administration's commitment to fair employment practices. If the president wished to dispel all such doubts, several committee members had argued at a meeting held only two weeks before MacLean assumed his new post, he should reconstitute the FEPC as an independent agency within the executive branch, provide a separate budget adequate to its needs, and arm it with the subpoena powers necessary to its investigative mission. David Sarnoff further proposed the issuance of a new executive order stipulating that the president would personally intervene in support of the FEPC when employers, unions, or federal agencies found to be in violation of the government's fair employment policy refused to comply with committee directives. Since it lacked the power to impose its own sanctions, Sarnoff argued, the FEPC could not reasonably be expected to prevail against the most unyielding violators of the president's order in the absence of a formal commitment from the White House to bolster the committee's actions.[51]

Uncomfortably wedged between a committee membership urging bolder action in support of its assignment and a sense of personal loyalty to a president whose closest aides had pointedly advised discretion in discharging a politically delicate task, MacLean charted a course that he apparently hoped would secure the confidence of his colleagues without incurring displeasure in the White House. Following a briefing on his new duties conducted by Mark Ethridge and presidential secretary Marvin McIntyre, a southern traditionalist whose reservations regarding the FEPC were never more than thinly veiled,[52] MacLean assured McIntyre, "I find myself now content and ready to go as fast and far as sound judgment on your part and the whole committee will go."[53]

If MacLean imagined that Roosevelt and his aides would adopt a more supportive attitude toward the FEPC once their political concerns were allayed by his cautious and deliberate leadership, he was mistaken. The committee's hope that it might be reconstituted as an independent, and presumably more effective, agency was extinguished when the War Production Board, created following the dissolution of the Office of Production Management in late January, assumed administrative supervision over the FEPC. Acutely aware that further resistance was futile, a majority of the committee perfunctorily consented to the transfer after Sidney Hillman, who had taken leave of the presidency of the Amalgamated Clothing Workers Union first to co-direct the OPM and then to head the Labor Division of the WPB, warned that "the Committee's effectiveness would be hampered if it were to be established elsewhere than in the War Production Board."[54] No one appears to have even ventured the possibility that the FEPC's effectiveness might be enhanced by its transfer to the WPB. "It is believed," Hillman sanguinely confided to the White House, "that the committee's effectiveness will not be decreased by this necessary re-organization."[55]

Constrained by a pathetically inadequate budget, submerged within a much larger agency that was, at best, oblivious to its mission, forced to work out of "dilapidated and ratty" quarters whose gloomy ambience sapped the morale of staff and visitors alike, and limited to holding public hearings whose findings it was powerless to act upon effectively, the FEPC was well on its way to becoming during the spring of 1942 what MacLean ruefully described as a "bastard agency."[56] Yet when MacLean sought to persuade the FEPC's figurative parent to confirm its legitimacy by lending the prestige of his name and the authority of his office to the committee's otherwise unavailing efforts to enforce Executive Order 8802, he found Roosevelt unamenable. MacLean suffered the first of several presidential rebuffs in this regard when he asked Roosevelt in mid-March to sign a directive to be sent to all federal agencies and departments requesting reports on the progress made by each in effectuating the president's order barring discrimination in government employment.[57]

Marvin McIntyre, through whom MacLean's request was transmitted to Roosevelt, set the tone for the White House's response to this and every subsequent FEPC plea for presidential assistance. "I don't know whether you want to follow this suggestion or not," McIntyre commented to Roosevelt. "Personally, I am a little leery for fear of stirring up the animals at this time."[58] Apparently agreeing with his secretary that the "animals" were best left undisturbed, Roosevelt instructed another close aide, federal budget director Harold Smith, to draft an appropriate reply to MacLean's request for presidential help. "It is my judgment," Smith dutifully advised his boss, "that the Committee should obtain under its own authority the information it desires and that you should not be called upon to ask the heads of departments and agencies to report directly to you the progress made on the subject of progress in the elimination of racial discrimination." A letter that Smith drafted "in keeping with this viewpoint" was signed by Roosevelt and promptly sent to MacLean.[59] Informing the FEPC that it was, in effect, on its own in trying to gain compliance with 8802, even within the federal government, Roosevelt's letter to MacLean patronizingly stated, "I am confident you will receive the full cooperation of the heads of departments and agencies in supplying the information you desire."[60]

To each of his subsequent requests during the spring for White House support in buttressing the committee's initiatives—in dealing with obdurate unions, in coordinating policies with various federal manpower agencies, in negotiating terms of compliance affecting defense industries and job training programs, in strengthening the fair employment practices provisions in government war contracts—MacLean received essentially the same response: the committee, notwithstanding its ultimate impotence, would have to go it alone. "I don't want to bother you any more than is necessary," MacLean had assured the White House, but there were cases "where we feel that we can't get down the road without your steam behind us."[61] What Roosevelt and his aides made clear was that the FEPC would have to progress under its own power, no matter how steep and seemingly impassable the road before it.

It is perhaps fitting, given the troubles that were to attend its efforts and the wreckage, of both hopes and intentions, that would be left in its wake in the Southwest at war's end, that the FEPC should have decided at a time when its own inherent untenability was becoming increasingly apparent to accept the challenge of relieving the employment discrimination against which Chicanos had contended almost from the moment that Anglo culture first invaded the region. That the committee finally took up the Chicano "problem" in the late spring of 1942 after having ignored it earlier was due to several factors: the continuing protests of Chicano leaders; the revelations of pervasive discrimination contained in the studies conducted in the Southwest by various federal agencies during the early spring; and, most important, the pressures exerted by the International Union of Mine, Mill and Smelter Workers (MMSW), whose campaign to organize copper workers in the Southwest rested, in large part, on a strategy of winning the allegiance of the thousands of Chicano workers employed in the industry by opposing the discriminatory practices of the dominant mining companies in the region.

As long as Chicano leaders had framed their complaints in ways suggesting that nothing short of comprehensive assault on the problem would satisfy their expectations of the federal government, they supplied administration officials accustomed to addressing only pieces of problems with a ready rationale for inaction. In contrast, the MMSW, because its narrower interests generated complaints of discrimination against Chicano copper workers that coincided with the precise jurisdiction of the FEPC, ultimately succeeded in prompting the federal intervention that equally worthy but less sharply focused complaints had failed to produce.

In deciding that the copper industry of the Southwest should be the focus of its initial attempt to deal with discrimination against Chicano workers, the FEPC was taking on what would prove to be one of the most formidable challenges of its brief but turbulent history. Indeed, the committee's three-year struggle to establish fair employment practices in the copper industry of the Southwest produced a record that discloses, as perhaps no other phase of its troubled career could, the extraordinary complexity attending the task of promoting fundamental change in a beleaguered democracy whose wartime preoccupations failed to incorporate a sincere commitment to economic justice for minority workers. It also reveals, in more particular ways, how bureaucratic inertia and moral apathy combined to impede reform, how the bitter internecine competition between affiliates of the American Federation of Labor and the Congress of Industrial Organizations alternately obstructed and aided the cause of fair employment practices, how irreconcilable approaches to combating discrimination caused the FEPC to limit its own effectiveness, and, finally, how the same wartime pressures that created the opportunity to launch a federal campaign against employment discrimination based on race, creed, color, or national origin also dictated the permissible limits of activism aimed at achieving that end.

2. *Last among Equals*

CHICANO WORKERS WERE indispensable to the establishment and expansion of the copper mining industry in the Arizona Territory in the late nineteenth century. They were also victims of discrimination from the earliest days of the industry's development in the region. Especially as the industry modernized, abandoning rudimentary techniques employed on a small scale in favor of highly capitalized, large-volume operations based on the most advanced mining and smelting technologies, the Chicano workers whose skills had helped unearth the early promise of Arizona's copper-rich future found their hopes for equal treatment in the mines sacrificed to employers' desires for a low-wage labor force and subordinated to an assertion of exclusive racial privilege by Anglo miners determined to reserve the most desirable and best-paying jobs for themselves.

So pronounced had this tendency toward racial segmentation of the labor force of the southwestern copper industry become by the turn of the century that Victor Clark, one of the earliest students of Chicano workers in the United States, described it as a principal characteristic of the job culture he encountered in the scattered mining camps of Arizona and western New Mexico. Clark found that "Mexican" wages were substantially lower than "American" (Anglo) wages throughout the copper industry of the Southwest (even though, as he noted, most Chicano workers were themselves native-born Americans), with the differential increasing as one moved from more northerly mines and smelters to those nearest the Mexican border. As the scale and technological sophistication of mining increased, Clark observed, "Mexicans have become in a way the scavengers of the mining industry, picking up the positions left vacant by other classes of workers, and supporting the least skilled and reliable Europeans and Asiatics. They mine both coal and shallow workings, and are extensively employed as muckers and surface men. The Mexican is a fairly good man for development work, or for cheap mining undertakings where a poor or a penurious company wishes to 'rat hole' a property; that is, work out the ore without scientific development or expert engineering advice."[1] Employers relegated Chicano workers to unskilled and semiskilled jobs, Clark reported, because they regarded them as culturally, even congenitally, unsuited to skilled work in the mines and smelters of the copper industry. He noted, however, that in the copper mines of Mexico, including the American-owned mines at Cananea only forty miles south of the Arizona border, Chicano workers were employed in every capacity, performing the most highly skilled jobs with notable efficiency. "In Old Mexico," Clark wrote, "native miners are employed exclusively in deep and dangerous workings that would try the skill of experienced white labor."[2]

Although his own analysis was laced with facile assumptions of Anglo superiority, Clark found little credible evidence that the economic and occupational subordination of Chicano copper workers was due to their alleged lack of innate ability or aptitude. He found, instead, that factors such as scale and profitability of operation were much more likely to determine whether or not Chicano workers were employed in skilled capacities. Chicano workers might be found, he reported, "mining copper and silver—that is, using drill and powder—in some new mine opened in a new district, to the entire exclusion of white labor, yet later, if the property proves valuable, [they] may be supplanted wholly by skilled American miners." Clark further observed, "In a district where white labor is chiefly used a few Mexicans will sometimes be found in smaller and less profitable workings. In most border districts large gangs of Mexican surface men, wood choppers, and often muckers are encountered."[3]

Motivated by mutually reinforcing considerations of race and economics, and favored by a labor market that permitted them to assert the inherent rationality of their employment policies, employers throughout the copper industry of the Southwest were able to institutionalize the subordination of Chicano to Anglo labor: to pay Chicano copper workers roughly half the wages of their Anglo counterparts for the same work, and, where both groups were employed, to relegate Chicanos to unskilled and semiskilled jobs. Anglo workers, partly out of self-interest and the same racist logic that informed the thinking of their employers, but also because of the fear induced by the proximity of a rival workforce, were generally willing collaborators in the fashioning and maintenance of a labor system that denied equal treatment and opportunity to workers for no reason other than that they were of Mexican descent.

Impressed by what he apparently regarded as the natural symmetry of the patently discriminatory labor system he observed in the copper mining camps of the Southwest, Clark approvingly explained, "This mingling of Mexican and white labor, without either supplanting the other entirely, comes from an equilibrium of competitive conditions, due to the general scarcity of labor, and the extensive development now occurring, and the easy adjustment of the wage of the Mexican to his true worth."[4]

If by orchestrating competitive tensions between Anglo and Chicano workers employers created conditions conducive to their economic self-interest, they also helped to extend and formalize existing patterns of social and cultural relations that disclosed the commanding influence of race and ethnicity in fixing the region's hierarchy of power and control. As a consequence of the labor policies adopted by the leading copper companies, the tendency toward separateness that had long marked Anglo-Chicano relations in the Southwest became obligatory practice as the sharpening distinction between "Mexican" and "American" insinuated itself into virtually every aspect of life in the region.[5]

The transcendent influence of this heightened racial and ethnic consciousness in the copper mining region of the Southwest revealed itself with particular clarity and force in the early efforts of workers to organize in the face of rising employer power, advancing technological change, and increasing competition between Anglos and Chicanos for job opportunities. The earliest unions to appear in the mining districts of the Arizona Territory, which, according to one source, "sprang more or less spontaneously out of the dangerous and semi-feudal conditions existing in most of the early mining camps,"[6] reflected a strong desire among the Anglos that comprised their membership to employ unionism as a means of achieving supremacy over rival Chicano workers no less than as a means to more conventional ends. Compounded of equal parts of bigotry, insecurity, and resentment over the use of Chicano workers as strikebreakers, the discrimination practiced by Anglo unions against copper workers of Mexican descent served to reinforce the biased wage and employment policies of employers while defeating any possibility of achieving the class solidarity that was a prerequisite to successful unionism in the industry.[7]

Even the radical Western Federation of Miners, whose professed devotion to industrial unionism ought to have rendered it immune to such divisive tendencies, was willing to exploit the racial and ethnic animosity of Anglo miners as a means of winning their allegiance. When a local of the WFM formed at Globe, Arizona, in 1896 to resist wage cuts imposed by the management of the Old Dominion copper mine, the union incorporated opposition to the employment of "Mexican" miners into its list of demands. The WFM was also active in an ultimately futile effort on the eve of Arizona's achievement of statehood to include a provision in the state constitution that would have severely restricted the employment opportunities of Chicano workers in the mining industry.[8]

Anglo miners did display a somewhat greater willingness to join forces with their Chicano counterparts as labor relations in the copper industry became more volatile and embittered in the period leading up to America's entry into World War I. Yet even when their common antagonism toward employers was forging an uneasy spirit of cooperation, the deeper traditions of economic competition and social separation upon which the insular work culture of southwestern mining communities rested remained in force. For the most part, Chicano copper workers trapped between the hostility of Anglo miners and the discriminatory policies of employers had no hope of protection beyond that which they were able to provide themselves. While nothing approaching durable organization grew out of their several efforts to fight the wage and employment discrimination confronting them at nearly every turn, Chicano workers were plainly willing to challenge the facile notion cherished by many of the region's mine owners that they would remain docile and uncomplaining in the face of the industry's exploitative policies.[9]

In the Clifton-Morenci mining district of southeastern Arizona, Chicano workers were especially active, if not particularly successful, in trying to combat the discriminatory wage and employment policies of the region's dominant copper companies. Assisted by the mutual aid societies that were active in the district, Chicano miners led a walkout by nearly 3,500 copper workers in the late spring of 1903. Although it was quickly broken by Arizona Rangers, state militiamen, federal troops, and a freak flood that devastated the ramshackle neighborhoods in Clifton where most of the strikers lived, the walkout exposed a strong undercurrent of militancy within the ranks of Chicano workers and the close-knit community they had helped to forge.[10]

Chicano workers in the Clifton-Morenci district provided still more emphatic evidence of their willingness to challenge the authority and discriminatory wage policies of mine owners in 1915, when, under the auspices of the Western Federation of Miners, which had overcome its earlier racist proclivities, they shut down the region's mines and smelters for five months. Their ultimate failure to eliminate wage and job discrimination rendered the victory they claimed at the strike's conclusion more symbolic than real, yet the several hundred Chicano copper workers involved had nevertheless demonstrated a remarkable degree of solidarity. When considered as an index of the militancy and organizability of Chicano copper workers in the Southwest, the Clifton-Morenci strike, and a brief walkout by Chicano miners at Ray, Arizona, during the same period, revealed that they, no less than their Anglo counterparts, were willing to contend against the redoubtable power of their employers whenever their collective discontent outweighed their individual fears.[11]

Despite the surges of labor activism that punctuated relations between copper workers and copper bosses in the Southwest during the volatile prewar period, neither Chicano nor Anglo miners succeeded in redressing the grievances that inspired their militancy. The beleaguered and factionalized Western Federation of Miners, which had belatedly disavowed its radical past and reconstituted itself in 1916 as the International Union of Mine, Mill and Smelter Workers (AFL), withered in the face of the determined antiunionism of Arizona copper companies. The discarded mantle of revolutionary unionism in the region was eagerly claimed by the Industrial Workers of the World (IWW), however, and as America went to war in the spring of 1917 the prospects for bitter labor conflict remained undiminished, especially given the IWW's resolve to accord militant Chicano workers equal standing with their like-minded Anglo counterparts in its drive to build a radical union among copper workers in the Southwest.[12]

Yet if the prospects for labor conflict increased as the IWW expanded its influence in the copper mining camps of Arizona, the rising tide of antiradical hysteria spawned by an often mean-spirited and expedient wartime patriotism afforded employers and their allies a singular opportunity to pursue their die-hard antiunionism behind a convenient façade of selfless loyalty to the nation's war effort and unwavering opposition to those threatening disruptions of a now strategic industry. The heightened risks of union activism were borne with generally bitter consequences by copper workers throughout Arizona whether or not they were affiliated with the IWW. Where Wobblies were conspicuous participants, however, the particular ferocity engendered by an antiunionism compounded of conventional employer self-interest and rabid patriotism became cruelly evident.

Copper miners in Bisbee, where the IWW enjoyed considerable support, acquired a special, if unwelcome, familiarity with this new strain of virulent antiunionism when, upon striking in the summer of 1917, more than 1,200 of them were herded into cattle cars at gunpoint, shipped into the New Mexico desert, and then abandoned without provisions. The hapless victims of the infamous Bisbee "deportation" also learned that, when the economic interests of the state's most powerful copper companies collided with their own supposedly inviolable civil liberties, the true loyalty of duly constituted local authorities was not to the abstract dictates of the Constitution of the United States but to corporate officials like Walter Douglas of the Phelps Dodge Corporation, whose personal will enjoyed the force, if not the legitimacy, of law. Any unease felt by Bisbee authorities and the small army of vigilantes that assisted them was apparently soothed by the knowledge that hundreds of those stripped of their rights were, in addition to being alleged radicals, also Chicanos.[13]

While the Bisbee episode revealed the unyielding antiunionism of mine owners in its most extreme form, it was but one of many assaults against organized workers, of whatever ideological bent, that accented wartime labor relations in the copper industry of the Southwest. Federal mediators hopeful of ensuring uninterrupted copper production in the region did seek to discourage the most extreme tendencies of antiunion mine owners, but they failed to establish the organizing and bargaining rights that were the promised keystones of the Wilson administration's wartime labor policy. In the war's aftermath, with employer opposition to unionism undiminished and a sudden plunge in the copper market propelling the industry toward depression, the last vestiges of effective worker organization in the mining camps of the Southwest quickly disappeared. The IWW, whose unhappy fate was sealed by the frenzied antiradicalism during and immediately after the war, was the first to disappear; however, the Mine, Mill and Smelter Workers was not far behind. Thwarted in its effort to project an image of responsible unionism by employers who were unwilling to tolerate unions of any kind, the MMSW descended during the 1920s into an organizational torpor from which it vainly struggled to extricate itself for more than a decade. "Only half a dozen weak local unions sustained the fading spark of life through the late twenties and early thirties," one scholar wrote of the MMSW. "A once powerful and proud international union had almost completely withered away."[14]

Because unionism had been the most promising vehicle available for advancing the struggle against discrimination in the copper industry, the withering of worker organizations in the principal mining districts of the Southwest following the war deprived Chicano workers of whatever chance they might have had to achieve equality on the job. Those workers fortunate enough to retain their jobs as the copper industry fell upon hard times invariably did so on terms dictated by employers. And for Chicanos the terms employers dictated ensured that the industry's tradition of wage and job discrimination against workers of Mexican extraction would continue in force.

The demise of unionism in the copper industry of the Southwest was symptomatic of the general decline of organized labor in the 1920s as the business culture of the decade restored the open shop as the basis of most industrial relations in the country. The onset of the Great Depression sent the labor movement careening into still more perilous circumstances during the early 1930s. But with the coming of the New Deal and the return of an economic and political environment more conducive to activism, the labor movement emerged from a decade of lethargy and despair to begin a period marked by a boldness and vitality destined to propel it far beyond the boundaries of its earlier achievements. The blighted fortunes of the Mine, Mill and Smelter Workers showed little improvement, however, even as the prospects for other unions brightened. In the copper industry of the Southwest in particular, the union had little cause for optimism. The industry's devotion to the open shop was undiminished as it began to shake off the worst effects of depression, and, with the giant Phelps Dodge Corporation leading the way, employers successfully blunted the feeble organizing campaigns of the Mine, Mill and Smelter Workers by launching their own company unions.[15] As a further discouragement to legitimate unionism, employers, again led by Phelps Dodge, routinely discharged workers who persisted in their activism even though the National Labor Relations Act of 1935 expressly prohibited such discrimination.[16]

Although the Mine, Mill and Smelter Workers was an original, if hardly indispensable, member of the insurgent faction within the American Federation of Labor whose championing of industrial unionism in the mid-1930s gave rise to the Congress of Industrial Organizations, its organizing record in the Southwest, as well as in equally important copper mining districts in Montana and Utah, was conspicuously devoid of the dramatic victories won by other CIO unions as the decade drew to a close. Not until the outbreak of war in Europe and the concomitant economic stimulation provided by America's own increasingly urgent defense preparedness effort was the copper industry, including its seemingly impregnable southwestern outposts, once again rendered vulnerable to unionism. Yet when the MMSW finally renewed its effort to gain a foothold in the mines, mills, and smelters of the Southwest, it faced opposition not just from employers, but also from

AFL craft and federal labor unions determined to contest their CIO rival's jurisdictional claims in the copper industry.[17]

As the often fierce jurisdictional rivalry that existed between the AFL and CIO nationally spilled over into the copper industry of the Southwest, it bred an activism that greatly enhanced the prospects for unionism in the region. As it intensified, it also became for those hoping to redress the problem of employment discrimination against Chicanos an increasingly influential factor, one that caused new attention to be focused on their cause even as it placed new obstacles in the path of their progress. As in the other industries in which this competition for bargaining rights arose, the rivalry between the AFL and CIO in the copper industry of the Southwest was significantly influenced by National Labor Relations Board determinations of appropriate bargaining units. Reflecting the CIO's devotion to industrial unionism, the MMSW petitioned the NLRB to create large, inclusive bargaining units that encompassed all nonclerical and nonsupervisory workers at each of the mines, mills, and smelters it sought to organize without regard to differences of craft and skill. In contrast, the AFL sought multiple bargaining units comprised of skilled workers represented by separate craft unions, with semiskilled and unskilled workers represented, if at all, by usually ineffectual federal labor unions under the federation's direct control.

Following its so-called Globe Doctrine, which afforded distinct crafts the right to settle questions of union representation through separate elections, the NLRB issued directives between 1940 and 1942 that effectively ensured that, to the extent they were organized, copper workers in the Southwest would be divided on the basis of occupation, with AFL craft unions that coordinated their activities through local metal trades councils representing skilled workers while either the MMSW or federal labor unions represented the unskilled and semiskilled. Since the industry's deeply rooted tradition of discrimination had fostered occupational segregation based on considerations of race and ethnicity, the organization of copper workers on the basis of skill ensured that the memberships of AFL craft unions would be almost exclusively Anglo, while those of the MMSW or federal labor unions would be largely Chicano.[18]

Like most CIO unions, especially those whose policies bore the imprint of left-wing leadership, the MMSW had long taken a strong stand in favor of equal opportunity in the workplace. As it became apparent that the organization of southwestern copper workers was proceeding on a basis that made it unlikely that the MMSW could compete successfully with the AFL crafts for the allegiance of the industry's skilled labor force, the union was quick to tailor its appeal to the Chicano workers who predominated in the ranks of the semiskilled and unskilled. Because the issues of greatest concern to Chicano copper workers continued to be the existence of discriminatory wage differentials and their virtual exclusion from skilled job classifications, the MMSW readily conceded that the success of its organizing campaign was inextricably linked to the union's willingness to commit itself to the redress of these historic grievances.[19]

The issuance of Executive Order 8802 and the creation of the President's Committee on Fair Employment Practice, which coincided with the MMSW's decision to embrace the issue of discrimination in the Southwest, afforded the union an unexpectedly convenient opportunity to support the new public policy enunciated by the Roosevelt administration as a function of both good citizenship and organizational self-interest. The MMSW's efforts to enlist the FEPC in a vigorous drive to eliminate discrimination against Chicano copper workers began in the fall of 1941 following the committee's Los Angeles hearings and continued into the following spring. The MMSW's "vigorous representations to the Committee," reported FEPC executive secretary Lawrence Cramer, insistently urged "that a public hearing be held at an early opportunity in the Southwest to consider complaints by persons of Spanish American origin."[20]

Preoccupied with the greater problem of job discrimination against blacks, and fighting an uphill battle to maintain a tenuous existence within a federal establishment that tended to view its mission with either hostility or indifference, the FEPC responded to the MMSW's requests with artful dodges rather than purposeful deeds.[21] To the extent that discrimination against Chicanos was a source of active concern to federal officials during the early months of 1942, it was in the Office of the Coordinator of Inter-American Affairs that the problem excited the greatest interest and disquietude. Within the OCIAA, however, discrimination against Chicanos in the Southwest was considered only in the narrow context of the potential threat it posed to hemispheric solidarity, and the remedial actions contemplated subordinated the enforcement of fair employment practices to "an educational campaign which would enlighten the dominant population groups on the background and the contributions of . . . Spanish-speaking peoples to the building up of this country, and particularly the Southwest, as well as their significant role in helping to spread the good neighbor policy in other Americas."[22]

With the FEPC seeming to lack both the resources and the ardor required for forceful action, and the OCIAA apparently determined to view discrimination in the Southwest as a problem whose solution lay in persuading Anglos to amend their offending and abusive ways, Chicano copper workers had little reason to believe in the spring of 1942 that the egalitarian sentiment embodied in Executive Order 8802 was anything more than beguiling rhetoric. The persistence of the Mine, Mill and Smelter Workers was suddenly rewarded, however, when the FEPC decided at its meeting on May 11 to hold a public hearing in the Southwest for the express purpose of exploring the nature and extent of job discrimination against Chicanos.[23] On the following day the committee announced that it would convene public hearings in the Southwest sometime during June in order to probe "charges of discrimination against Spanish-speaking people because of their national origin."[24]

In the wake of the committee's announcement that it was finally prepared to investigate the problem of discrimination in the Southwest, the MMSW and those Chicano organizations that had previously lobbied for federal action began to marshal evidence of job bias in the copper industry. For its part, the FEPC, whose understanding of discrimination against Chicanos was severely limited by its own studied neglect of the problem, was forced to acquaint itself with the situation in the Southwest by consulting the studies that other federal agencies had prepared earlier in the spring.[25]

The committee also sought to gain a better sense of how its efforts in the region were likely to be received by soliciting the advice of Maury Maverick, a former Texas congressman whose earlier enthusiasm for reform had marked him as one of a rare political breed: an authentic southern liberal.[26] Yet if the committee believed that Maverick's reputedly liberal outlook disposed him toward a sympathetic reaction to its proposed hearings in the Southwest, it was badly mistaken. Maverick, who headed the War Production Board's Bureau of Governmental Requirements, not only advised the committee to abandon its planned hearings, but also denied the existence of widespread discrimination against Chicanos in the Southwest. "Many complaints are made of discrimination against 'Mexicans,'" Maverick acknowledged, but there was in fact, he declared, "no economic discrimination against Latin-Americans hardly anywhere in Texas and none in New Mexico." He added, "I doubt if any man with the ability to do a job would be turned down anywhere in Texas on account of being a Mexican." In Arizona, he somewhat grudgingly conceded, "you will find the Anglos dominate and *I have heard* there is some discrimination there."

That the Southwest was burdened with an undeserved reputation as a region where discrimination flourished was largely due, Maverick suggested, to the rabble-rousing of irresponsible "Mexican racial agitators . . . who will bellow that the Mexicans are being treated badly" when, in actuality, the alleged offense usually amounted to nothing more than that "somebody didn't speak politely to a Mexican at a skating rink or something of that kind." For its own sake, Maverick urged, the FEPC should abandon its misguided plan to conduct unnecessary and potentially injurious public hearings in the Southwest. He patronizingly admonished the committee:

> Sometimes I used to get mad (that was a long time ago) and write very mean letters. I have a drawer in my desk in which I place these letters for cooling off. Several days later I would read them and in practically every case never send them. After you've thought over calling this meeting [hearing], I would like for you to place it in that same drawer and let it cool off for a while for it's my candid opinion that such an open meeting would do nothing towards helping the war effort but cause dissension and maybe trouble.

Whatever the real or imagined grievances of the FEPC's clients, Maverick bluntly concluded, "America is worth fighting for as it is—racial and religious minorities are better off here than anywhere else in the world."[27]

While the committee could hardly have been cheered by Maverick's disapproving reaction to its proposed foray into the Southwest, it remained committed to its announced plan of action, designating El Paso, Texas, as the hearing site. Yet because it was preoccupied until the latter part of June with the planning and conduct of its first public hearings in the heart of the deep South, in Birmingham, Alabama, the committee found it necessary to push back the tentative date for its hearings in the Southwest from June to mid-August.[28] Not until mid-July did Lawrence Cramer finally advise Senator Dennis Chavez of New Mexico, a staunch advocate of the planned hearings, that the committee was at last prepared to dispatch its field investigators to the Southwest.[29]

What Cramer failed to tell Chavez, or anyone else looking forward to FEPC action in the Southwest, was that powerful forces within the Roosevelt administration had already acted decisively to ensure that the committee's promise of public hearings in the Southwest would not be honored. Leading this effort to forestall a public inquiry into alleged discrimination against Chicanos was the undersecretary of state, Sumner Welles, who advised President Roosevelt on June 20 that the Department of State was "strongly opposed to the public hearings which the

Committee on Fair Employment Practices proposes to hold in the Southwest." The State Department's opposition to the El Paso hearings, Welles explained, derived both from a concern that America's enemies would exploit public disclosures of discrimination against those of Mexican heritage in the Southwest to the detriment of the Good Neighbor Policy and from a conviction that the provocative method the FEPC had chosen to discharge its mandate in the border region was ill-conceived.

"Axis agents and others seeking to discredit this country in Mexico and the other American republics," Welles wrote, "have been and are making effective use of racial discrimination in this country." He warned, "It would be most unfortunate, if through the record of public hearings conducted by an agency of this Government, we should afford them further material which because of its official character could be used even more effectively against us." Welles readily conceded that discrimination against Chicanos in the Southwest was "in a very definite sense a negation of the Good Neighbor Policy," and one that was "frequently cited as such in the other American republics." Indeed, he insisted that the problem was already so apparent that the FEPC's proposed hearings would accomplish nothing more than to disclose the obvious. "I believe," Welles argued, "that there exists an abundance of evidence of racial discrimination against citizens of the other American republics residing in the Southwest and that, accordingly, the holding of public hearings is unnecessary to gain an adequate understanding of the problem." If in the future "additional factual information" was needed in order to address the problem, he observed, "such information could best be secured by discreet investigation rather than by holding public hearings."

The discrimination that the FEPC was proposing to remedy plainly had an "adverse effect" on America's relations with southern neighbors, Welles acknowledged, and was therefore a subject with which the Department of State was "naturally very much concerned." Yet it was a problem, he told Roosevelt, whose solution lay in a dispassionate educational campaign rather than a headline-grabbing publicity campaign. Apparently referring to the still plodding efforts of Nelson Rockefeller's office, which he exaggerated out of all proportion to their actual effects, Welles asserted, "The conclusion has been reached after careful study that the problem can be solved only by means of a long range program embracing the education and improvement of the standard of living of the alien population involved and education of both aliens and citizens to a better understanding of each other. Much has already been accomplished along these lines, but time, tact and patience will be required in order to bring about a permanent solution."

Curiously, Welles made only a cryptic reference to what was probably the State Department's most immediate source of concern regarding the FEPC's planned hearings in the Southwest. Without explaining why, he warned Roosevelt that the Mexican government was anxious that the hearings not be held. "In a recent discussion of this subject with our Ambassador," Welles confided, "the Mexican Under Secretary for Foreign Affairs emphasized the belief that any publicity in connection with our efforts to combat racial discrimination against Mexicans in this country would be most harmful."[30] Whether because he knew that Roosevelt required no further explanation or because he felt that the case against the El Paso hearings was already so compelling that a more detailed argument was unnecessary, Welles made no effort to explain that the Mexican government's concern arose out of a fear that public disclosures of discrimination against Chicanos in the Southwest would force it to cancel final negotiation of an unpublicized bilateral agreement permitting the importation of thousands of its citizens into the United States to alleviate shortages in the depleted agricultural labor force of the western states.[31]

Responding to the increasingly insistent entreaties of western agribusiness interests, the State Department had agreed in May, shortly after the FEPC announced its intention to hold hearings in the Southwest, to join forces with several other interested federal agencies, including the Department of Labor, the Department of Agriculture, the Department of Justice, the War Manpower Commission, and the Office of the Coordinator of Inter-American Affairs, to explore the possibility of contracting for Mexican workers to satisfy the growing manpower needs of farm employers. In early June the American ambassador to Mexico formally broached the subject with the Mexican government, which reluctantly agreed to consider supplying workers to farm employers in the United States as part of its contribution to a war effort that it had only recently joined. The ensuing negotiations, which resulted toward the end of July in a labor-contracting arrangement popularly known as the "bracero program," took place just as the FEPC was moving ahead with its plans for public hearings in the Southwest. Because the Mexican government was obliged by domestic political considerations to insist that all imported workers would be treated in a manner consistent with the provisions of Executive Order 8802, the prospect of public hearings that were almost certain to reveal endemic discrimination against Chicanos in the Southwest was one that both governments found intolerable.[32]

Consequently, blocking the hearings commended itself to the Department of State as the surest means available to avoid embarrassing the Mexican government and thereby jeopardizing the success of its negotiations.

Without bothering either to inform the FEPC that a controversy had arisen in regard to its proposed El Paso hearings or to afford the committee an opportunity to counter the arguments advanced by Welles, Roosevelt immediately acceded to the State Department's demand. Referring to Welles's letter, Roosevelt instructed presidential aide Marvin McIntyre on June 23: "Take this letter up today with [FEPC Chairman Malcolm] McLean [*sic*] and tell him really for international reasons public hearing should be stopped. And tell Sumner Welles that you are doing so and that he also may do it."[33]

Armed with the president's authorization, Welles wasted no time in notifying Malcolm MacLean that the committee's El Paso hearings would have to be canceled. Although he was apparently unaware that the committee had already publicly announced its intention to hold hearings in El Paso, Welles was unmoved by MacLean's claim that canceling them would severely damage the FEPC's credibility with those individuals and groups who had been led to believe that the federal government was, at long last, ready to tackle the problem of job discrimination against Chicanos. Welles did suggest that, once the FEPC abandoned the highly publicized inquiry it had initially intended, the State Department would have "no objection to the Committee proceeding with its investigations or with any steps looking toward a solution of the problem short of holding a public hearing."[34]

Suddenly, and arbitrarily, denied the use of the only real weapon in its otherwise puny arsenal, the FEPC was powerless to do anything more than register its displeasure and disappointment. Following a meeting of the FEPC on July 6, Lawrence Cramer wrote to Roosevelt advising him of the committee's readiness to accede to "any plan which will eliminate unnecessary friction with neighboring governments." Cramer's thinly veiled contentiousness, however, communicated the committee's resentment rather than its concurrence. Forcing the FEPC to cancel its El Paso hearings without regard to the resultant dilemma such an action posed was, Cramer intimated, a particular source of concern to the committee. Should the committee be forced to declare "that a scheduled hearing, publicly announced, has been cancelled . . . ," he warned Roosevelt, "our enemies can assert, without the possibility of convincing contradiction on the part of our Government, that the hearing was cancelled because so much that was unsavory was discovered in the course of preliminary investigation that our Government found it necessary to suppress the evidence."

Cramer also objected that, if the State Department's reasoning in opposing the El Paso hearings was followed to its logical conclusion, the FEPC would be forced to treat complaints of discrimination lodged by Chicano workers differently from those filed by non-Chicano complainants. "The committee," he observed, "cannot determine in advance in what city in which it may hold a hearing valid complaints from Spanish Americans may arise. If all cases involving Spanish Americans are to be treated differently from other cases, this would necessitate a considerable change in its procedures." The State Department's apparent unwillingness to disclose that its objection to the El Paso hearings derived, in large part, from a concern that nothing interfere with its recruitment of Mexican labor placed the FEPC at a distinct disadvantage in answering Welles's criticism. Yet even if it had been fully informed it is unlikely that the committee would have agreed that exposing discrimination against Chicanos threatened to do more harm than good to Mexican-American relations. Claiming that the War Department's recent public disclosure of its success in redressing a "particularly glaring case of discrimination against persons of Mexican origin" at a Colorado military camp proved that forthrightness in dealing with such matters was a strength rather than a weakness, Cramer insisted that, contrary to the State Department's view, "such information is precisely of a character to improve our relations with Mexico rather than to disturb them."[35]

Apparently hopeful that by forcing the president to act personally in the matter the committee's position might command more sympathetic consideration, Cramer wittingly concluded, "The Committee requests . . . that you advise it if you desire to have it announce the cancellation of its scheduled hearing in El Paso, Texas. Also it requests your directions as to whether it shall refuse to consider cases of discrimination involving Spanish American in any of its public hearings in the future."[36]

If members of the committee expected to maneuver Roosevelt into a political corner by insisting that he personally decide the fate of the El Paso hearings, they grossly underestimated his legendary talent for insulating himself from such potentially nettlesome issues. The response to the FEPC's letter, the White House promptly decided, should be drafted by Sumner Welles, the person whose rigid views the committee hoped to change by enlisting Roosevelt's support.[37] Predictably, Welles found nothing in the committee's argument to warrant a reconsideration of the opinion he had expressed earlier. That the FEPC's credibility would be endangered if it abandoned its El Paso hearings was, Welles suggested, a manufactured concern. "So far as the Department is aware," he wrote, "there has been no adverse publicity arising from the fact that the public hearings have not yet been held. If this is the case, it would seem likely that if the holding of public hearings continues to be postponed indefinitely there may be no adverse publicity." When the situation was considered in that light, he argued, there was "no particular reason . . . why there should be any public announcement that the public hearings are not to be held." Ignoring the FEPC's lack of an effective alternative to publicity in enforcing its mandate, Welles concluded, "Those who seek rectification of such cases of discrimination as may exist should have no objection if their objective can be accomplished through non-publicized efforts of suitable representatives of appropriate agencies of this Government." In response to Cramer's claim that publicity had proven beneficial in the case of the War Department's recent efforts in behalf of Chicano workers in Colorado, Welles rather abstrusely observed, "While the publicity given to the correction of the situation . . . may have been beneficial, the fact remains that there had previously been adverse publicity. This Department would approve publicity regarding the adjustment of incidents such as that in question, if there had previously been adverse publicity but it would prefer that the adverse publicity be forestalled by administrative action preventing such incidents."

Nothing in Cramer's letter, he reiterated, altered the fact that the Mexican government had forcefully expressed the belief that "any publicity in connection with our efforts to combat racial discrimination against Mexicans in his country would be most harmful." From the State Department's point of view, Welles implied, this factor deserved greater weight than any others in determining administration policy. "It has been observed," he quoted the Mexican ambassador as having written, "that in certain places, signs are posted, announcements published and lectures and talks given proclaiming the end of certain specific acts of discrimination and the coming of a new sort of fraternal and friendly treatment for the Mexicans. This manner of approaching the racial problem, although well intentioned, nevertheless has the defect of being indiscreet, since it places emphasis on the existence of such discriminations, calling them to the attention even of individuals who have nothing whatever to do with them."[38]

With Welles unwilling to reconsider his opposition to the El Paso hearings and the White House committed to letting the State Department have its way in the matter, the FEPC confronted an increasingly familiar predicament: having to do its work without the means necessary to success. Never formally consulted by either the White House or the State Department at any stage of the decision-making process that sealed the fate of the El Paso hearings, the FEPC was still innocently "looking forward to further discussion on the matter" even as Roosevelt was disposing of it once and for all on the basis that Welles had recommended.[39]

The cancellation of the El Paso hearings, though important in itself, was symptomatic of a far more profound and increasingly apparent debility affecting the FEPC as it limped toward the end of its first year of operation. Unable to acquire the authority it needed to be taken seriously, starved of the resources its task required, and incapable of defending its role and its prerogatives within an administration alternately hostile and indifferent to its purpose, the FEPC was by the summer of 1942 drifting into a state of impotence that the forced, though never formally announced, cancellation of its proposed El Paso hearings only confirmed. Never unmindful of its precarious status and always acutely conscious that in seeking to implement Executive Order 8802 it was running against a current as powerful and relentless as any affecting the course of American history, the FEPC had from the first endeavored to remain as cautious as it could without betraying its essential purpose. In both its pronouncements and its policies the committee had resolutely resisted the temptation to regard the promotion of fair employment practices as an end in itself. Instead, in recognition of the special circumstances under which the president's nondiscrimination order was promulgated, and in deference to the public's continuing ambivalence toward the idea of equal opportunity, the FEPC had scrupulously adhered to the position that its specific function was to aid the war effort by encouraging the fullest possible utilization of minority workers.[40]

During each of the public hearings it conducted between the fall of 1941 and the summer of 1942, the commitee's sensitivity to charges that it was stirring up the "race question" led it to issue reassuring disclaimers. In its most extreme form, this determination to dispel all fears that it was promoting "social equality" served to undermine the committee's credibility rather than to enhance it. During the committee's ultrasensitive public hearings in Birmingham, Alabama, Mark Ethridge, who stayed on as one of its members after stepping down as chairman, sought to allay the acute concern of white southerners by stoutly defending the sanctity of segregation and assuring his listeners that Jim Crow had nothing to fear from the FEPC.[41]

For all its caution, however, the FEPC remained controversial if for no other reason than because its existence excited the hopes of aggrieved minorities and the fears of those who, out of whatever motives, found the prospect of an effective campaign against unfair employment practices intolerable. The Roosevelt administration, whose preference was for a committee that encouraged fair employment practices through grandiloquent appeals to patriotism and the people's sense of fairness rather than confrontation and coercion, grew uneasy in the face of any FEPC action that even remotely threatened to impinge upon either the war effort or the president's political standing.

The committee's repeated requests for more authority, a realistic budget, and strong White House backing when violators of Executive Order 8802 defied its orders were routinely denied by the administration, which never lost sight of the fact, as some others were prone to, that Roosevelt was responding to a political rather than a moral imperative when he reluctantly created the FEPC. Thus, even under the most tranquil conditions, the FEPC could not expect, in light of the incommodious circumstances of its birth, anything more than perfunctory loyalty from the White House. And when its actions or announced intentions rendered it impolitic or indiscreet in the administration's judgment, the committee found to its chagrin and disappointment that even the wan gestures of support it had earlier received from the White House were no longer proffered.

While the members and staff of the FEPC were acutely aware that fair employment practices did not enjoy a high priority on the Roosevelt administration's domestic agenda, they were never sufficiently well acquainted with the prevailing currents of opinion inside the White House to appreciate just how far down the list of work to be done the committee's mission was actually situated. When Roosevelt and his advisers refused throughout the spring to augment its authority and budget, the committee's disappointment never diminished its determination to do what it could with the meager resources it did command. Similarly, when Roosevelt denied the FEPC's request in early July to publish a summary of its findings of widespread discrimination in defense job-training programs financed through the federal Office of Education, the commitee apparently took the setback in stride.[42] Even the forced cancellation of the El Paso hearings, though deeply troubling, bruised the committee's morale more than it deflated its will to carry on.

That the committee remained undeterred in the face of so many rebuffs was a tribute to the resilience of a minor agency that was chronically beleaguered. Yet the FEPC's otherwise too sanguine outlook may have also derived from the mixed signals it received from the White

House. Roosevelt was usually generous in his endorsements of the FEPC during the first year of the committee's operation, even as he regularly refused to take the specific steps required to facilitate its success. The president was also lavish in his praise of the committee when its Alabama hearings were conducted in mid-1942 without provoking the vitriolic reactions from southern politicians that many anticipated when the FEPC first proposed its risky foray into Dixie.[43] The most important antidote to despair within the tacky confines of the FEPC headquarters, however, came in the form of an apparently vague pledge from Roosevelt in early summer that the committee's tattered status was in line for renovation. At a meeting with Malcolm MacLean and Lawrence Cramer following the Birmingham hearings, the president seemingly endorsed the committee's previously thwarted plans "for a broad offensive to enforce 8802." In addition to affording the FEPC the independent status it had earlier sought within the Office for Emergency Management, the scheme that Roosevelt reportedly sanctioned also envisaged, according to staffer John Beecher, a large enough appropriation of new resources to permit the committee at long last to break out of its Washington beachhead and to establish a permanent presence in every region of the country. "The prospective budget came to more than $1,000,000 as against the first year's $80,000 pittance," Beecher claimed. "Twelve adequately staffed regional offices were to be established for the prompt investigation of complaints, holding of hearings and routine policing of war industries."[44]

Buoyed by what it believed was a promise from the White House both to expand the scope of its operation and to reinforce the importance of its mission, the committee could accommodate itself to the cancellation of the El Paso hearings without concluding that its prestige and credibility had been irreparably harmed. The committee's morale and self-image were not strong enough, however, to withstand Roosevelt's totally unexpected announcement on July 30 that the FEPC had been transferred "as an organizational entity . . . to the direction and supervision of the Chairman of the War Manpower Commission."[45]

Shocked by the president's decision, which he dejectedly described as "a reversal, without discussion or warning," of the pledge of greater White House support for the FEPC made only a few weeks earlier, MacLean was at last forced to a conclusion that he and his committee colleagues had previously resisted: the Roosevelt administration's announced commitment to fair employment practices was fraudulent. "Minorities will feel," MacLean ruefully advised Marvin McIntyre, "that this transfer negates Executive Order 8802 and deprives them of the only Federal agency that gives them a voice in this crisis."[46]

When divorced from the political context that explained it, a feat that the administration vainly attempted, Roosevelt's decision to place the FEPC under the control of the War Manpower Commission reflected a certain organizational logic. Created in April 1942 "to bring about the most effective mobilization and the maximum use of the nation's manpower in the prosecution of the war," the WMC represented a necessary effort to integrate and consolidate the functions of several disparate federal agencies crowded into the same general jurisdiction.[47] Among the agencies absorbed by the WMC was the Labor Division of the War Production Board, under whose nominal auspices the FEPC operated following the abolition of the Office of Production Management at the beginning of 1942. For the FEPC the elimination of the War Production Board afforded a welcome opportunity to press again for the independent status it had earlier sought within the Office for Emergency Management.[48] In the view of WMC chairman Paul McNutt, however, the logical placement of the FEPC was within his own expanding domain. Noting that there was "some ambiguity as to what the relationship between the President's Committee on Fair Employment Practice and the War Manpower Commission is," McNutt proposed to Roosevelt on May 29 that the FEPC be transferred to the WMC's authority and control "so that all of the related activities" of the two agencies "may be properly integrated."[49]

The dilemma created for the president by the contest that arose over the proper location of the FEPC within a vastly expanding and constantly shifting wartime bureaucracy was neatly summarized by Harold Smith, director of the Bureau of the Budget and a White House insider, who informed Roosevelt that "Governor McNutt has requested you to transfer the Committee to the War Manpower Commission since full utilization of manpower is the goal of both groups. Mr. MacLean indicates that the Committee wishes to be an independent agency in the Office for Emergency Management and, further, expand its scope of activity to include non-war industries as well as broaden its enforcement aspects in furtherance of the national policy of non-discrimination." Smith perhaps betrayed his own preference in the matter by pointedly adding, "A very real policy question is whether the Committee should confine its action to holding hearings and reporting to you, to the appropriate agencies, or to the public its findings, or whether it should be granted authority to issue orders to the various agencies which might affect their relationships with war contractors." He concluded, "Because of the implications in this situation I should like to discuss this with you."[50]

If McNutt, Smith, or other opponents of a stronger and more independent FEPC made any headway during the early summer of 1942 in winning the president over to their point of view, Roosevelt gave no outward indication that such was the case. Indeed, to the extent that Roosevelt had signaled his intentions regarding the committee's status there was reason to believe, as both Malcolm MacLean and Lawrence Cramer plainly did believe after meeting with him, that the president was committed to a more powerful and independent role for the FEPC.[51] The probability that the FEPC would continue to function outside the WMC's orbit was further suggested by the negotiations that the two agencies conducted through mid-July in order to resolve the jurisdictional conflicts existing between them. Had WMC officials anticipated the president's decision to place the FEPC under McNutt's authority and supervision, it is unlikely that they would have proceeded with negotiations that clearly contemplated the committee's continuing independence.[52]

The fact that Roosevelt ultimately decided to subordinate the FEPC to the WMC when the available evidence suggested that such a course of action was unlikely tends to confirm the important influence exerted by two unanticipated political controversies: one arising out of the internal dispute between the Department of State and the FEPC over the propriety of the proposed El Paso hearings, the other fueled by southern politicians whose vehement objections to the committee's recently concluded Alabama hearings quickly achieved a cumulative significance within the White House. The wrangling between the State Department and the FEPC over public hearings into discrimination against workers of Mexican ancestry in the Southwest revealed the potential foreign policy complications threatened by vigorous implementation of Executive Order 8802—Roosevelt's personal involvement in the dispute may well have persuaded him that if similar conflicts were to be avoided in the future the time had come to restrict the committee's independence rather than to increase it.

The bitter complaints of FEPC "meddling" that southern politicians and editors lodged in the wake of the Birmingham hearings were probably of even greater importance in promoting a belief within the White House, where sensitivity to the feelings of white southerners was usually acute, that the committee's enthusiasm for its work needed to be dampened in the interest of political tranquillity and wartime unanimity.[53] Coming when they did, just as Roosevelt was being pressed to resolve the FEPC's ambiguous status, these protests almost certainly prompted the administration's dubious effort to depict a highly charged political decision as nothing more than a routine judgment commended by sound organizational considerations.

Within those constituent groups that regarded a strong and independent FEPC as the "brightest hope" of America's minority workers in their struggle to achieve equal opportunity, the surprise that greeted Roosevelt's announcement of the committee's transfer to the WMC quickly gave way to angry protest. Forecasting the tenor and focus of these protests, FEPC chairman MacLean warned the White House that critics of the president's decision were certain to regard it as "appeasement . . . of white Southern political pressure which has been building up to maintain 'discrimination as usual' even at the cost of losing the war." MacLean further advised that critics were likely to charge that placing the FEPC under the control of WMC chairman Paul McNutt was "election window dressing," since they believed that "under a political head" the committee "cannot . . . become other than a small Federal bureau without power." Under the circumstances, MacLean concluded, minorities were bound to "feel that the Boss has deserted them."[54]

MacLean's dire predictions proved remarkably accurate. Walter White, who in his capacity as secretary of the National Association for the Advancement of Colored People had shared leadership with A. Philip Randolph of the nervy agitation that produced Executive Order 8802, bitterly complained to Roosevelt that his "abolition of the independent status" of the FEPC violated the agreement that spawned the committee a year earlier. "Doing this without, so far as we know, having consulted with the committee," White protested, "is not only a reflection upon the responsibility of the committee but also an abrogation of the assurances made by you to Mr. Randolph and myself at the White House on June 18, 1941, that the committee would be and would remain an independent agency responsible only to yourself." Abruptly dismissing the administration's claim that the FEPC transfer was merely an organizational decision, White continued, "Your action of July 30, following as it does the bitter opposition of reactionary southern politicians to the Birmingham and proposed El Paso hearings, indicates that the principle of Executive Order 8802 is in danger of being surrendered to southern political considerations."

Firmly convinced, as he informed Roosevelt, that McNutt lacked both the will and the competence to conduct the committee's affairs in a way that affirmed the letter and spirit of 8802, White implored the president to rescind his action. "If all the good accomplished thus far by the committee is not to be negated, and if reactionary southern politics are not to be considered paramount to the federal government and our entire war effort," he caustically declared, "then it is imperative that you take immediately such action as will restore the Committee on Fair Employment Practice to the independent status which it occupied previously."[55]

Although most of the protests against the FEPC transfer came from black activist groups and the black press, the committee's white supporters were no less critical of the president's action. For example, New York City's Mayor Fiorello LaGuardia, who had played a crucially important role in the negotiations that led to the issuance of 8802, advised the White House that he was "inclined to agree" with A. Philip Randolph's angry assertion that in submerging the FEPC within the WMC the administration was pursuing a policy "which completely emasculates and destroys [the] usefulness" of the committee.[56]

Confident that they could ride out the brief storm the transfer had provoked without giving in to their critics, Roosevelt and his advisers steadfastly denied any intention to curtail the FEPC's effectiveness because of political concerns. Responding to Mayor LaGuardia's protest, White House assistant Marvin McIntyre, whose antipathy toward the FEPC had led some to believe that he had personally "maneuvered" the transfer,[57] reassuringly wrote, "Frankly, I think there is quite a misunderstanding about the so-called submergence of the Committee, and I hope very soon to see this misunderstanding cleared up."[58] The decision to treat criticisms of the transfer as misguided interpretations of the president's action was made after the White House had rejected Malcolm MacLean's urgent proposal that "the Boss go on the air with a powerful fireside talk to minorities" that included "a statement about the Committee, the transfer to War Manpower and what the Boss expects the Committee still to accomplish." "I am sure that unless something strong and sure is done quickly all hell will break loose," he forebodingly advised McIntyre. "I and others can take it, but I don't want the Boss to have to."[59]

Guided by his own more practiced political instinct, the "Boss" dismissed MacLean's ominous assessment, concluding instead that "this whole thing" excited by his transfer of the FEPC amounted to "a lot of smoke and very little fire."[60] Accordingly, he ignored MacLean's impolitic proposal of a soothing fireside chat in favor of a press release sent out over an aide's signature expressing the president's "regrets that this transfer and the reasons therefor have been so widely misunderstood" and reassuring blacks and other minorities that he had acted "to strengthen—not to submerge—the committee, and to reinvigorate—not to repeal—Executive Order 8802."[61]

As their continuing, if less frequent, protests indicated, the administration's most ardent critics summarily rejected the official explanation of the president's action and reiterated their demand for a restoration of the FEPC's independence.[62] Just as summarily, the White House brushed aside all such protests.[63] Finally conceding, as NAACP secretary Walter White informed Roosevelt almost five months after the dispute first arose, that opponents of the FEPC transfer had "no other alternative than to bow to your decision," the administration's critics reluctantly allowed the controversy surrounding the committee's diminished status to die out.[64]

With its freedom of action sharply curtailed by an unwelcome reorganization that vested control over every important aspect of its operation in administration functionaries apparently determined to mitigate the political dangers posed by excessive activism in the cause of fair employment practices, the FEPC's fear that "submergence" within the WMC would have the practical effect of nullifying Executive Order 8802 was realized. Throughout the fall of 1942 the committee waged a hopeless struggle to withstand the debilitating effects of the administration's studied neglect of its mission.

For those in the Southwest who cherished the hope that the problem of discrimination against Chicano workers would, at long last, be addressed by a federal agency consecrated to equal opportunity in the workplace, the FEPC's slow descent into impotence was destined to become a source of especially bitter disappointment.

3. *No Small Task*

HAD THE FEPC launched its investigation of employment discrimination in the Southwest still in possession of what Malcolm MacLean described as its "greatest force," the power to expose violators of Executive Order 8802 through public hearings, it would have had at least a fighting chance of gaining its ends. Deprived of that prerogative because of the State Department's opposition to public hearings, and forced to surrender control over its operations to officials in the War Manpower Commission whose commitment to fair employment practices was tempered by conflicting concerns, the FEPC dispatched its field investigators to the Southwest in mid-summer of 1942 armed with nothing more formidable than an overworked claim of moral authority.

From its temporary field office in El Paso, which was also to be the site of public hearings before the State Department intervened, the FEPC hoped to carry out its preliminary investigations without attracting undue attention to its activities in the region. Yet when James Fleming, the committee's field investigator, reached El Paso on July 21 he was surprised to find front-page articles in both of the city's daily newspapers reporting his arrival.[1] Already suspicious of the FEPC's intentions, local authorities were outraged when they discovered that Fleming was black. A quick telephone call to a member of the Texas congressional delegation, however, prompted an immediate decision by the FEPC to replace Fleming with a white investigator.[2]

That the FEPC's first act in the Southwest was to defer to the racist sensibilities of the local white establishment hardly bolstered the committee's reputation among those expecting it to combat discrimination. Ernest Trimble, the white investigator hastily instructed to replace Fleming, advised his superiors shortly after arriving in El Paso that their ready capitulation to local prejudice had disappointed and distressed the committee's prospective clients, including representatives of the

Mine, Mill and Smelter Workers Union. "Some of these Union boys," Trimble reported, "feel that in sending me to supersede Fleming the Committee made too much concession to local opinion. They seem anxious that the Committee take a very aggressive policy. They feel this is necessary in order to give workers courage to 'stick their necks out' by filing complaints."[3]

A much more serious threat to the committee's credibility, however, was posed by the issue of public hearings. Having announced earlier that it would be undertaking an investigation of alleged discrimination against Chicanos in the Southwest as a necessary prelude to the convening of public hearings, the committee found itself in the awkward position of having to carry out the first phase of its inquiry while no longer possessing the authority to carry out the second. Yet, perhaps because it hoped that the State Department might drop its objections or that even an ultimately empty threat could have a salutary effect in the short run, the committee made no effort to inform the public that its announced plans for the El Paso hearings had been abandoned. Even Ernest Trimble, whose job it was to direct the committee's investigative activities in the region, was initially told only that there was a possibility the hearings would not be held. In his instructions to Trimble, Lawrence Cramer strongly hinted that the committee's representatives in the Southwest should say as little as possible about its plans for public hearings. "We should avoid the issuance of publicity releases," Cramer cautioned. "If you are questioned as to the Committee's plans for its hearings, you should state that the Committee has announced its intention to hold a hearing on August 14 and 15 and should give general information as to the Committee's techniques and purposes to any person who properly may inquire. In other words, you should not seek publicity, but you should not arouse people's curiosity by being evasive or secretive."[4]

As the investigation was getting underway Cramer did suggest to Manuel Gonzales, who had earlier lobbied for FEPC action in the Southwest on behalf of the League of United Latin American Citizens, that the status of the committee's plans for public hearings in the region was unsettled. "As our preliminary findings merit," Cramer obliquely explained, "the Committee may hold public hearings in El Paso at a future date, similar to hearings held in other parts of the country. As you already know, the dates for such public hearings have been given as August 14 and 15, but the scope of our preliminary investigations and certain other unforeseen changes may compel us to shift the dates to a few weeks later."[5]

While the members and staff of the FEPC hardly needed to be persuaded that public hearings were critically important to the committee's success, Trimble warned Cramer that the level of intimidation was so high in the company towns of the southwestern mining industry that Chicano workers would be unwilling to file formal complaints of discrimination against the major copper firms if they suspected that the El Paso hearings were in jeopardy. The typical Chicano worker felt he "was taking a big chance in complaining against the corporation," Trimble reported, and would feel "definitely let down if the hearings are not held." He further warned that regional representatives of the MMSW, whose frustration over the federal government's slowness in tackling the problem of discrimination against Chicano copper workers left them in "a rather belligerent mood," would be especially offended if the committee reneged on its promise to hold public hearings.[6]

Trimble's fear of alienating the MMSW derived from a realization that the committee's investigation of discrimination against Chicano workers in the Southwest was dependent upon the union's active cooperation. From the time that the MMSW made equal job opportunity for Chicano copper workers a primary feature of its organizing campaign in the Southwest, the union took the lead in pressing for federal action. Forty locals of the union from Arizona, New Mexico, and western Texas banded together during the spring of 1942 to form the Southwest Industrial Union Council and immediately announced a program of action that included an attack on discriminatory employment practices. Following the FEPC's announcement of its intention to hold hearings in El Paso, the newly formed council established its own Fair Employment Practices Committee to amass "documentary evidence of the very real discrimination which exists and which is particularly vicious in the copper industry."[7] As a result of the MMSW's preliminary efforts, Trimble was able to report that "a bunch of affidavits containing complaints against Copper Mining concerns" were in the committee's hands even before its own field investigation began.[8]

Because it was the only organization in the region that had prepared itself for the FEPC's arrival, the MMSW was able to influence the character and focus of the committee's investigation to a significant degree. Confronted by uncooperative local authorities and a business community that was, at most, only grudgingly tolerant of the committee's mission in the Southwest, Trimble and his colleagues, some of whom were on loan from other federal agencies, ended up focusing their attention almost exclusively on the employment practices of the leading copper companies not only because they represented the dominant defense industry in the region, but also because the union's preparatory work clearly channeled the investigation in that direction.

At the earliest stage of its southwestern investigation, the FEPC relied heavily upon information provided by Harry Hafner and Leo Ortiz, two of the officials in charge of the MMSW's own inquiry into discrimination against Chicano workers.[9] In their detailed statement to committee investigators, Hafner and Ortiz described an industry whose work culture was infused at every level and in every aspect—recruitment, job assignments, wages, training, promotions, company housing, and medical benefits, subsidized leisure—by considerations of race and ethnicity. Almost without exception, they asserted, the mines, mills, and smelters operated by the major copper companies of the Southwest comprised two separate but coexistent worlds, one Anglo and the other Chicano. While employment conditions in the region were distinctly inferior in most regards to those that prevailed in the copper industry's other centers, in Utah and Montana, any advantages available to copper workers in the Southwest were nearly always reserved to Anglos only.

In making their case, Hafner and Ortiz sought to document the endemic character of discrimination against Chicanos by taking Trimble and his field staff on what amounted to a guided tour of the unfair employment practices that prevailed in the copper camps of the Southwest. At both the open pit mine and smelter operated in the Silver City area of New Mexico by the Nevada Consolidated Copper Company, a subsidiary of the Kennecott Copper Corporation, Chicano workers, along with Spanish American workers descended from the earliest Spanish settlers in the region, were, according to Hafner and Ortiz, routinely denied equal treatment. "This company," they asserted, "has always maintained a special rate for Mexicans,[10] has refused them promotions, and has refused to hire them for certain jobs in open pit mines, such as shovel operations, drivers, craftsmen, mechanics, locomotive engineers, and firemen." In the smelter, they added, Anglos only worked as "craftsmen, mechanics, furnace men, tappers, . . . mill operators" and in "jobs of like category." Chicano and Spanish American workers, who comprised 60 percent of the company's 2,000 employees, were relegated to jobs as trackmen, powdermen, mechanic's helpers, and general laborers in the mines and to similar low-wage jobs as laborers and helpers in the smelter.

"In many instances," they maintained, "Mexican workers have trained Anglo workers to do certain jobs in [the] mine and smelter, while the Anglo student was getting a higher rate of pay than the man who was training him. The Anglo was promoted to the vacant job. The vacant job is denied to the qualified Mexican worker." Even when it was critically short of labor, Hafner and Ortiz charged, the Nevada Consolidated Company refused to promote fully qualified Chicano and Spanish American workers. "New Anglo workers are imported from the outside to fill vacant jobs, and are trained by qualified Mexican workers who are available to fill these jobs." Finally, they insisted, there was "a difference in what an Anglo laborer is paid and what a Mexican laborer is paid for the same job."

The tradition of discrimination that the company enforced in the workplace was, Hafner and Ortiz claimed, matched by an equally rigid policy of segregation in its housing, recreational, and medical facilities. The housing made available to Chicanos and Spanish American workers was "not as well maintained or as well provided for" as that reserved to Anglo workers, they reported, while company recreational facilities consisted of a "luxurious two-story clubhouse for Anglos" and "an old canteen" for non-Anglos. The company hospital, they added, maintained separate wards for the two groups of workers.[11]

According to Hafner and Ortiz, the discriminatory practices that obtained at Nevada Consolidated's mine and smelter were merely representative of the abuses that confronted Chicano workers throughout the copper industry of the Southwest. Whether they worked for the Miami Copper Company, the Inspiration Copper Company, or the International Smelting and Refining Company in the Miami-Globe area of south-central Arizona; for the Magma Copper Company at Superior, Arizona; for the Phelps Dodge Corporation at mines, mills, and smelters scattered throughout Arizona and at its refinery in El Paso, Texas; or for the American Smelting and Refining Company, at its El Paso refinery, Chicano workers allegedly faced what was by the time Hafner and Ortiz completed their tour a familiar litany of unfair practices: denials of equal wages for equal work; denials of promotion to skilled-job classifications; denials of equal access to employer-owned housing, recreational, and medical facilities—in short, denials of equal treatment in every important aspect of employment. Only at the Shattuck-Denn Company mine in Bisbee, they concluded, could one find a major employer in the industry who was according Chicano copper workers treatment equal to that enjoyed by Anglos.[12]

Beyond the continuing force of those obvious economic motives that led the major copper companies in the region to fashion discriminatory labor policies in the first place, the occupational captivity of Chicanos was reinforced, Hafner and Ortiz charged, by both the bigotry of Anglo workers and the cynical opportunism of AFL craft unions that willingly and profitably accommodated themselves to the industry's segregationist tradition in the Southwest. Most of the Anglo copper workers in the region, they insisted, were not drawn from "the natural labor supply" of the region, but had been recruited from southern states where the transcendent force of Jim Crow shaped values and habits as profoundly in the workplace as in every other setting. This preconditioning, they implied, ensured that most Anglo workers adjusted easily and naturally to the race-conscious job culture administered by the dominant copper companies in the region.[13] To the extent that AFL craft unions had established bargaining rights on behalf of the Anglo workers who comprised the skilled labor force in the industry, they functioned, according to Hafner and Ortiz, as staunch defenders of employment policies that systematically excluded Chicano workers from the skilled job classifications they represented.[14]

The sweeping allegations of discrimination lodged by Hafner and Ortiz against the major copper companies of the Southwest, while they suggested the broader dimensions of the problem that FEPC investigators had been sent to explore, were not a satisfactory substitute for the specific individual complaints that the committee required before it would act.[15] In the wake of the committee's announcement that it intended to hold public hearings in the Southwest, a handful of individual complaints found their way to its Washington headquarters. Upon arriving in El Paso, committee investigators were presented with additional individual complaints by MMSW representatives. While these early complaints rarely contained precise details of the sort the committee hoped to have in its files before proceeding against alleged violators of the president's nondiscrimination order, they corroborated the broader charges lodged by union activists and the leaders of various Chicano civic organizations in the region.[16]

Persuaded that the copper industry was the logical place to start in dealing with the problem of discrimination against Chicano workers, Trimble dispatched his field investigators to the region's major mining districts at the end of the first week of August. Still unsure about the fate of the committee's planned hearings in the Southwest, Trimble nevertheless instructed his field agents to conduct their investigations in anticipation of such an eventuality. Based upon the information supplied by MMSW officials, investigators were informed that they should "be concerned largely with two types of discrimination: (1) Wage differentials, and (2) Refusal to up-grade workmen or hire them for certain jobs." But while he stressed the importance of securing formal complaints from those individual workers alleging discrimination, Trimble also instructed field investigators to collect wage and occupational data from each employer "in order to ascertain whether there is a pattern of . . . discrimination" and to determine if companies had resorted to "token" compliance as a means of evading their obligation to comply fully with the terms of Executive Order 8802.[17]

By suggesting that formal complaints from individuals were unlikely to provide an adequate basis for assessing the extent of employment discrimination against Chicanos, Trimble was apparently reacting to warnings given by Hafner and Ortiz that in many cases prospective complainants were simply too fearful of employer retaliation to come forth. Describing to Lawrence Cramer one of the more extreme examples of intimidation mentioned by MMSW officials, Trimble wrote, "Hafner . . . says that in Miami, Arizona the Chief of Police, who incidentally is a brother of the employment officer of the copper concern which dominates the town, has a record of having killed six Latin-Americans and that as a result of this the Latin-Americans in that section are intimidated."[18]

Although it was completed within a few weeks, the FEPC's investigation of the occupational status of Chicano workers in the copper industry of the Southwest disclosed the complexity—historical, political, social, economic, cultural—of the discriminatory tradition that governed relations between Anglos and those indiscriminately lumped together as "Mexicans" because more precise distinctions as to race, ethnicity, and nativity were apparently irrelevant to most members of the dominant culture. It also revealed, however, that a tendency among most Anglos to ascribe the unarguably degraded status of Chicanos to the operation of natural, and thus inherently rational and immutable, sociobiological mechanisms rather than to willful discrimination ensured their resistance to any remedial action the committee might propose.

Working simultaneously in New Mexico and Arizona, FEPC field investigators quickly discovered that evidence of discrimination against Chicano copper workers was not hard to come by. At the facilities of the Nevada Consolidated Copper Company in Hurley and Santa Rita, New Mexico, James Fleming, who had stayed on as an investigator after being superseded by Trimble, and Daniel Donovan, a longtime labor activist whose experience was to prove especially helpful in sorting out the interaction between union rivalry and discrimination, readily substantiated the allegations made earlier by MMSW officials, Chicano leaders, and individual complainants. Based on their investigation, Fleming and Donovan reported that Chicano and Spanish American workers, who constituted 60 percent of the company's workforce at its open pit mine in Santa Rita and 40 percent at its mill and smelter in Hurley, were systematically victimized by unfair wage differentials, arbitrary work assignments, specious job classifications, and denials of promotion or upgrading to any skilled work that tradition defined as an "American" or "white man's job." They further observed that the pattern of discrimination found in the workplace extended to most other aspects of community life in Santa Rita and Hurley.[19]

While noting that such discrimination was deeply embedded in the history and traditions of the region, Fleming and Donovan argued that unfair employment practices, especially those related to promotions and upgrading, were reinforced by the bitter rivalry that existed between craft and industrial unionism at the Nevada Consolidated facilities. Where no unions had existed previously, the National Labor Relations Board certified eleven separate bargaining units in the spring of 1942. Ten of the units—two railroad brotherhoods and eight AFL craft unions—represented skilled trades comprised almost exclusively of Anglo workers. The eleventh unit, represented by the CIO's Mine, Mill and Smelter Workers Union, was dominated by Chicano and Spanish American workers employed in relatively low-wage semiskilled and unskilled jobs.[20] As a consequence of union rivalries that served to divide the workforce along lines of race and ethnicity as well as skill and craft, discrimination against Chicano and Spanish American workers in matters of promotion and upgrading had, according to Fleming and Donovan, become both more pronounced and less amenable to corrective action. With only rare exceptions, they explained, the promotion or upgrading of Chicano and Spanish American workers necessitated their moving from the CIO bargaining unit covering unskilled and semiskilled job categories to one of the ten craft bargaining units represented by either AFL unions or railroad brotherhoods. Because the Anglo-dominated craft unions either barred Chicano and Spanish American workers from membership or were unwilling to accord them fair and equal representation, the discriminatory promotion and upgrading practices the company had long employed were, Fleming and Donovan concluded, reinforced and perpetuated.

The AFL unions, whose contracts with Nevada Consolidated prohibited discrimination on the basis of "race, creed or color" but not national origin, were reportedly content to block the promotion or upgrading of Chicano and Spanish American workers to "Anglo jobs" through informal means. According to Fleming and Donovan, the railroad brotherhoods, whose contracts failed to include any kind of an antidiscrimination clause, erected formal barriers by entering into a contractual arrangement with the company that specified that car droppers, the only category of mining-related railroad work in which Chicano and Spanish American workers were employed, were ineligible for promotion to any of the more lucrative and desirable job classifications traditionally reserved to Anglos.[21]

When confronted by Fleming and Donovan, Nevada Consolidated's managers staunchly denied that the company engaged in any form of discrimination against Chicano or Spanish American workers. That such workers were concentrated in semiskilled and unskilled jobs at or near the bottom of the company's wage ladder—and that few if any could be found working in those skilled occupations in which Anglos were concentrated—was, management officials rather nebulously explained, a function of long-standing regional traditions reflecting differences in cultural values and natural racial and ethnic aptitudes. Yet, notwithstanding their claim that occupational and wage patterns did not result from discriminatory practices, Nevada Consolidated managers did admit a reluctance to disturb those patterns. Most of the company's Anglo workers, they explained, came from Texas and Oklahoma and were imbued with racial attitudes that caused them to "object to working with 'Mexicans.'" Thus to promote or upgrade Chicanos and Spanish Americans into the midst of Anglo workers who would not accept them, company officials implied, was to pursue a policy that was at once futile and disruptive. Add to this the fact that promotions or upgradings of Chicano and Spanish American workers would only exacerbate the conflict between rival unions, company managers observed, and there was even less to commend such a course of action.[22]

Although their investigation confirmed the existence of systematic discrimination against Chicano and Spanish American workers at Nevada Consolidated's Santa Rita and Hurley facilities, Fleming and Donovan made no direct effort to press for compliance with the president's order. That responsibility resided with FEPC officials in Washington, who were, following the cancellation of the El Paso hearings and the committee's unexpected and unwelcome transfer to the War Manpower Commission, struggling to ascertain just how much of their already meager authority they still retained.[23] Fleming and Donovan did take it upon themselves, however, to promote more cooperative relations between the AFL and CIO at Santa Rita and Hurley. Convinced that any effort the committee might undertake to force the company's compliance with 8802 was likely to fail as long as the existing union rivalry facilitated discrimination, Fleming and Donovan initiated an ambitious, if unauthorized, plan to foster a "labor unity program" in the area. Since both the company and the unions acknowledged that "the jurisdictional rivalry between the AFL and the CIO is a barrier to fair upgrading on the basis of merit," they reasoned, it made sense that FEPC representatives should "offer their services to bring the two labor groups together for conversations which might result in upgrading and pay on merit and without discrimination based on race, creed, color, or national origin."

If the jurisdictional rivalry between the AFL crafts and the MMSW could be reduced or eliminated, Fleming and Donovan believed, unionism could function as a powerful ally of fair employment practice at Nevada Consolidated, and throughout the rest of the copper industry in the Southwest, rather than as a major impediment to it. They argued in defense of their actions:

> Your investigators fully believe that a large portion of discrimination practiced against Spanish-speaking peoples at Nevco [Nevada Consolidated] can be corrected through the usual grievance channels, if the several unions are placed in [a] position to represent adequately all the men in their units, even those who were once, or still are, members of the rival labor organizations; if each union encourages each of its members to affiliate with whichever local has jurisdiction over him, and, therefore, can represent him before management; if each faction agrees not to raid or invade the other, and if each could present a united interest to management in full observance of Executive Order 8802.[24]

A "unity program" of the kind they were proposing, Fleming and Donovan suggested, had the potential to benefit everyone: the AFL, the CIO, the FEPC, Nevada Consolidated, and, especially, the Chicano and Spanish American copper workers who were unable to contribute fully to the war effort as long as job discrimination persisted. "Management also agrees," they concluded, "that labor peace between the CIO and AFL would greatly improve management labor relations in matters of fair promotion opportunities, etc. Both factors of labor agree that a 'unity program' would also prevent management from using the union situation as an alibi for refusing, or failing, to give all workers employment opportunities without discrimination based on race, creed, color, or national background."[25]

Encouraged by Nevada Consolidated's acknowledgment that greater cooperation between the AFL and CIO "would greatly contribute towards [a] more harmonious relationship between management and labor unions" and thus help to alleviate the problem of discrimination,

Fleming and Donovan pressed their unity program on representatives of the rival unions. Not surprisingly, they found MMSW leaders, who had already strongly endorsed the FEPC's investigation, willing to consider any suggestion that promised to reduce discrimination against Chicano and Spanish American workers. Their own preference, MMSW leaders stated, was for the establishment of a "Joint Committee" of all unions at Nevada Consolidated that would afford special assistance to any worker who felt that he was "not getting adequate representation" from the union "which has jurisdiction over him." Leaders of the Chino Metal Trades Council, which represented the various AFL unions at Hurley and Santa Rita, also endorsed the concept of labor unity, but displayed little enthusiasm for proposals aimed at eliminating all barriers to the promotion and upgrading of Chicano and Spanish American workers. As a counter to the CIO's position that all promotions and upgradings should be made without regard to considerations of race, ethnicity, or national origin, AFL representatives proposed that workers seeking advancement to higher job classifications should "be subjected to an aptitude test, so as to insure selection of a man who can advance to a craftsman." The idea of an aptitude test was rejected by CIO spokesmen as "a streamlined way to discriminate against 'Mexicans' whose background and lack of facility with the English language might handicap them disastrously." Yet despite the inability of rival union officials to agree on a common plan of action in dealing with discrimination at Nevada Consolidated, Fleming and Donovan were sufficiently encouraged by the initial responses to their unity campaign to report that local leaders of the AFL and CIO had taken "the first steps toward eliminating jurisdictional conflict as a barrier to fair employment and upgrading practices."[26]

In light of what they regarded as overwhelming evidence of discrimination against Chicano and Spanish American workers by the Nevada Consolidated Copper Company, Fleming and Donovan recommended that the FEPC take vigorous action to enforce Executive Order 8802. As the committee's investigation progressed, however, it became increasingly apparent that the pattern of discrimination uncovered at Nevada Consolidated's facilities in western New Mexico extended to virtually every corner of the copper industry of the Southwest. Barron Beshoar, an investigator on loan to the FEPC from the War Manpower Commission's Denver office, found that discrimination against Chicano workers was a common denominator of the labor policies in force throughout Arizona's immense copper industry, which in 1941 had led the nation in production.[27]

Armed with "a large number of individual complaints as well as general complaints" alleging discrimination against Chicano workers by the region's major copper companies, Beshoar arrived in the Globe-Miami copper district east of Phoenix in early August. While noting that complaints were "most openly expressed . . . where the International Union of Mine, Mill and Smelter Workers is active," Beshoar reported that among the "scores" of workers he interviewed, "both Mexican and Anglo," there was an "almost unanimous belief that both of the general complaints are true—namely that Mexicans are paid at a lower scale than Anglos for the same or similar work, and that there is a general failure to upgrade or promote qualified Mexican workers to the higher classifications and better paid jobs."[28]

At the Inspiration Consolidated Copper Company's mine and ore-processing facilities in the hills north of Miami, Beshoar readily uncovered evidence that appeared to confirm allegations of widespread discrimination against Chicano workers. Except for those Chicanos employed underground, where the common dangers of mining copper deep beneath the surface had forged a tradition of equal treatment, Beshoar found that workers of Mexican ancestry, who comprised approximately 30 percent of the company's 1,500 employees, occupied a collective status distinctly inferior to that of their Anglo colleagues. Chicano workers, he noted, were generally excluded from skilled occupations and frequently denied wage parity with Anglo workers performing the same or similar tasks at or near the bottom of the company's job hierarchy. In some of the company's operations—the power plant and security department, for example—Beshoar found that Chicanos lacked even token representation. Where Chicanos were employed, he reported, they were concentrated in the lowest job classifications and tended to earn the lowest wages paid within those classifications. Of the 208 workers employed in the company's mechanical department, for example, he noted that only 24 were Chicanos and of that number 21 worked as "laborers at the lowest possible scale of pay." Similarly, in the crushing plant, where Chicanos outnumbered Anglos by roughly two to one, Beshoar found that, while half of the Chicano workers were in the lowest wage category, not a single Anglo worker was at the bottom of the wage scale. Overall, he observed, the markedly uneven distribution of Chicano and Anglo workers across the wage spectrum at Inspiration Consolidated tended, at the very least, to raise suspicions regarding the fairness of the company's employment and wage policies. Of the company's 476 Chicano employees, 229 of them, or just under 50 percent, were in the lowest wage classifications. In contrast, only 53 of the company's 1,092 Anglo employees, or slightly less than 5 percent, were in the same low-wage classifications.[29]

When Beshoar questioned Inspiration Consolidated's managers, they stoutly rejected the notion that discrimination had played a part in determining the job assignments or wages of Chicano workers. Richard Newlin, the company's general superintendent, asserted that both job assignments and wages were governed by considerations of merit only. To the extent that Chicano workers employed on the surface were concentrated in the least desirable jobs and at the lowest wage classifications it was, he claimed, a function of their physical and mental shortcomings rather than purposeful discrimination. When asked to explain why some surface work gangs were comprised exclusively of Chicanos while others were made up entirely of Anglos, Newlin contended that "it just happened to be that way." While Newlin professed bewilderment that any of Inspiration Consolidated's Chicano employees should have thought themselves victims of discrimination, the company's lawyer charged that the FEPC's plainly misguided and unwarranted investigation represented "an attempt by the International Union of Mine, Mill and Smelter Workers to use discrimination as a lever against the company for organization purposes."[30]

In denying that the company engaged in any form of discrimination against Chicano employees, its managers did acknowledge that in determining job assignments they were not unmindful of the alleged unwillingness of Anglo craftsmen to accept workers of Mexican ancestry into their ranks. Because its workers were unorganized, however, the company could not argue, as the managers of Nevada Consolidated Copper Company had, that unions were responsible for enforcing Anglo claims of normative racial or ethnic hegemony over skilled work. Nor could the company claim that the patently discriminatory employment orders it routinely placed with the Globe office of the U.S. Employment Service derived from other than its own authority. When he consulted with a USES official in Globe, Beshoar found that on every occasion that Inspiration Consolidated requested government assistance in filling vacancies in skilled, clerical, or professional job classifications between April and July 1942 it specified that referrals should be of "White" or "White American" workers only. Conversely, when the company sought the help of the USES in recruiting surface laborers or mine muckers, its employment agent either asked for "Latin Americans" only or failed to specify a racial or ethnic preference.[31]

At the nearby mine and mill of the Miami Copper Company, Beshoar found Chicanos working under the same disadvantages that obtained throughout Inspiration Consolidated's facilities. Remarkably, however, he also found that the company's local managers, unlike their counterparts at Inspiration Consolidated, were willing to admit openly that the relatively few Chicano workers they employed were denied equal treatment in nearly every regard, including hiring, job assignments, promotions, or upgradings and wages. Richard Hughes, the mine superintendent, expressed his personal reservations about such discriminatory practices, which he attributed to policies dictated by the company's New York headquarters and to the racism of Anglo workers. Despite such refreshing candor, however, he gave Beshoar no reason to believe that the situation was likely to change.[32]

Although officials of the Mine, Mill and Smelter Workers had alleged that the employment policies of both the Magma Copper Company in Superior, Arizona, and the Nevada Consolidated Copper Company in Ray, Arizona, reflected the same broad pattern of discrimination against Chicano workers found in the other principal mining districts of the state, the absence of individual complaints against either company apparently persuaded Beshoar to limit his inquiries. Officials of each company assured Beshoar that Chicano employees received fair and equal treatment, and his rushed and perfunctory investigations failed to establish a conclusive basis for challenging their facile assertions.[33]

When he arrived in the Jerome-Clarkdale mining district of central Arizona, however, Beshoar encountered a corporate and community atmosphere so heavily laden with the signs and symbols of racial and ethnic bigotry that reaching definitive conclusions required little in the way of probing inquiry or analytical rigor. As the site of the legendary United Verde Mine, which contained some of the richest copper deposits in the West, Jerome had been one of the leading mining camps of the Southwest since the late nineteenth century. Describing the town's singular geographical setting, one writer observed:

> Jerome, the camp—or town, city, or what you will—that the United Verde called into being, was one of the most distinctive mining communities in the United States. Like Jerusalem of old, it was in truth a city that was compact together. Built on the slopes and ridges of a not inconsiderable mountain, its steep, narrow, winding streets were the wonder and alarm of the chance visitor from the cities of the plains; the roof line of one of its houses often lay many feet below the ground floor level of its neighbor; and a number of vantage points in the town brought vividly to mind Kipling's description of the Wonders of Shamlegh's village in the heart of the Himalayas—"a swallow's nest under the eaves of the roof of the world."[34]

After extracting more than a hundred million dollars' worth of copper, gold, and silver from the wide veins of ore that coursed through the mountain below the streets of Jerome, the heirs of W. A. Clark, the pioneering entrepreneur who had developed the property, agreed in 1935 to sell the United Verde mines, and a companion smelter located five miles down the canyon at Clarkdale, to the Phelps Dodge Corporation, Arizona's largest and most powerful copper concern.[35] If Jerome's unique setting conjured up romantic allusions among some of its visitors, the town's look and feel prompted a distinctly less positive and generous reaction from Beshoar. Describing a place he found more forbidding than scenic, Beshoar wrote, "Jerome is dirty and squalid. There are large numbers of unpainted, weather-beaten frame houses perched precariously on the mountain side. Private citizens can only purchase 20 feet of the surface. The entire mountain upon which Jerome stands is owned by the Phelps-Dodge Corporation and there is a mine directly under the town. The town is closely supervised by police and the influence of the Phelps-Dodge Corporation is everywhere and in every aspect of Jerome life. The population of the town of Jerome is 50 to 60 per cent Mexican."

While he noted that the pervasive influence of Phelps Dodge ensured that "the atmosphere [was] the same in both," Beshoar was impressed with the aesthetic and demographic contrasts between Jerome and Clarkdale, where the company maintained its smelter. Describing the self-contained community as "strictly a company camp," he wrote, "Clarkdale is clean and modern. There are well-constructed brick houses which are rented to the workers, and the streets are wide and clean. There are simple facilities such as schools, a theater, a park, etc. I was unable to discover if any Mexican or Indian workers live in Clarkdale, but it is my opinion there are none. The Mexicans and Apache Indians, of whom there are large numbers, live in either Jerome or Cottonwood, a small community south of Clarkdale."[36]

When he sought to determine the extent to which the racial and ethnic consciousness that governed local patterns of living mirrored the labor policies of Phelps Dodge, Beshoar soon discovered that a climate of fear among its workers insulated the company from open criticism. "Workers in Jerome," he reported, "are perfectly aware of the company influence and the policy [of] supervision and are not disposed to talk to any person from the outside about themselves or their work." Yet if fear discouraged workers from cooperating with his investigation, Beshoar soon learned that the company's refusal to cooperate derived, in roughly equal measures, from a well-practiced style of combative management and an undisguised contempt for the FEPC's mission.

At each of his stops prior to arriving in the Jerome-Clarkdale area, Beshoar had met with copper company officials who exhibited a reasonably cooperative attitude even as they remained distrustful of his purpose and harbored an abiding conviction that his investigation was another example of unwelcome and unwarranted federal meddling. Yet in dealing with Charles Kuzell, who served both as the manager of the Jerome-Clarkdale operations and as "the representative of the Phelps-Dodge general management on all problems relating to labor in the Southwestern copper-producing area," Beshoar was confronted by a corporate representative who made no effort to mask his disdain for the FEPC, whose addressing of the "race question," he bluntly observed, amounted to nothing more than "a lot of sons-of-bitches . . . trying to stir up trouble."

Described by Beshoar as "belligerent when he discussed employment practices," Kuzell was nevertheless candid in acknowledging the company's use of ethnic and racial criteria in making job assignments. "Many jobs in the copper mines are traditionally white and I wouldn't think of putting a Mexican on them," he told Beshoar. "If I put a Mexican in the electrical shop the whites would walk out. They might not make a big fuss about it, but they would simply pick up their tools and walk out." That Anglo workers approved of the company's practices, he informed Beshoar, was confirmed during recently concluded contract negotiations with their unions, which "wanted to include language that would discriminate against Mexicans." Kuzell reported that the company had rejected the Anglos' demand in order "to keep our skirts clean," but when pressed for details he brusquely advised Beshoar that it was "none of [his] business." Unable to overcome the unwillingness of Phelps Dodge workers to confide in a stranger, and stymied in his attempt to collect employment and wage data relating to Chicanos by the company's bellicose management, Beshoar left Jerome with little to show for his efforts. Yet if the committee lacked the information required to assess the extent of discrimination against Chicano copper workers in the area, Charles Kuzell's defiant admission that Phelps Dodge segregated its labor force through the maintenance of separate "Anglo" and "Mexican" job categories plainly confirmed the existence of discrimination.[37]

As the largest employer of copper workers in the Southwest, the Phelps Dodge Corporation's labor policies served as an informal standard for the other mining companies in the region. And to the extent that Phelps Dodge officials, including the company's chief spokesman in matters of labor policy, made plain their intention to resist what they regarded as unjustified interference by federal "do-gooders," they put the FEPC on notice that discrimination against Chicano workers was a tradition that would not be abandoned without a fight.

The depth and force of the company's commitment to business as usual despite the existence of Executive Order 8802 was further impressed upon committee investigators when they extended their inquiry to other Phelps Dodge operations in the region. In the Clifton-Morenci district along Arizona's eastern border, where the company's massive open pit mine and ore-reduction works accounted, directly or indirectly, for nearly every job in the region, committee investigator Daniel Donovan found that the "empire and sovereignty of the Phelps Dodge Corporation" extended to every aspect of life. He reported after interviewing various community leaders, "it is apparent that segregation and discrimination against Spanish-speaking Americans is an established policy of the Phelps Dodge Corporation in the Morenci area." Donovan's interviews also disclosed a strongly held belief among many local residents, both Chicanos and Anglos, that as Phelps Dodge expanded its operation and extended its authority in the region during the late 1930s the company's policy of segregation "had been greatly intensified."

On the job, Donovan noted, Chicano workers faced a familiar assortment of unfair practices. "In reference to discrimination in employment," he wrote, "the same practice so generally evident in other Phelps Dodge plants is apparent in Morenci—a 'Mexican wage,' discrimination as to promotion of qualified workers to higher job classifications, and the general policy of favoritism to 'Anglos.'" Beyond the obvious disadvantages facing workers who were routinely relegated to the lowest wage and skill classifications, Donovan also discovered that because the local Selective Service Board typically granted draft deferments only to those Phelps Dodge employees working in skilled occupations Chicanos were more likely to be drafted for military service than were Anglos.[38]

Finally, in addition to reporting the existence of discrimination against Chicano workers by Phelps Dodge at its facilities in the Clifton-Morenci areas, Donovan pointedly advised his superiors that the prevailing employment practices in the region apparently resulted as much from deliberate corporate policies dictated by the company's New York headquarters as from the residual influences exerted by long-standing customs and traditions. Among those local residents who were willing to discuss the sensitive subject of discrimination, Donovan reported, there was a resolute consensus that Phelps Dodge president Louis Cates was personally "responsible for the intensified . . . segregation policy of the company."[39]

Simply by addressing the problem of employment discrimination against Chicanos in the Southwest, Donovan noted, the FEPC had aroused hope among workers whose historic subordination to Anglo power and control had long militated against optimism. Yet its success in exciting a collective sense of hope among Chicano copper workers, he warned, conferred a solemn obligation upon the FEPC to take decisive action against Phelps Dodge and the other mining companies whose discriminatory employment practices had been exposed by the committee's southwestern investigation. "The Spanish-speaking Americans with whom I have had contacts . . . will be greatly disappointed," he cautioned, "if a public hearing is not held regarding . . . discrimination in employment by Phelps Dodge and other industries in the Southwest."[40]

The emerging conviction that the Phelps Dodge Corporation was the key to remedying discrimination against Chicano copper workers was reinforced when committee investigators shifted their inquiry to the company's operations in the Bisbee-Douglas area along Arizona's southeastern border. At the company's legendary Copper Queen mining operation, whose fame derived from the prodigious quantities of copper, gold, and silver gouged from its deep passages, Donovan and Barron Beshoar found that only 15 percent of the more than 1,600 workers employed there were Chicanos and that, with the exception of about 30 who worked underground, they were confined to low-wage jobs as surface laborers in what the company itself designated as the "Mexican gang."[41] Bisbee, the site of the Copper Queen, had in its early years enjoyed a reputation as a riotous, rough-and-tumble mining town whose widely advertised inhospitability to non-Anglos, particularly to Chinese and Chicano workers, earned it the dubious distinction of being the "last white man's camp" in the West.[42] While the unwillingness of Phelps Dodge officials to provide information relating to the company's employment and wage policies made their job more difficult, Donovan and Beshoar were not long in concluding that insofar as the treatment of Chicanos was concerned Bisbee's reputation as a "white man's camp" remained largely intact.

Confined for the most part to neighborhoods on the edge of town, Chicanos also complained bitterly of being consigned to the fringes of opportunity by Phelps Dodge's employment policies. The company employed only Anglo workers in skilled occupations, its critics asserted, and ensured that such jobs remained off limits to Chicanos by denying them admission to the apprenticeship programs that supplied its needs for skilled labor. Even in the face of critical shortages of skilled labor, Donovan and Beshoar learned, Phelps Dodge refused to abandon its discriminatory recruitment policy. Referring to information provided by a local representative of the U.S. Employment Service, they reported, "Mr. Puckett said the company is always searching for men with ability, but that it does not look among the Mexicans for ability."[43]

As the investigation proceeded, it also became increasingly apparent to Donovan and Beshoar that Phelps Dodge maintained its policy of preferential treatment of Anglo workers with the help of the Bisbee Metal Trades Council, which coordinated the activities of the various AFL unions that had won bargaining rights at the Copper Queen mining division only a few weeks earlier.[44] That the Bisbee Metal Trades Council was involved in a collusive arrangement was confirmed by the president of the AFL Building Trades Council in nearby Douglas, who not only asserted that it had "a company-union relationship" with Phelps Dodge, but also claimed that the organizing drive that established its bargaining rights at the Copper Queen was sponsored and paid for by the company. Without admitting the truth of these allegations of collusion, an official of the Metal Trades Council did readily acknowledge that "there was definitely a double scale for [the] same or similar work in the Bisbee mines" and that Phelps Dodge maintained a discriminatory wage differential through the use of arbitrary job titles that meant "absolutely nothing."[45]

Given the relatively small number of Chicanos employed by Phelps Dodge at Bisbee, and the fact that the Anglo-dominated unions there appeared to share the company's interest in defending existing employment policies, Donovan and Beshoar found that the issue of discrimination against workers of Mexican descent was largely ignored. Only a few miles away in Douglas, however, where Phelps Dodge operated its huge Copper Queen smelter, they quickly discovered that the presence of a large Chicano work force represented by the Mine, Mill and Smelter Workers Union ensured intense interest in the issue.

Like their counterparts in Bisbee, and throughout the southwestern copper industry in general, Chicano workers at the Copper Queen smelter in Douglas were victimized by two particularly common forms of discrimination: a wage differential that denied them equal pay for equal work and a steadfast refusal by the company to promote or upgrade them into skilled occupations traditionally reserved to Anglos.

Yet, unlike their counterparts in most of the other centers of the Southwest, where fears of employer retribution tended to discourage formal complaints to the FEPC, Chicano smelter workers at Douglas were distinctly unbowed. Comprising roughly 60 percent of the smelter's 1,000-man work force and emboldened by a union that had made the elimination of discrimination one of its principal objectives, Chicanos greeted the appearance of committee investigators in Douglas with undisguised enthusiasm.[46]

Already well acquainted with the general character of discrimination against Chicano copper workers in the Southwest, Donovan and Beshoar were able to acquire through their interviews with disgruntled Phelps Dodge employees in Douglas the detailed evidence of unfair practices that had previously eluded them. Typical of the complaints they received was that filed by Jose Chavez, an Arizona native who, since going to work for Phelps Dodge in 1936, had discovered that once relegated to the smelter's lowest wage classification—"the so-called Mexican rate"—Chicano workers were systematically denied advancement. Chavez complained:

> During the six years I have been employed by the Phelps Dodge Corporation I have frequently asked for promotion to better jobs. Each time I have been told there were no openings available, but to my positive knowledge others, who were Anglo-Americans, have been promoted. In many instances these Anglos had less seniority than I had. Furthermore, I have had to train Anglos for particular jobs. These Anglos whom I trained received $6.22 per day from the day they started to work. At the time I was training these men I was receiving the so-called Mexican scale of $4.90 per day. Many of these Anglos, receiving $6.22 when they started to work, were then advanced to even higher rates of pay.

"To my positive knowledge," Chavez asserted, "the Phelps Dodge Corporation keeps Latin-American workers in the cheap labor classification while deliberately advancing Anglos into the higher paid jobs. Due to this racial discrimination, workers of Spanish extraction are kept in the lowest wage scales as a matter of company policy." As long as race and ethnicity determined eligibility for advancement at Phelps Dodge, Chavez concluded, Chicano workers would continue to languish at the bottom of the company's payroll "even though they have ability which warrants their receiving better pay and promotion."[47]

Still earning "the lowest wage in the plant" after seventeen years on the job at the Copper Queen smelter, Jose Estrada was equally critical of the company's employment policies. Embittered by the company's rejections of his repeated requests for promotion, and by its routine advancement of less senior Anglo workers to jobs that his ancestry rendered him ineligible to hold despite his demonstrated ability, Estrada related a plight common to Chicano workers on the Phelps Dodge payroll. "Since I have worked at the plant," he declared, "I have broken in fifty or sixty Anglos. I taught them their jobs, but I got the Mexican scale while I was teaching them their work and they got the so-called white scale. The Anglos got approximately $1.52 per day more while I was breaking them in." Explaining this otherwise paradoxical circumstance was, according to Estrada, quite simple. "I feel I am subjected to discrimination because of my race."[48]

Another veteran Chicano employee, Carlos Rivera, complained that job segregation at Phelps Dodge was so rigid that neither ability nor length of service mitigated the influence of race and ethnicity. Recalling an incident in 1936 when a momentary labor shortage resulted in his being assigned to a "white man's job," Rivera reported that the company's anxiety over such a breach of policy led the general foreman to remove him from the job within less than an hour. When Rivera asked why he was being replaced by an Anglo worker who, like himself, was classified as a laborer, the foreman explained that he was simply "putting an American in the American job." "I told him," Rivera stated, "I was born and raised here in the United States of America and that I was an American. He said: 'I don't care if you were born in China, you are still a Mexican and I am putting a white man in the job.'" Even after sixteen years on the job, Rivera ruefully observed, there was nothing but the "pick and shovel for Mexicans" at the Copper Queen smelter. "As a result of my own experiences and those of other Latin-Americans at the plant who I know well," he concluded, "it is perfectly plain to me that Mexican workers are held in the cheap labor class and are denied promotions even if they have ability with a view to exploiting them by keeping cheap labor. All of us Latin-Americans are discriminated against."[49]

In addition to the complaints they received from the alleged victims of discrimination at Phelps Dodge, Donovan and Beshoar found that the union's concern with the issue also led some Anglo smelter workers to denounce the company's employment practices. R. C. Carter, a union shop steward who had worked as a carpenter in the smelter's mechanical department since 1925, told Donovan and Beshoar that when he asked a Phelps Dodge supervisor why a job in the blacksmith shop had been given to an Anglo worker with less seniority than a Chicano worker who had applied for the opening the company official replied, "We have to save all of the best jobs for the Americans because they pay more money and that's the rule of the Company." "This was a confession of discrimination as far as I was concerned," Carter declared, "as I understood the term American, as he used it, to mean Anglo-American."[50]

Carter's allegation was confirmed by William Bates, another skilled Anglo smelter worker whose twenty years on the job, including thirteen years spent in a supervisory capacity, rendered him "thoroughly familiar with the employment policies of the company." Bates stated:

> To my positive and personal knowledge, the Phelps Dodge Corporation uses both a Mexican and a white scale . . . for the same or very similar work requiring no additional skill. I know that Anglo-Americans who have never worked in a smelter are brought in at higher wages than are paid to Latin-Americans who have been on the job as long as 20 years. From personal observation and acquaintance I know that many of these Mexican workers have capabilities which entitle them to promotion to better jobs, but they are denied such promotions because of their race.
>
> In my years with the company I know that it has been the policy of the company to pay a higher rate to Anglo-Americans than to Latin-Americans and to deny Latin-Americans promotions.[51]

When Donovan and Beshoar asked Stewart Carpenter, the superintendent of the Copper Queen smelter, for information regarding the company's wage and promotion policies, he responded, as had his counterpart at Bisbee, that only Harrison Lavender, the official in charge of all Phelps Dodge mining operations in the Southwest, could authorize cooperation with the committee's investigation. Speaking "off the record," however, Carpenter did confide his belief that "the Mexican people were not yet advanced enough to handle more money than they were receiving and that higher wages would be a corrupting influence."[52]

Given the cumulative weight of the evidence, it is doubtful that Phelps Dodge officials, even if they had been more forthcoming, could have explained the company's policies toward Chicano workers in a way that might have led Donovan and Beshoar to retreat from their conviction that discrimination permeated employment relations in Bisbee and Douglas as completely and insidiously as it did the whole of the copper industry in the Southwest. Nor is it likely that they could have been persuaded to abandon their belief that discrimination against Chicano copper workers was, despite a robust tradition of racial and ethnic bias in the region, fostered and perpetuated by compelling economic motives. In their report to Ernest Trimble on the wage differentials between Anglo and Chicano copper workers that appeared to exist throughout the Southwest, Donovan and Beshoar noted, "In all instances where the wage differential between Mexican and Anglo workers has been discussed with company officials, we have been given the idea that the differential is based upon tradition and a historical pattern. It is our belief that there is an economic factor." Elaborating this thesis, they wrote:

> Assuming that there are 5,000 [Chicano] workers in the copper mine labor class in the two states [Arizona and New Mexico], and many believe this is a fairly accurate estimate, a wage differential of $1.52 [per day] between the Mexican scale and the Anglo scale would be important from an economic point of view.
>
> If 5,000 Mexicans are paid a scale that is $1.52 per day less than that paid to Anglos, that would mean an aggregate saving to the copper companies of:
>
> | | |
> |---|---|
> | Per day . . . . | $ 7,600 |
> | Per week . . . . | 45,600 |
> | Per year . . . . | 2,371,200 |

"Many of these companies," they concluded, "have been operating more than 20 years; some for as long as 35 and 40 years. Taking 20 years as an average the condition described above would mean an aggregate saving in wages of: $47,424,000."[53]

In the end, however, documenting the existence of discrimination against Chicano copper workers in the Southwest was more important to FEPC investigators than discerning the motives of the companies that practiced it. After several weeks in the field surveying the employment and wage policies of the leading copper companies in the region, Trimble and his staff were fully persuaded that industry practices with regard to the treatment of Chicano workers constituted clear violations of Executive Order 8802. Based on the assessments provided by his field investigators, as well as the emphatic impression imparted during his own unavailing discussions with the recalcitrant officials of the company's El Paso refinery, Trimble was also convinced that eliminating discrimination against Chicano workers by the Phelps Dodge Corporation was the key to gaining compliance with the president's order throughout the remainder of the copper industry in the Southwest.

In Jerome, Morenci, Bisbee, and the other sites of Phelps Dodge's major operations, Trimble observed, the company's pervasive control and influence over nearly every aspect of industrial activity and community life bred a climate of fear and suspicion that he likened to "Harlan County, Kentucky, transferred to Arizona." "This Phelps Dodge Company is a tough one," he advised his superiors, and it appeared "very doubtful" that anything short of the maximum pressure the committee could bring to bear would produce necessary reforms.[54] As the largest copper producer in the Southwest, and the industry's "biggest offender" insofar as discrimination against Chicanos was concerned, Phelps Dodge posed what Trimble regarded as both the greatest challenge and the richest opportunity confronting the FEPC in the Southwest. "It is the toughest company we have to deal with," he confided to FEPC executive secretary Lawrence Cramer, "and if we could whip it into line, I think we would not have any difficulty with the other companies."[55]

But as Trimble plainly recognized, deciding where pressures for change could be most profitably applied was considerably easier than determining how, in light of the committee's enfeebled condition, such pressures might be generated. To the extent that the committee's investigation of discrimination against Chicanos in the Southwest was intended to reinflate the sagging hopes of those who had earlier lobbied for vigorous enforcement of Executive Order 8802 in the region, it had succeeded admirably. Yet in the course of restoring the faith of Chicano activists and CIO leaders in its resolve to implement the president's order, the committee necessarily reinforced its obligation to take forceful corrective actions once its investigation disclosed that there was, indeed, "considerable discrimination against Mexicans in the copper fields."[56]

Confessing to Cramer that the morale of the El Paso staff "dropped almost to zero" when it belatedly learned of the FEPC's transfer to the War Manpower Commission, Trimble was acutely aware from the moment of his arrival in the region that an even deeper disappointment awaited those who were trusting in the committee to redeem its promise of public hearings in the Southwest. "If these hearings are permanently called off," he only half-jokingly importuned Cramer, "give those of us here in the office time to get out of town before it is announced."[57] If Trimble truly hoped that he and his staff could complete their investigation and "get out of town" before the committee's local clients discovered that the El Paso hearings had been canceled, he was disappointed. Reports in the black press that the hearings had been postponed at the insistence of the State Department came to the attention of CIO officials in the region by mid-August, and their confidence in the committee, according to Trimble, quickly began "to wane." In order to keep the committee's credibility from eroding further, however, he strongly advised against an official announcement that the El Paso hearings had been called off. The major copper companies in the Southwest still appeared to be ignorant of the committee's diminished authority, he sanguinely informed Cramer, and "the threat and possibility of a hearing may correct the situation in regard to discrimination as well as a public hearing would."[58]

Notwithstanding the influence he hoped to exert through audacious bluffs and hollow threats, Trimble was keenly aware that, in the end, he would have to confront the redoubtable power of Phelps Dodge and the other copper companies in the Southwest with nothing more formidable than an appeal to patriotism and good corporate citizenship to sustain the committee's authority. As daunting as the challenge posed by the Southwest's biggest copper companies appeared to be, however, they—and the various interest groups, including AFL unions, that shared their aversion to change—merely symbolized the far more powerful forces of history and tradition that stood in the way of the committee's efforts to achieve equal treatment for Chicano workers within a regional culture founded upon a seemingly immutable assumption of Anglo dominion.

4. *Retreat from Fairness*

IN LIGHT OF the critical manpower shortages that faced copper companies in the Southwest during the summer and fall of 1942, full utilization of the available labor supply was more important than ever as the industry, along with the rest of the country's burgeoning strategic industries, struggled to meet rising wartime production goals.[1] While disquieted federal manpower officials cited high labor turnover resulting from relatively low wages and poor working conditions in the mines, mills, and smelters of the Southwest as the principal reason for the industry's deepening crisis, they privately acknowledged that endemic wage and employment discrimination against Chicano workers significantly increased the already serious labor shortages confronting the region's major copper companies. Even before the FEPC began its investigation in the Southwest, officials of the War Manpower Commission concluded that industry proposals to import Mexican nationals to ease labor shortages had little to commend them as long as copper producers in the region failed to utilize fully the Chicano workers already available to them.[2] In a subsequent report, the War Production Board reached a similar conclusion: "In some mining areas, particularly in the Southwest, Mexican mine workers constitute a substantial proportion of the total employment. The wage treatment which is accorded to these Mexican workers in some mining properties, however, acts as a deterrent to effective utilization of Mexican workers. In some properties the differentials between Mexican and American white workers is as high as $1 per shift for common labor. Moreover, in some properties there is a tendency to keep Mexican workers employed as common laborers even if they are skilled miners."[3]

Despite increasingly frequent and urgent declarations that forceful federal action was required to solve their growing manpower problems, industry spokesmen refused to acknowledge that the inability of southwestern copper companies to attract the labor that their expanding operations required was connected in any way to their continuing discrimination against Chicano employees. Throughout the fall of 1942 copper producers also continued to argue that their labor shortages should be alleviated, as had those of agribusiness in the Southwest, by importing Mexican workers.[4] Alarmed by falling copper production, federal officials readily agreed that immediate action was required to ease the industry's manpower problems, but multiplying reports of the discrimination against Chicano copper workers in the Southwest, including those generated by the FEPC's investigation, led them to sidestep employers' demands for a contract labor program with Mexico similar to that approved only a few weeks earlier for western agriculture.[5]

Carefully avoiding any reference to the issue of discrimination against Chicano workers, industry spokesmen complained, rather ironically, that the Roosevelt administration's refusal of its request for Mexican labor constituted a clear case of "outrageous discrimination" against the beleaguered copper companies of the Southwest. "From all parts of the nation," the *Mining Congress Journal* indignantly editorialized, "come cries of manpower shortages, some of the most frantic appeals coming from the southwestern states where so much of the nation's copper is produced. Our State Department and Department of Labor have arranged for the immigration of 2,000 workers from Mexico to help relieve the manpower shortage in western agriculture. Puzzling the mining industry . . . is the fact that the Mexican miners, long asked for, have not been permitted entrance to work in our copper mines under a similar arrangement." "Can it be," the journal's editor scornfully observed, "that New Deal pussyfooting 'power politics' supports the position of union leaders in that an influx of Mexican miners would weaken the union's bargaining power which capitalizes on maintaining a scarcity of labor in the copper mines?"[6]

The suspicion among employers that their proposal to import Mexican workers was being blocked by the Mine, Mill and Smelter Workers Union was not entirely unfounded. In preliminary discussions with the War Manpower Commission, MMSW officials did express serious reservations about the importation of Mexican workers. Their concerns, however, did not derive from a fear that "an influx of Mexican miners would weaken the union's bargaining power." Rather, the union advised WMC officials that it would not oppose the importation of Mexican copper workers if "all possible methods of filling the manpower shortage with American workers [were] exhausted" and if the government would "guarantee that Mexicans would not be brought into the U.S. to work in operations where discrimination is practiced."[7] And because the union endorsed the position that, in the end, winning the war against fascism overrode every other consideration, its own frequently voiced concern that copper production be increased at whatever cost suggested that even these two conditions were subject to compromise. Indeed, when the union approvingly reported to its membership in late October that the WMC was contemplating the importation of 1,200 Mexican miners to fill labor shortages in the copper industry of the Southwest, it made no mention whatever of the need for guarantees regarding the full utilization of existing manpower or the prior elimination of all wage and employment discrimination against Chicano workers by those companies intending to employ imported labor.[8]

The major copper companies in the Southwest would almost certainly have succeeded in their effort to recruit contract labor from Mexico had they agreed to eliminate discrimination against their Chicano employees. Yet their stubborn refusal to depart from wage and employment policies that the FEPC and other federal agencies found patently discriminatory even at the cost of continuing manpower shortages and lost production confirmed the depth of their commitment to business as usual. The employers' resolve also ensured that Ernest Trimble's efforts to eliminate discrimination against Chicano copper workers would be met by unbending resistance.

Trimble warned his superiors even before the committee's southwestern investigation was completed that gaining voluntary compliance with Executive Order 8802 was unlikely, given the unwillingness of the region's leading copper companies to acknowledge the existence of discrimination against Chicanos. While he still intended to threaten public hearings in the hope of persuading obdurate employers to reform their employment practices, his inability to go beyond threats left him convinced that the FEPC's prospects in the Southwest were uncertain at best.[9]

To avoid having to negotiate from a position of conspicuous weakness, Trimble sought both to enhance his authority and to enlist the support of potential allies before he confronted employers. Neither undertaking, however, produced the results he had hoped for. Having failed earlier in his attempts to persuade unsympathetic local representatives of various federal agencies, including the Social Security Board and the U.S. Employment Service, to assist the committee's investigation of unfair employment practices affecting Chicanos, Trimble's efforts to cloak his mission with the authority of the War Manpower Commission, the

FEPC's newly designated parent agency, proved similarly unavailing. Until the FEPC's relationship with the WMC was clarified, and the sharp differences between the two agencies over questions of jurisdiction and authority finally resolved, any possibility that the committee might employ the vastly greater influence of its new parent in support of its own puny enforcement power was, Trimble discovered, clearly forestalled.[10]

Marshaling the unified support of a bitterly divided labor movement behind the committee's enforcement campaign in the Southwest proved an equally elusive goal. Convinced that the "rivalry between the CIO and AFL . . . actually tended to promote discrimination" against Chicano copper workers, Trimble hoped that a "unity program" similar to that which committee investigators had urged upon rival unions at the Nevada Consolidated Copper Company's operations in the Hurley–Santa Rita region of New Mexico might be inaugurated in Arizona, where competition between AFL craft unions and the Mine, Mill and Smelter Workers appeared to buttress the discriminatory labor policies of the Phelps Dodge Corporation. Referring to the negotiations he proposed to conduct with the head of Phelps Dodge's scattered operations, Trimble hopefully reasoned, "If we could get the wholehearted cooperation of both the AFL and the CIO it is possible that we could exert enough pressure on the company's representative in Arizona to get some concession from him."[11]

With the MMSW's support assured, the success of Trimble's strategy depended on the disposition of AFL unions, whose fulsome endorsements of the committee activities in the Southwest belied collusive arrangements with Phelps Dodge that subordinated the interests of Chicano copper workers to those of the company and their own overwhelmingly Anglo memberships. Commenting on the ambivalent outlook of local AFL officials regarding the FEPC's mission in the region, one of Trimble's staff noted that they were "seemingly in accord with the objectives of our Committee, but the long established and profitable policy of a 'Mexican wage' classification by the Copper Companies in the Southwest and the attitude of many workers in the crafts can lead to concessions in line with traditional practice."[12]

To gain the cooperation he considered vital to his success in the region, Trimble instigated an appeal to Frank Fenton, the AFL's national director of organization. Fenton was in a position to be especially helpful since, following the departure of original committee member William Green in the fall of 1941, he served as the federation's representative on the FEPC. Hoping, as he explained to his superiors, to persuade

Fenton "to send a wire to the AFL representative in the Southwest . . . ordering him to cooperate with us in eliminating discrimination," Trimble delegated the task to committee investigator Daniel Donovan, whose credentials included a lengthy stint as a federation organizer.[13] Gently reminding Fenton that he was "to a considerable degree responsible for [the committee's] investigation . . . in the Southwest," Donovan reported that conditions in the copper industry merited forceful action. "There is no doubt," he wrote, "of a long existing practice of discrimination in the matter of wage rates for Mexican workers and a policy of holding such workers, regardless of length of service or qualification, to the 'Mexican' wage." While he was careful to apportion the largest share of responsibility for discrimination to the region's major copper companies, Donovan informed Fenton that the committee's investigation had plainly revealed that AFL unions, notably those dealing with Phelps Dodge, were consciously abetting employer violations of Executive Order 8802. Even AFL building trades officials in the region, he assured Fenton, readily corroborated charges "that the Phelps Dodge Company has an understanding with the AFL crafts to support the double scale of wages and that Mexicans are kept from jobs in the higher wage groups by this understanding."

Purposefully noting that the company's "hostility to Organized Labor over the years is well known," Donovan claimed that eliminating discrimination at Phelps Dodge's various operations was not only the key to establishing fair employment practices throughout the copper industry of the Southwest, but an essential prerequisite to more far-reaching improvements in the collective status of the region's Chicano population. "The whole system of Mexican discrimination as it shows itself by segregation in schools, restaurants and Anglo clubs," he argued, "will be to a great extent removed when the wage scale for the job is the same for Anglos and Mexicans, and when promotion on the basis of qualification is also equal." "The authority to deal with any collusion to retain the existing wage discrimination existing between the copper producing companies in the Southwest district and the AFL crafts is in your hands to an unusual degree," Donovan observed. By using that authority in a way that might encourage AFL officials in the region "to cooperate with us to remove this Mexican discrimination," he concluded, Fenton could make an invaluable contribution to the committee's success.[14]

Although Paul Peterson, the AFL's representative in the region, advised Trimble that he would "agree to a unity program if Fenton says so," no such pressure was exerted from the federation's Washington headquarters. Whether Fenton's apparent disinclination to intervene in the Southwest was due to policy considerations or to a simple lack of authority on his part to take the forceful action the FEPC requested is unclear. Yet, whatever the reasons, the AFL made no significant effort to assist the FEPC's enforcement activities in the Southwest and the goal of a labor unity program, though it initially won the cautious endorsement of a few craft union officials in the region, was never achieved.[15] That is not to say, however, that AFL representatives in the region were invariably unsympathetic to the committee's efforts in behalf of equal opportunity for Chicano copper workers. Commenting on the Phelps Dodge Corporation's treatment of Chicano workers at its mine and smelter in the Jerome-Clarkdale district, O. A. Dever, an AFL organizer, confessed to committee investigators, "We all know that the Phelps Dodge Corporation takes the position that they will not advance these people. This seems to me to be decidedly unfair to our Latin American workmen. . . . They are competent and efficient men and thru the action of the corporation the incentive to try for a higher position and to really demonstrate what they are capable of doing has been taken from them." Yet, despite his sympathetic disposition, Dever—and like-minded AFL leaders similarly immobilized by their apparent sensitivity to Anglo constituents in the skilled trades—regarded discrimination against Chicanos as a problem for the FEPC alone to solve. "Should your committee be able to eliminate this unfair practice . . . ," he observed, "you will have done a great service not only to the Latin-American people, but to the Anglo races as well. As long as the corporation continues this policy they can use this lower paid group as a club over the heads of the other group, and in this way keep one group working against the other."[16]

Except for the Mine, Mill and Smelter Workers Union, whose still precarious position in the copper industry of the Southwest made it a somewhat feeble ally, the FEPC quickly discovered that it was on its own in trying to alleviate the problem of discrimination against Chicano workers. That Chicano activists within struggling MMSW locals throughout the Southwest were passionate in their commitment to eliminate discriminatory employment practices was never in doubt. They were, however, well aware that, until the MMSW succeeded in overcoming the fierce opposition of both employers and its AFL rivals, the union power they hoped ultimately to wield in the cause of equal treatment on the job could not be secured. And because the determined and relentless opposition meant that victories were almost never easily or finally won by their union, Chicano loyalists of the MMSW were under pressure throughout the war to be trade unionists first and members of an aggrieved minority second.

In much the same way, the MMSW, as ardently as it wished the committee to succeed in combating discrimination against Chicano copper workers, was too busy with the consuming challenges of union building to take on any more of the FEPC's work than it already had.[17] The relatively few Chicano organizations active in behalf of equal employment opportunity in the region were also unable to offer the committee anything more than moral support. To be sure, they had eloquently expressed the historic grievances of those victimized because of their racial and ethnic heritage, but their collective capacity to effect change in an Anglo-dominated society was not perceptibly greater than the sum of their members' individual powerlessness. Even such groups as the Texas-based League of United Latin American Citizens, perhaps the best-organized and most visible of the middle-class organizations active in behalf of equal rights for Chicanos, were generally too limited in their political influence and circumspect in their agitational tactics to add much in the way of effective support to the FEPC's enforcement efforts in the Southwest. Their contribution had been in helping to apprise federal officials of the discriminatory practices that confronted Chicano workers, and they believed, not without justification, that it was the government's responsibility to enforce the national policy promulgated to end those abuses.[18]

Once it became apparent to him that the FEPC could not expect much help in trying to eliminate discrimination against Chicano workers, Ernest Trimble sought to accomplish what he could with the meager resources at hand. To start with, he encouraged his superiors to adopt a strategy designed to exert simultaneous pressures against offending copper companies at their New York corporate headquarters as well as at their southwestern operations. Such a strategy was particularly desirable in dealing with the Phelps Dodge Corporation, he argued, since it was apparent that officials in Arizona would "make no move on employment matters" without the prior approval of the company's president, Louis Cates. "It seems obvious," he advised Lawrence Cramer, "that the key to the whole southwestern copper situation is Mr. Louis Cates." While confessing that he "would very much like to see this Phelps Dodge Company whipped," Trimble warned that if such a result was to be achieved "strong measures will have to be taken against Cates."[19] If the committee agreed that Phelps Dodge "might be handled from the top easier than from the bottom," he wrote, "it might be well for us to have pressure being exerted from both the top and the bottom at the same time."[20]

While the committee was apparently willing to confront the New

York–based corporate managements of Phelps Dodge and other copper companies when and if it became necessary, Cramer instructed Trimble to begin direct negotiations with the firms' regional representatives as a first step toward adjusting individual complaints of discrimination and securing pledges of future compliance with the president's order. He also authorized Trimble to issue separate warnings to officials of each of the companies against whom complaints had been filed that public hearings would "have to be held either in El Paso or Washington if no satisfactory adjustment is made." While the committee no longer had the authority to convene public hearings in the Southwest on the general subject of discrimination against Chicano workers, Cramer apparently believed that its power to conduct public hearings involving individual employers remained in force. Yet despite his seeming determination to pursue complaints against the region's major copper companies, even to the extent of conducting public hearings, Cramer instructed Trimble to close the committee's El Paso office and return to Washington as soon as his efforts to negotiate settlements were completed.[21]

Armed with little more than an ardent conviction that the company was "as guilty as hell," Trimble began his negotiations with representatives of Phelps Dodge at the end of August. During a lengthy meeting with Charles Kuzell, the tough-talking head of labor relations for Phelps Dodge in Arizona, Trimble suggested that if the company was interested in "settling out of court" it would have to "accept Executive Order 8802 and be guided by it in its future dealings" with all employees; to post notices throughout its facilities that all hiring, promotion, and wage policies would operate "without regard to race, color, creed or national origin"; to submit "periodical reports to the Committee"; and to dispose of existing individual complaints of discrimination "in accordance with the spirit of the Executive Order."

Kuzell, whose amiability during the day-long discussions contrasted sharply with his earlier belligerence, responded that, since Phelps Dodge was already "following the spirit of the Executive Order" and would continue to do so in the future, agreeing to Trimble's proposed terms for a settlement "would be a confession of guilt." As an alternative, he suggested that all complaints of discrimination filed by Chicano workers at the company's Copper Queen smelter in Douglas should be resolved through the operation of grievance procedures previously agreed to in the collective bargaining agreement between Phelps Dodge and the Mine, Mill and Smelter Workers Union. Such an approach, he asserted, had already been endorsed by the National War Labor Board, which had, in the course of its intervention a few months before in contract negotiations that had bogged down over the issue of promotion policies at the Douglas smelter, ordered that all complaints of discrimination lodged by Chicano workers should be settled through the grievance process that the parties had adopted.[22]

In relaying Kuzell's counterproposal to Cramer, Trimble left little doubt as to his own skepticism, especially since the grievance machinery in place at Phelps Dodge's unionized operations was noticeably inert. Trimble also voiced his suspicion that Kuzell's proposal was based on a cynical assumption that the company's collusive relationships with Anglo-dominated AFL unions at several of its biggest operations would continue to discourage the filing and processing of grievances by Chicano workers. "Kuzell now takes the position," he reported,

> that we ought to wait and give the grievance machinery a chance to solve these complaints before we intervene, and because we have come here, he is injecting a little activity into the grievance machinery, at least at the Douglas, Arizona, operation. He seems to feel more guilty in connection with that operation than any of the others, that is, he thinks we can make our strongest case there. Since in the other operations he is dealing with AFL unions which have been accused of being largely company unions, I think he hopes to prevent any serious complaints arising in the rest of the field outside of Douglas. Then, if he could get us to stay out of Douglas and give the grievance machinery a chance to operate, he thinks he can get by without being involved with a public hearing.

As long as there was "collusion between the company and the [AFL] unions and a lack of interest in the [Executive] Order on the part of the unions," Trimble observed, there was no reason to believe that discrimination against Chicano workers would be eliminated through the operation of existing grievance procedures. "I am sure he does fear a public hearing," Trimble wrote in reference to Kuzell, "but he is by nature a fighter," and his unwillingness to accept the committee's terms for a settlement suggested that "he is bluffing or else he has heard something that makes him think that we will not go through with the hearing." Kuzell's unrepentant attitude reflected the uniformly defiant mindset of Phelps Dodge's corporate management, Trimble believed, and even if public hearings were held he remained reluctant to predict the company's ultimate submission to FEPC dictates regarding the treatment of its Chicano employees. "I think this company is guilty as hell," he bluntly informed Cramer, "but it will be hard to prove. They will bribe and intimidate, and they often give old jobs new names to justify paying Anglos a higher wage. The result is that one must know the inside operations of the plant well in order to pass upon the company's defense."[23]

Operating for the most part without helpful instructions or useful advice from his superiors in Washington, who were preoccupied throughout the fall of 1942 with the increasingly urgent need to defend the committee's freedom of action,[24] Trimble quickly accommodated himself to the necessity for compromise in dealing with Phelps Dodge. In a letter to Harrison Lavender, the top Phelps Dodge official in the Southwest, Trimble reiterated the terms of settlement he had earlier suggested to Kuzell, but added, despite his private reservations, that complaints of discrimination already filed against the company could be settled through existing grievance procedures, with an FEPC representative "sitting in" to ensure compliance "with the spirit of Executive Order 8802." Rebutting Kuzell's earlier contention that accepting that the committee's terms was "tantamount to a confession of guilt," Trimble assured Lavender of the FEPC's willingness "to let by-gones be by-gones" and to regard Phelps Dodge's acceptance of the proposed terms of settlement as "evidence of good faith without any imputation on the part of the Committee itself that the company was guilty." Raising once again the specter of public hearings, Trimble observed that "it would be much better for all concerned" if the company voluntarily agreed to comply with the president's nondiscrimination order.[25]

While Phelps Dodge and the other copper companies on the committee's list of offending employers were clearly desirous of avoiding the adverse publicity that would result from public hearings, their dread of such an eventuality was not great enough to induce submission to Trimble's terms. Apparently convinced that their strategic importance made it unlikely that the Roosevelt administration would permit the FEPC's enforcement efforts to jeopardize copper production,[26] the companies had little to lose by resisting Trimble's overtures. By steadfastly denying all allegations of discrimination against Chicano workers, Phelps Dodge and the other copper companies that Trimble confronted placed the burden of proof on the committee, whose inability to subpoena pertinent employment records placed it at an obvious disadvantage.

The committee's investigation of employment practices in the Southwest had confirmed the existence of pervasive discrimination against Chicano copper workers, but a strict construction of Executive Order 8802 limited the FEPC to acting only on behalf of individual complainants. While discriminatory wage and employment policies in the southwestern copper industry were directed against Chicano workers as a class rather than as individuals, Trimble found that his effective authority to confront violators of the president's order existed only in proportion to the willingness of individual victims of discrimination to come forth, at real or imagined personal risk, for the purpose of lodging specific complaints of mistreatment on the job. Even when the committee succeeded in persuading aggrieved workers to come forward, Trimble soon realized that individual complaints could be fully investigated and properly adjudicated only if the employers against whom they were lodged voluntarily agreed to cooperate with his efforts to effect settlements. With the copper companies in anything but a cooperative mood, Trimble was forced to proceed on the basis of what was attainable under distinctly unfavorable circumstances rather than with an intention of uncompromisingly enforcing the letter of Executive Order 8802.

In the hope of strengthening his hand in dealing with Phelps Dodge, Trimble asked both AFL and CIO officials to supply him with information relating to internal employment practices that was inaccessible to him because of the company's uncooperative disposition. Since few if any formal complaints had been received from Chicano workers employed at those Phelps Dodge operations where AFL unions alone enjoyed bargaining rights, Trimble urged local trade union leaders to solicit affidavits from known victims of the company's discriminatory practices. To O. A. Dever, an AFL organizer who had earlier acknowledged that Chicanos at the company's Jerome-Clarkdale facilities were afraid to protest their mistreatment, Trimble wrote:

> Your report on conditions in Jerome-Clarkdale supports the other reports which we have received from several sources about discrimination against Latin-American people in this section. In order, however, for the Committee on Fair Employment Practice to take any effective steps to correct the situation, we must have specific affidavits setting forth how each particular individual has himself been discriminated against. . . .
>
> I readily understand the fear of the workers that signing such a complaint might bring some kind of a penalty. Can you not, however, overcome this fear on the parts of workers by assuring them that their union will protect them against any punitive action on the part of their employer?[27]

While Trimble believed that having formal complaints of discrimination from Chicano workers employed at each of the various branches of the Phelps Dodge complex in the Southwest might strengthen the committee's case against the company if public hearings were eventually held, his increasingly solicitous efforts to arrange a settlement that would make such a potentially volatile confrontation unnecessary yielded little. On the instructions of Lawrence Cramer, Trimble softened his initial terms even further by suggesting that Phelps Dodge and the other copper companies with which he was negotiating could satisfy the requirements of the president's order by formally announcing their commitment to fair employment practices and notifying their own personnel officers and supervisors, as well as the unions, employment services, and job-training agencies they dealt with, that all workers would be recruited, trained, paid, and upgraded "without regard to their race, creed, color or national origin."[28]

After outlining the committee's presumably less onerous terms to Charles Kuzell at a largely unproductive meeting held in Phoenix during the second week of September, Trimble rather plaintively added, "You will note that nothing is said about the past policy of the Company and as far as I can see there is no implication of guilt. Such an agreement would, however, give the committee definite assurance of the Company's good faith." So anxious, in fact, was he to reach an agreement with Phelps Dodge that he accepted Kuzell's argument that compliance with the committee's fair practices guidelines should be expected only to the extent that it could be accomplished without jeopardizing the "harmonious operation" of the company's facilities. By expressing his willingness to accept such a condition, which was prompted by the company's unproven claim that Anglo workers would not tolerate the intrusion of Chicanos into certain skilled trades, Trimble, who was acting on his own authority, made plain his determination to achieve a settlement in the Southwest even at the expense of the committee's credibility. Not much of that credibility was retrieved by his rather lame stipulation that the committee would expect the company to "do everything reasonable to bring about cooperation on the part of any recalcitrant employees in applying Executive Order 8802 in the hiring and promoting of employees."[29]

Despite Trimble's offer of a settlement so generous that it would have permitted Phelps Dodge to determine the extent of its compliance with the president's order, Kuzell's belief that the War Production Board could be counted upon to block the public hearings the FEPC had threatened apparently convinced him that even a token concession to the committee's authority was unnecessary. Dejectedly confessing to Lawrence Cramer in mid-September that he was "not very hopeful of a satisfactory agreement" with the company, Trimble wrote, "In case I fail to reach an agreement with the Phelps Dodge Corporation I think we ought to proceed at once with a public, not a private, hearing. It is only a public hearing that the corporation dreads and that will have any influence on the corporation." Even though Kuzell was "hoping that enough pressure can be exerted to prevent a hearing," Trimble predicted that the committee might still achieve a partial victory if it made good its threat to expose Phelps Dodge's discriminatory employment practices to public scrutiny. "I have the evidence in my files," he assured Cramer, "to convict the company of discrimination in the Douglas-Bisbee area and I believe also enough to convict the refinery here in El Paso. The policy of the company in the A. F. of L. sections is of course the same but I am unable to get the specific affidavits to convict the company in these areas."[30]

Trimble's view that Phelps Dodge was unlikely to reform its employment practices in the Southwest in response to any pressures short of public hearings was heartily endorsed by many civic and trade union leaders throughout the region. Reflecting the opinion of those whose hopes for change had begun to fade as the inefficacy of the committee's discreet and dilatory methods became increasingly apparent, Rabbi Wendell Phillips of El Paso urged the FEPC to bring the problem of job discrimination "into the open" by subjecting Phelps Dodge to immediate public hearings. "It would be a great blow," Phillips declared, "to realize that Phelps Dodge, one of our leading industries and a long time offender in matters of discrimination, was able to dominate the scene today."[31]

Reid Robinson, the president of the Mine, Mill and Smelter Workers Union, issued an even more forceful demand that the FEPC get on with its public hearings into the discriminatory employment policies of copper companies in the Southwest. Addressing delegates to the union's 39th convention in early September, Robinson declared, "It is unfortunate that the Fair Employment Practices Committee was prevailed upon by vested interests and by old-time politicians in the State Department to call off its announced hearings in El Paso, Texas, in August to consider the question of discrimination against our Spanish-American brothers. . . . The failure of this committee to carry out its commitments is a victory for the reactionary forces of the Southwest." "It is still possible," he suggested, "for the committee to hold such hearings and I recommend that this convention call upon the Fair Employment Practices Committee to fulfill its function by so doing."[32]

Since the committee had earlier authorized the threats of public hearings that Trimble repeatedly employed in his negotiations with Phelps

Dodge and the other copper companies, it was hardly in a position to reject his recommendation to proceed with them. But while the committee agreed that public hearings would be scheduled if Trimble was unable to reach satisfactory settlements, Lawrence Cramer informed him that hearings involving Phelps Dodge and the other copper companies with "eastern headquarters" would be held in Washington rather than in the Southwest.[33] Whether Washington was selected as the proposed hearing site because of its proximity to the corporate offices of Phelps Dodge and the other companies or because the committee believed that holding hearings in the Southwest constituted an unacceptable political provocation is not clear.

Yet whatever the committee's reasons for designating Washington as the site of any future hearings into the problem of discrimination against Chicano copper workers, Trimble expressed immediate reservations. "I am wondering about the nature of the public hearing in Washington that you contemplate. I am wondering, for instance, if you are planning to present my record only to the company's representatives there, or if you plan to transport some witnesses. I wonder if the former plan would be satisfactory. What would happen, I believe, is that [Louis] Cates would have Kuzell come to Washington, and he would merely enter a denial except as to some failure to up-grade. This failure to up-grade, he would attribute to opposition on the part of the rank and file of the A. F. of L. unions." He added, "I wonder if the result of this type of hearing would not be inconclusive. To actually convict the company in the eyes of the Committee, I believe it would be highly desirable that we be able to put good witnesses on the stand, both Anglos and Mexicans, who know in detail the operations of the plant and the policy of the company. They could expose much better than I any defense that Kuzell would offer."

Perhaps to remind Cramer of just how defiant and intransigent Phelps Dodge remained in the face of the committee's inquiry into its treatment of Chicano workers, Trimble pointedly added:

> The C.I.O. organizer, with whom Mr. Kuzell conferred last week, is in town here now. He tells me that Kuzell, during the discussion and in the presence of Stanley White, Conciliator for the Department of Labor, suggested that certain jobs in his smelter at Douglas be reserved for Anglos. This is in itself a confession of discrimination and is in line with the company's past policy of reserving the best jobs for Anglos. Kuzell told me also that he had proposed to Mr. Larson, the C.I.O. representative, that Mexicans and Anglos be promoted on a 50-50 basis. Since the Anglos

would necessarily come from the outside, that too is a confession of discrimination.[34]

Trimble's pessimistic assessment of the committee's chances for reaching a satisfactory agreement with Phelps Dodge was confirmed when Charles Kuzell formally rejected his proposed terms for settlement on September 23. As far as Phelps Dodge was concerned, Kuzell declared, the FEPC had manufactured an "issue" based on allegations of employment discrimination that were wholly unfounded. "There is no issue between us that we know of," he argued, "except your proposed treatment of the matter and your threat to hold a hearing, or, as you express it, settle the issues in court if we do not follow a procedure suggested by you." Referring to the alleged discrimination against Chicano workers at the company's Copper Queen smelter in Douglas, the only Phelps Dodge operation in Arizona from which the committee had received formal complaints, Kuzell claimed that to the extent disputes existed they were matters to be resolved through grievance procedures already in place.

"During the negotiations of a contract between the Smelter Division of the Copper Queen Branch of the Phelps Dodge Corporation and the International Union of Mine, Mill and Smelter Workers, C.I.O.," Kuzell stated, "the latter raised the issue that workers of Mexican origin did not have equal promotion rights." With the help of a federal conciliator, he explained, the company and the union agreed on a contract provision stating that "equal opportunity for employment and advancement . . . shall be made available to all to the fullest extent and as rapidly as is consistent with efficient and harmonious operation of the plant." "This clause," he continued, "was reviewed and approved by the War Labor Board, who, to implement the clause, provided for an arbitrator to decide any unadjusted grievances arising over the application of the clause. The War Labor Board panel hearing the disputes between the Company and the C.I.O. was also fully aware of the President's Executive Order 8802 and recommended that should any question of the proper application or interpretation of the clause arise that the arbitrator should be guided by the spirit and language of the executive order."

Implicitly disputing the FEPC's jurisdiction over claims of employment discrimination that had become a subject of collective bargaining and contract administration, Kuzell also argued that arbitration under the auspices of the War Labor Board was a far better method of deciding the company's contractual obligations to its Chicano employees than the coercive and disruptive means that the committee had threatened to employ. "Arbitration appears to us," he sternly lectured Trimble, "to be a very practical and sensible way to implement the clause. It is preferable to a public hearing or a trial, as you refer to it, since the arbitration hearing differs from the trial since it is private and not public, is creative and not destructive, restores good will and friendship instead of destroying them, works toward an elimination of disputes and not a creation of disputes, creates understanding and not partisanship or prejudice, heals wounds and does not create wounds."

"I think we all agree," he asserted, "that a 'trial' is not necessary; however, you express a desire to enforce some form of paper action, which desire, you say, is predicated upon your wish that we give your committee some definite assurances of the Company's good faith. This good faith is surely proved by the contract and arbitration and our statement that we will abide by the decisions of the arbitrator." Lest the FEPC's ardor blind it to the fact that winning the war remained the federal government's essential goal, Kuzell concluded, "Our war efforts require copper. The war policies and orders of the President require compliance by everyone, so the maximum contributions can be made toward the war. We intend to so conduct our operations that these results will be accomplished."[35]

While Phelps Dodge, because of its dominant position in the copper industry of the Southwest, was the focus of Trimble's enforcement activities, his negotiations with the other companies suspected of discriminating against Chicano workers also proved difficult. The Nevada Consolidated Copper Company, with operations in Santa Rita and Hurley, New Mexico, as well as Ray, Arizona, continued to deny that its employment policies were discriminatory and thus rejected Trimble's proposals for reform as unnecessary.[36] The other two major companies against which the committee had complaints of discrimination, the Miami Copper Company and the Inspiration Copper Company, jointly adopted a less confrontational strategy, one intended to mollify Trimble without actually requiring significant modifications of their employment practices in regard to Chicano workers. Appropriating to their own needs the notion of conditional compliance originally formulated by Phelps Dodge, representatives of both companies pledged following joint conferences with Trimble in late September to recruit and promote their employees "without regard to race, creed, color or national origin." Emphasizing the grudging and conditional nature of their decision, however, each company, in language that Trimble had apparently approved in advance, pointedly stipulated, "It was the understanding gained at our conferences that it is not the purpose or intent of the President's order to interfere with or disrupt the orderly and maximum production of copper, and therefore, such order should be observed insofar as it is consistent with the efficient and harmonious operation of the Company's business."[37]

In accepting a compromise settlement providing for conditional compliance with Executive Order 8802, a course of action he had expressed a willingness to follow during his earlier negotiations with Phelps Dodge, Trimble was acting without the prior approval of his superiors. Consequently, he set about the task of selling the idea to Washington even before it had been reduced to writing. Readily acknowledging to Lawrence Cramer that the proposed settlement was based on "weasel words" that permitted the managements of Miami and Inspiration to determine the extent to which fair employment practices would be observed at their operations, Trimble nevertheless defended his action as necessary and reasonable.

"These words were suggested by the War Labor Board in a recent case before it," he wrote in defense of the dispensation he had worked out with representatives of the Miami and Inspiration companies, "and these men wanted these phrases included because they contend that there are some cases in which the promotion of a Mexican worker would cause some of their Anglos to walk out of the plant." In light of the worsening manpower shortage confronting them, he advised Cramer, the companies were justified in their concern. "At the present time," he explained, "there is a scarcity of workers in the copper mining industry. . . . These companies are, therefore, not in a position to take a chance on causing some of their employees to leave." He contended, "I think there is some basis for the belief that some of these Anglos might walk out if Mexicans were promoted into the crafts."

While he was well aware that conditional compliance created opportunities for abuse, Trimble assured Cramer that both companies had promised to "make every reasonable effort to induce any recalcitrant employees to cooperate fully in applying the Executive Order in hiring and promoting workers. . . . The important thing is that the Company not use this as an excuse. I told them that we were very much interested in continued and efficient operation of the mining industry, but that we wanted to be assured that the Management would cooperate with the committee in applying the Executive Order." A promise of good faith, he admitted, was not a guarantee, since "in interpreting and applying this agreement the honesty and integrity of the Management will be very important." "But," he added, "that would be true with any agreement that we made."

Trimble's personal frustration and acute sense of impotence after several weeks of fruitless negotiations had led him to acquiesce in an agreement that he knew was problematical. He recognized that in the end the arrangement he had worked out with Miami and Inspiration might not win committee approval. Yet while he plainly believed that he had accomplished as much as was possible under the circumstances, he dutifully invited Cramer to "chuck the whole agreement if you wish to."[38]

On September 25, a little more than two months after he opened the FEPC's temporary office in El Paso, Trimble returned to Washington. Prevented from carrying out the original purpose of his mission, the holding of public hearings into allegations of discrimination against Chicano workers in the Southwest, he departed the region with little to show for his efforts. In an industry found to be rife with employment discrimination, Trimble's lone success was in eliciting vague promises from two companies that they would abide by the letter and spirit of Executive Order 8802 as long as they could do so on their own terms. Shortly after his return to Washington, Trimble saw even this dubious accomplishment negated.

Concluding that the agreement Trimble had negotiated with Miami and Inspiration represented a transparent effort to skirt the requirements of the president's order, Lawrence Cramer promptly voided the section providing that the companies were obliged to observe fair employment practices only when doing so was "consistent with the efficient and harmonious operation" of their businesses. In the wake of Cramer's decision, Trimble was forced to notify officials of both companies that the crucial basis of their agreement had been nullified. In separate letters to each company, Trimble somewhat apologetically explained:

> You will recall that I pointed out at our first meeting that I did not have authority to bind the Committee by an agreement, but could only make a tentative agreement subject to the approval of Mr. Cramer, Executive Secretary of the Committee. . . . He approves of it except in one respect. He objects to the qualification implied in the statement that "such Order should be observed insofar as it is consistent with the efficient and harmonious operation of the company's business." He appreciates the difficulty of the employer's position, but feels that since the Order is law, the agreement should provide for its unqualified acceptance by the company.

"If an interruption of the company's operation should occur or be seriously threatened by observing the Order," he wrote in further explanation of Cramer's attitude, "such fact, he feels, should be reported to the Committee. By this method the unions or employees responsible for a violation of the Order could be isolated and the Committee could proceed directly against them. It would also have the effect of relieving the company of any responsibility or blame." While Trimble was keenly aware that conditional compliance was the feature that had made the original agreement palatable to each company, he nevertheless sanguinely requested that "this qualifying provision be dropped from our proposed agreement and that instead your company agree to hire, promote and pay its employees in accordance with Executive Order 8802, and that it report to the Committee on Fair Employment Practice any interruption or serious threat of interruption of the company's operations resulting from such a policy."[39]

As formidable as his task had proven to be during his stay in the Southwest, Trimble had at least been in a position to deal directly and personally with both supporters and opponents of the committee's mission. With his return to Washington, the immediacy and gravity that had attached to the issue of job discrimination as a result of his presence in the region quickly dissipated. To the extent that his presence had communicated the resolve of the FEPC to establish equal opportunity on the job as effective public policy, his departure tended to symbolize to both workers and employers alike the committee's retreat from vigorous remedial action. On a more practical level, however, Trimble's departure from the region meant that the committee was once again forced to rely upon local informants, both friendly and unfriendly, as a basis for monitoring compliance with the president's order by copper companies in the Southwest.

Despite the committee's conspicuous failure to achieve its announced purposes in the Southwest, neither Trimble nor Cramer was willing to admit defeat. Instead, they sought a new face-saving arrangement that would not, as Trimble's proposal of conditional compliance had, require the committee to submit to terms that might be interpreted as a capitulation to recalcitrant employers or an accommodation to discriminatory practices. The approach they chose to follow, which was embodied in proposals Trimble made to the Inspiration Copper Company and the Miami Copper Company in mid-October, consisted of nothing more than a requirement that each company state in writing that it "stands behind the President's Order and has directed strict compliance with adherence thereto."[40] When the companies readily accepted the proposal,

Trimble was apparently content to regard the question of their compliance with the president's order as having been settled to the committee's satisfaction.[41] Such an arrangement, while it may have served the purposes of both the companies and the committee, failed to ensure that discrimination against the Chicano workers it affected would, in fact, be either reduced or eliminated. Indeed, even as he fashioned the settlement with Miami and Inspiration officials, Trimble was drafting a final report on his southwestern investigations in which he unequivocally asserted that discrimination against Chicano workers by the region's leading copper companies was so pervasive and deeply rooted that nothing short of public hearings was likely to generate the pressure required to ameliorate the problem.[42]

In light of his inability to project the committee's authority with enough credibility to chasten defiant employers, an already familiar problem that had become more frequent and pronounced during the fall of 1942 as the FEPC floundered under the ambivalent stewardship of the War Manpower Commission, Trimble's eagerness to settle for vague promises of compliance with the president's order is not surprising. Once the decision was made, he sought to reach a similar accommodation with Phelps Dodge, whose continuing opposition to even a token settlement threatened to undermine the committee's claim that it was making progress in eliminating discrimination against Chicano workers in the Southwest.

Phelps Dodge, however, presented special problems for Trimble. With complaints of discrimination still coming in from various company operations, especially those at Morenci and Douglas, where the independent activism of local community leaders and the Mine, Mill and Smelter Workers Union had created especially keen expectations of the committee among aroused Chicano workers, proposing a settlement that was more cosmetic than substantive ignored Phelps Dodge's defiant commitment to business as usual.[43] Except for what one union activist characterized as a few token upgradings of Chicano workers at its Douglas smelter, which occurred in response to direct pressures exerted by the MMSW rather than by the FEPC, Phelps Dodge's policies in regard to wages, job assignments, and promotions, each of which Trimble had found to be discriminatory, remained fully in force.[44]

Still, since he could not reasonably expect Phelps Dodge to accept more stringent terms than those embodied in the committee's freshly concocted arrangements with Miami and Inspiration, Trimble was in the ironic position of having to ignore the company's unabated defiance of the committee in order to reach a nominal settlement designed to salvage what remained of the FEPC's sagging credibility rather than to eliminate discriminatory employment practices. Perhaps because Phelps Dodge officials, despite their previous resistance to compromise, sensed that the committee was now willing to content itself with what Charles Kuzell had earlier described as "some form of paper action,"[45] the company was not long in adopting a more conciliatory posture.

Kuzell remained insistent, however, that any settlement reached with the committee should treat discrimination as a labor relations issue rather than as a subject necessitating special agreements beyond the realm of collective bargaining. In response to Trimble's request that Phelps Dodge agree to a settlement similar to those reached with Miami and Inspiration, Kuzell proposed an alternative arrangement whereby compliance with the spirit of Executive Order 8802 would be achieved through strict adherence to the "antidiscrimination" provision of the company's union contracts. Such an approach was now possible, Kuzell explained, because the company had negotiated new contracts with its AFL unions that included a promise of "equitable opportunity . . . to all with respect to employment and advancement without discrimination because of race, creed, color or national origin."

With the inclusion of this provision in each of its AFL contracts, Kuzell stated, the company was now in a position to accede to an FEPC request that it was forced to reject earlier—that is, "to give formal notice that we intended to comply with such a contractual provision." To ensure a uniform policy, he added, the company was willing to notify the Mine, Mill and Smelter Workers Union, which represented its smelter employees at Douglas, that it intended "to comply fully with our contract obligation not to discriminate" against Chicano workers.

Finally, in an apparent attempt to assure the committee of the company's good faith in addressing the substance of the president's order, Kuzell declared, "We are also willing to instruct our employment agents to carry on their activities in the recruitment, training and upgrading of workers on the basis of the qualifications and seniority of such workers or applicants without regard to race, creed, color or national origin, and further to apply this policy in such a manner that the hiring of any new non-Mexican workman possessing no skill or qualifications for occupations better than common labor shall not result in the circumvention of Mexican employees possessing qualifications for filling such better occupations."[46]

Although Trimble had hoped to devise a settlement that obliged Phelps Dodge to defer to the committee's authority even if it failed to ensure compliance with the president's order, Kuzell's proposal afforded the committee a face-saving opportunity too tempting to resist. Accordingly, Lawrence Cramer immediately accepted Kuzell's offer without qualification, adding only that the committee still intended to seek "appropriate adjustment [of] all specific complaints which have been made to it."[47]

Based on the information available to the committee as a result of its own investigation in the Southwest, as well as on a careful reading of the terms set forth in Kuzell's proposal, Cramer and Trimble were overly sanguine if they truly believed that they had finally arrived at a formula for reducing or eliminating the discrimination that Phelps Dodge had long practiced against Chicano workers. For, beyond affording the company exclusive authority to define and assess all qualifications for employment, job placement, and promotion or upgrading, the agreement entrusted the equitable adjustment of discrimination complaints to previously negotiated processes of dispute resolution whose reliability and efficacy the committee already had reasons to doubt. Committee investigators were unanimous in their conclusion that Anglo-dominated AFL unions had conspired with the management of Phelps Dodge to maintain the company's discriminatory practices toward Chicano workers, and AFL officials had done nothing to suggest that they were now prepared to abandon collusion in favor of a policy of equal advocacy on behalf of Chicano grievants.

The grievance machinery provided for in the contract between the Mine, Mill and Smelter Workers and Phelps Dodge at its Douglas smelter was no less problematical as a means of adjusting discrimination complaints, although for different reasons. Union officials at the smelter could be counted upon to act in behalf of Chicano complainants, but, as one explained to Trimble only a month before the committee's settlement with Phelps Dodge, badly strained relations between the MMSW and the company had resulted in a nearly complete breakdown of the grievance machinery they had agreed to earlier.[48] Moreover, since the contract between Phelps Dodge and the MMSW at Douglas stipulated, despite the FEPC's objection, that equal opportunity would be accorded Chicano workers only when it was "consistent with the efficient and harmonious operations of the plant" to do so, even a fully functional grievance process could not ensure compliance with the president's order.

Although the agreements that the committee reached with Phelps Dodge, Miami, and Inspiration created the illusion of progress, they failed to offer Chicano workers and their supporters the real improvements that Executive Order 8802 promised. Presumably, however, the committee benefited even if Chicano workers did not, since each of the three companies, while refusing to submit to its authority, did concede its jurisdiction at least to the extent of negotiating with its representatives.

In contrast, the FEPC was unable to claim even symbolic successes in its dealings with the Nevada Consolidated Copper Company and the Phelps Dodge Refining Corporation, whose large refinery in El Paso operated under a management that was independent of those officials in charge of the parent company's mining and smelting operations in Arizona. By steadfastly denying that its Chicano employees were unfairly treated, Nevada Consolidated claimed that the FEPC lacked a legitimate basis for intruding upon its operational routine. As long as the committee was unable or unwilling to carry through on its threat to convene a public hearing, the company succeeded in effectively nullifying the president's order. Adopting a similar strategy, the Phelps Dodge Refining Corporation responded to the committee's preliminary finding of discrimination against Chicanos at its El Paso refinery with a defiant assertion that its employment policies were "beyond criticism." When Trimble suggested that the company's refusal to cooperate with the committee's probe might necessitate a public hearing, its management, ominously observing that such an action "might endanger [the] present peaceful operations" of its strategically important refinery, virtually dared the FEPC to make good its threat. After several months of ineffectual appeals and fainthearted threats, none of which induced the company to adopt a more cooperative attitude, the committee simply let the issue rest.[49]

Beyond disclosing the depth and formidability of Anglo opposition to reforms intended to afford the region's Chicano workers equal treatment on the job, the FEPC's difficult and demoralizing experience in the Southwest during the fall of 1942 was indicative of the increasingly beleaguered and precarious condition in which the committee found itself following its involuntary transfer to the authority and control of the War Manpower Commission. To be sure, its jurisdiction had been far from precise prior to the transfer. Yet the scope and magnitude of the committee's authority to effectuate the president's order became even more nebulous and confused in the wake of it as adjacent agencies within an unruly and diffuse wartime bureaucracy sought to discharge overlapping functions.

In the course of its troubled venture in the Southwest, the FEPC, which had grown increasingly sensitive to issues of jurisdiction as the uncertainty of its role within the WMC mounted, was confronted by the narrow limits of its authority. Yet beyond the challenge it faced in trying to discipline obdurate employers without the authority the task required, the committee also saw its jurisdiction invaded by a new rival: the National War Labor Board.

Created at the beginning of the war to regulate labor-management relations—especially collective bargaining—in the interest of uninterrupted industrial production and wage stability, the War Labor Board's jurisdiction did not extend to the elimination of unfair employment practices as an end in itself. Only when it became a point of contention, and a source of potential conflict, between labor and management did the WLB address the issue of discrimination, and even then it did so for the expedient purpose of ensuring labor peace rather than with the intention of enforcing the policy of fair employment practices embodied in Executive Order 8802.[50]

The conflict between the WLB and the FEPC, which arose in the fall of 1942 over the wording of a seniority clause included in the contract between the Mine, Mill and Smelter Workers and Phelps Dodge's smelter division at Douglas, Arizona, provides a classic example of how two federal agencies, each acting in good faith and within the confines of its prescribed jurisdiction, could end up at loggerheads when a problem cut across the boundaries of a jerry-built wartime bureaucracy. The conflict also revealed, however, that the FEPC's lack of genuine authority and an influential leadership handicapped it in dealings with other federal agencies no less than in dealings with employers.

The committee's differences with the WLB might have been resolved without difficulty had it been more confident of its status and secure in its jurisdiction. Yet while the committee readily accommodated itself to the need for compromise in dealing with intransigent copper companies in the Southwest, Lawrence Cramer was determined to defend the FEPC's imperiled jurisdiction against the WLB's apparent encroachment. The WLB's endorsement of contract language that appeared to circumvent the president's order merely reflected its determination to ensure industrial peace. According to Stanley White, the federal conciliator dispatched to Douglas in November 1941 to assist Phelps Dodge and the MMSW negotiate the first contract covering workers at the company's Copper Queen smelter, "discussion of the seniority clause brought up racial discrimination sharply." Recalling the particular contentiousness that suffused the issue, White wrote, "The Company desired explicit statements to the effect that Mexicans would not benefit under promotional seniority. The Union fought this on principle and because its constitution does not allow discrimination." "To break the deadlock," White explained, "I advanced a phrasing which eliminated any specific reference to discrimination. At that time, I obtained the reluctant consent of Management to the phrase 'In all cases of curtailment, promotion, or restoration of force, length of continuous service shall govern where ability and efficiency are equal, and where consistent with working harmony. . . .' I separately advised the union that its battle against discrimination could not end with any such phrase which would require pressure to back the company away from a discriminatory interpretation in particular situations."[51]

When the still unresolved dispute came before the WLB in February 1942, the parties were directed to adopt a seniority clause that included a provision that "equal opportunity for employment and advancement under this clause shall be made available to all to the fullest extent and as rapidly as is consistent with the efficient and harmonious operation of the plant."[52] Four months later, when differences arose between the company and the union over the interpretation of this provision as it pertained to the promotion rights of Chicano workers, the WLB sustained the propriety of the seniority clause, but added, "Should there arise any question of its proper interpretation or application, the arbiter should be guided by the spirit and language of the President's Executive Order on Fair Labor Practice issued on June 25, 1941, wherein the policy of the United States regarding this question is set forth. . . ."[53]

Despite the WLB's amplification, the promotion rights of Chicano smelter workers at Douglas remained a source of bitter disagreement between Phelps Dodge and the MMSW. When Stanley White was once again sent to Douglas in mid-September to facilitate a settlement of the issue, he found Charles Kuzell still determined "to reserve certain jobs for Anglo-Saxon employees" and MMSW officials equally determined "to combat the die-hard stand of Phelps Dodge."[54] Reporting that the issue would have to be submitted to arbitration, White rather belaboredly noted that in light of the WLB's recent clarification the "ruling of the arbitrator finally selected will have to go against the Company unless it goes against the President's Fair Labor Practices order. . . ."[55]

The threat posed to the FEPC by the WLB's assumption of authority in dealing with the issue of employment discrimination at Douglas became apparent when Phelps Dodge challenged the committee's jurisdiction over matters whose resolution was properly pursued, the company insisted, through collective bargaining procedures. The committee's concern was heightened further when both the Miami Copper Company and the Inspiration Copper Company sought to base their compliance with Executive Order 8802 on the condition of "efficient and harmonious operation" incorporated at the WLB's direction into the contract between Phelps Dodge and the MMSW at Douglas.

Yet, in raising the issue with the WLB, Lawrence Cramer was at least as interested in resolving the larger question of jurisdictional primacy in the area of employment discrimination as he was in eliminating language in the collective bargaining agreement at Douglas that appeared to compromise the integrity of the president's order. The committee's objections to the offending seniority clause, Cramer informed WLB chairman William H. Davis, were rooted in an acute concern that high principle had been sacrificed to mere expediency. Suggesting to Phelps Dodge that compliance with Executive Order 8802 was required only when it did not diminish efficiency or harmony at the company's Douglas smelter, he complained, wrongly implied "that opportunities for promotion may legitimately be closed to workers of Mexican and Spanish origin." Furthermore, he lectured Davis, the WLB's action in the Phelps Dodge case was objectionable because it "makes the employer alone or the employer and the union officials rather than the Committee the judge as to whether an employer is fulfilling his obligation to observe the Order."

At the very least, Cramer insisted, the WLB had handled the issue in a manner that "gives a color of justification to an employer who may wish to evade his obligation to obey the Order." That copper companies in the Southwest were already seeking "to qualify their obligation to observe the Order by the use of this phrase," was, he noted, proof of the flaw inherent in the WLB's response to the problem of employment discrimination at Phelps Dodge's Douglas smelter. "The Committee is sure that members of the Board do not wish to encourage disobedience to Executive Order 8802 or to be parties to its evasion by employers," Cramer wrote. "It is regretted, therefore, that the Board approved a contract which contained this phrase."

To compromise the principle of equal employment opportunity embodied in the president's order was to violate it, Cramer asserted, and the WLB's decision in the Phelps Dodge case did obvious violence to a policy whose ultimate value to the war effort would be determined by the constancy of its application. Reminding Davis that the WLB had recently decided another case in which it "categorically ordered that a contract . . . be modified to include a provision according pay for women employees equal with that for men doing the same work," Cramer proposed that the board adopt the same "unequivocal position" in upholding the principle of equal employment opportunity for Chicano copper workers. From the committee's point of view, he concluded, a satisfactory disposition of the case would not be realized until the WLB directed both Phelps Dodge and the MMSW "to modify all existing contracts between them to eliminate any reservations in such contracts which are inconsistent with the provisions of Executive Order 8802."[56]

In replying to Cramer's protest, WLB chairman Davis rather impatiently suggested that the FEPC's dissatisfaction with his agency's handling of the Phelps Dodge case derived from the committee's apparent ignorance of the factors that informed the board's decision. "This case," Davis declared, "was considered at length by the entire membership of the Board. Both union and industry representatives were consulted regarding the particular clause to which your letter refers. The phrasing of the clause had their full agreement. It was the considered judgment of the Board that such a clause was necessary in order to avoid the possibility of wasteful interruptions of essential war production."

Above all, however, it was the committee's presumptuousness in questioning the propriety of the WLB's disposition of the Phelps Dodge case that annoyed Davis. "Because of our thorough study of this particular situation," he bluntly informed Cramer, "we are at a loss to understand why your committee should undertake to make recommendations to the Board regarding this matter without first obtaining full information from us as to the reasons for our decision." "I can assure you," he added, "that we would be glad to cooperate with your committee if we were given the chance."[57]

Notwithstanding Davis's unceremonious rejection of its complaint, and despite its own ratification of a settlement that exacted nothing more than a vague promise of future compliance with Executive Order 8802 from Phelps Dodge, the committee persisted in its effort to reverse the WLB's decision in regard to the Douglas contract. The WLB's explanation of its action, FEPC chairman Malcolm MacLean advised Davis on November 23, had "not disclosed any fact which in the judgment of the Committee justifies a withdrawal of its recommendation to you." Citing evidence provided by Stanley White that Phelps Dodge was continuing to oppose equal promotion rights for Chicano workers at its Douglas smelter, MacLean pointedly challenged Davis's assertion that the WLB had already satisfied the legitimate concerns of the FEPC by directing that arbitrations of grievances arising under the disputed seniority clause "should be guided by the spirit and language" of the president's order. In light of the evident ineffectiveness of the board's directive, and the fact that its decision in the Phelps Dodge case was being relied on by other copper companies in the Southwest "to justify non-compliance with Executive Order 8802," the FEPC was, MacLean explained, compelled to renew its recommendation that the WLB remove from the Douglas contract any language that was "inconsistent with the provisions" of the president's order.[58]

While MacLean succeeded in persuading Davis to bring the issue to the attention of the full board once again, his demand for remedial action was finally rejected. Arguing that the record of the board's involvement in the Phelps Dodge case "clearly shows that the operation of the contract clause in question was to be in conformance with the provisions of Executive Order 8802," WLB vice-chairman George Taylor informed MacLean that no further action in the matter was justified. Ignoring evidence provided by the FEPC that the disputed seniority clause was not operating in conformity with the president's order no matter what the WLB's original intention had been, Taylor adamantly declared, "The National War Labor Board holds the view that its order and the accompanying panel report clearly show that the seniority clause in question is to be interpreted and applied in conformance with the terms of Executive Order 8802."[59]

Although the WLB vigorously asserted that it had handled the issue of equal promotion rights for Chicano workers at Douglas in a way that was sensitive to the requirements of the president's order, the board's unwillingness to subordinate its essential purpose to that of another federal agency presented a familiar dilemma to the FEPC. Given the wide disparity between its own resources and authority and those of such agencies as the WLB, the FEPC was never in a position to go beyond the force of argument in pressing its case. The committee's dispute with the WLB was finally rendered moot when the MMSW succeeded in negotiating a new contract with Phelps Dodge that did away with language that compromised the promotion rights of Chicano smelter workers at Douglas, but the essential jurisdictional conflict out of which the dispute arose remained unresolved.[60]

In the end, the FEPC's inability to resolve its differences with the WLB on a basis that might have confirmed its primacy in defining and implementing federal policy regarding employment discrimination conformed to the general pattern of discreet backtracking and inevitable compromise that characterized the committee's troubled sojourn in the Southwest. Having failed in its ambitious mission to dislodge a tradition of employment discrimination that reached to the bedrock of social and cultural relations in the Southwest, and thus to secure the equal job rights of Chicano workers employed in the region's dominant industry, the FEPC's forced retreat into ambiguous settlements with recalcitrant copper producers entrusted the immediate future of fair employment practices to hope rather than certainty. To the regret of both the committee and expectant Chicano workers, that hope was not long in being disappointed.

5. *From Bad to Worse*

NOTWITHSTANDING ITS FEEBLE authority and anemic resources, and the growing disquietude fostered by strategic retreats of the sort that it awkwardly executed in the Southwest, the FEPC had survived its first year and a half of operation with its credibility largely intact. The highly publicized hearings the committee conducted in various regions of the country, including the South, had had little if any ameliorative effect on the widespread employment discrimination they disclosed, but they nevertheless imparted an impression of activism that helped to allay the concerns of those who doubted the FEPC's fortitude. Similarly, the committee's well-advertised success in extracting promises of compliance with the president's order from a handful of prominent employers had also helped to counter suspicions regarding the force and legitimacy of its mandate. Even its unavailing efforts in behalf of Chicano workers in the Southwest, when considered on the basis of the positive intentions they disclosed rather than the negligible gains they produced, enlarged the body of evidence available to those determined to put the best possible face on the FEPC's performance.

Convinced that its early record of apparent progress warranted a more ambitious campaign in support of fair employment practices, the committee and its staff had sought White House authorization in the late spring of 1942 for a greatly expanded effort. While the initial response from the White House was sufficiently ambiguous to excite the committee's hopes, the shallowness of the Roosevelt administration's commitment to fair employment practices was revealed with numbing force in its arbitrary decisions to cancel the proposed El Paso hearings and to place the FEPC under the inimical authority of the War Manpower Commission.[1]

Despite its uncertain status and dwindling morale, however, the committee and its staff had doggedly persevered in the largely unrewarded service of Executive Order 8802. The committee had largely exhausted the force of its now tattered moral authority, and the expedient claim that a successful war effort depended upon full utilization of all available labor had generally failed to deter employers whose discriminatory labor policies were rooted in long-standing custom and crass self-interest. Still, the FEPC, though its function and jurisdiction within the WMC became subjects of protracted and rancorous negotiations during the fall of 1942, had done what it could to carry on its increasingly arduous work.

Although the political controversy inherent in public hearings was especially obvious in the wake of its unhappy experience in the Southwest, the committee remained convinced, as Malcolm MacLean informed WMC chairman Paul McNutt, that public exposure was the "greatest force" available to it in fighting job discrimination.[2] As the committee soon discovered, however, persuading the White House to accept the political risks associated with public hearings was an impossible task.

In response to mounting evidence of particularly egregious discrimination against blacks by railroad companies and unions, the committee had announced in October its intention to hold public hearings on the industry's employment practices. Apparently hoping both to convince the White House of the need for such action and to enlist the president's support, Lawrence Cramer outlined the committee's plans in a letter to presidential aide Marvin McIntyre. "In the course of preparations for this hearing," Cramer wrote, "the Committee's staff has found that the most important railroad unions have a definite ban against the admission of non-Caucasians into their membership. The agreements entered into between railroad managements and the unions in many cases make special provisions to limit the types of jobs to which Negroes can be promoted. This is done through the so-called 'non-promotable men' clause."

The need for public hearings was obvious, he claimed, since "the Committee is in a position where it must take jurisdiction over the complaints which have reached it and must undertake to do something about a problem that is of long standing and has, so far, not been solved."

The committee was well aware, Cramer confessed, that it "would face a rather imposing array of railroad managements and railroad unions who may present a united front and thus not make the Committee's job easier." Yet, with the president's help, he noted, especially in gaining the cooperation of A. F. Whitney, president of the Brotherhood of Railway

Trainmen and a Roosevelt loyalist, the committee's chances for realizing its aims would be greatly enhanced. Whitney had already confided that he was "in full accord with the letter and spirit of Executive Order 8802," Cramer sanguinely reported, and "a bit of encouragement from the President would be all that was necessary" to persuade him that "a dramatic repudiation of the color bar by his organization would have repercussions throughout the railroad industry."[3]

McIntyre, whose personal disdain for the FEPC's work made him an unpromising ally, acted at once to undermine the committee's plans by surreptitiously providing a copy of Cramer's memorandum to George Harrison, president of the Brotherhood of Railway Clerks and a staunch opponent of the proposed railroad hearings. Predictably, Harrison strongly urged the White House to reject Cramer's appeal for support. The railroad unions, Harrison declared, were united in their belief that "agitation [of the] Negro question" was "unfortunate and . . . creating dissension among the people" and that the FEPC was "being used by certain ambitious negroes to promote negro labor unions," an apparent reference to the continuing activism of A. Philip Randolph and the Brotherhood of Sleeping Car Porters in behalf of fair employment practices.[4] While disingenuously assuring Roosevelt that he was "taking George's advice and keeping my fingers out of the pie," McIntyre nevertheless made sure that Harrison's vehement objection to the proposed railroad hearings was brought to the president's personal attention.[5]

Despite its frail condition, the obvious formidability of its unified opposition, and the studied disinclination of the Roosevelt administration to assist its efforts, the committee was undeterred. With its credibility sagging, the committee recognized the need for a new enforcement initiative sufficiently ambitious in scale and impressive in result to restore the badly depleted authority of Executive Order 8802. Because of the blatantly discriminatory employment practices that prevailed in the railroad industry, its selection as the focus of the committee's efforts made sense objectively even if it posed obvious dangers politically. In standing by its decision to proceed with public hearings, the committee was reflecting its deepening conviction that redressing the problem of discrimination in the railroad industry constituted an appropriate test of whether or not the president's order was still a viable basis for the Roosevelt administration's fair employment policy.

In the end, however, the bankruptcy of Executive Order 8802 was confirmed by White House action rather than by the failure of the FEPC to survive a fair test of its capabilities. On January 11, only two weeks before the committee's proposed railroad hearings were scheduled to begin, any remaining doubts regarding the depth of the Roosevelt administration's commitment to fair employment practices was finally dispelled. Acting at the direct behest of the White House, WMC chairman McNutt announced that the hearings had been "indefinitely postponed." The action was taken, he explained during a subsequent press conference, in order that the WMC might pursue a more "normal way" to redress the problem of job discrimination in the railroad industry, one that could be followed "without using force."[6]

McNutt's announcement, which was made without prior consultation with either the membership or the staff of the FEPC, effectively demolished what remained of the federal antidiscrimination policy proclaimed in Executive Order 8802 only eighteen months earlier. A flurry of resignations followed the cancellation of the railroad hearings, including those of chairman Malcolm MacLean and member David Sarnoff. Charles Houston, a prominent Washington attorney and civil rights activist who had been engaged by the committee as special counsel for the railroad hearings, also resigned, as did his staff. In his letter of resignation Houston, whose views reflected the thinking of black leaders nationally, expressed the particular bitterness and frustration that the administration's actions fostered among once hopeful black activists. Explaining his resignation to MacLean, Houston angrily wrote:

> The action of Mr. Paul McNutt . . . in calling off the public hearings of the President's Committee on Fair Employment Practice concerning discriminations against Negro railway workers, without even conferring with the Committee beforehand, exposes the hollow pretension of the government's pledge that the Committee would still function as an independent body after transfer to the War Manpower Commission. Mr. McNutt's action followed the traditional pattern of sacrificing the Negro whenever an attempt to do him justice antagonizes powerful reactionary forces in industry and labor. The railroad industry, the railroad unions and the Government itself are afraid to permit these public hearings to be held because they know the charges of discrimination are true.

While noting that the administration was apparently convinced that it had "purchased domestic peace and . . . satisfied the reactionaries" by calling off the railroad hearings, Houston argued that such a "surrender of principle" exposed an unregenerate racist mindset that would "rise to plague the Government in North Africa, China, India, South America and every other place where colored populations predominate." Suggesting the broader implications of the administration's political faintheartedness, he declared, "Mr. McNutt has not merely repudiated the Negro; far worse for the future of this country he has made a mockery of the nation's war aims. As spokesman for the Government he has in effect proclaimed that the four freedoms do not cover Negroes. . . ." Asserting that the administration's action "disappoints but does not discourage us," Houston promised that blacks would "work all the harder to rally the liberal forces of this country behind a program which works by principle and not by panic."[7] In a separate letter of protest to Roosevelt, Houston solemnly concluded, "I respectfully submit that the time when Negro issues can be disposed of without first conferring with Negroes themselves has passed, and it is important that government officials begin to realize that Negroes are citizens, not wards."[8]

By canceling the railroad hearings, the administration validated the claims of those who had warned six months earlier that the committee's transfer to the WMC was a transparent act of political containment. Still more importantly, however, the administration's action sealed the fate of Executive Order 8802. In the wake of McNutt's announcement the White House was bombarded by urgent calls for a complete renovation of the administration's policy in regard to fair employment practices. Lawrence Cramer, whose work as the committee's executive secretary afforded an intimate perspective on its troubled operation, advised Marvin McIntyre on January 15 that the FEPC would have to be fully reorganized if it was to continue to function. Outlining his views in a "personal and confidential" memorandum, Cramer wrote:

> The postponement by order from above of the railroad hearings scheduled by the Committee, added to the postponement of the El Paso hearing and the transfer of the Committee to the War Manpower Commission, has raised many and serious questions as to the intention of the Administration to carry into effect the policy of Executive Order 8802. The way in which decisions on these matters were made, the lack of preparation for their announcement, and the failure to take the Committee into deliberations leading to those decisions have all tended to raise doubts and increase bitterness.

"Any solution that is offered, if it is to reduce heat and passion," he insisted, "must on the one hand carry conviction to the minority groups that they are not the victims of a plot to 'sell them down the river' and, on the other hand, remove so far as is possible the particular causes of concern of those who have objected to procedures employed by the Committee."

A clear consensus existed among its supporters, Cramer argued, that the FEPC could be made effective only by granting it "independent status with direct responsibility to the President, an adequate staff and field force . . . and adequate sanctions to compel compliance with the Order." In contrast, he noted, nothing short of its dissolution was likely to satisfy the committee's enemies. Since the administration could not abandon its avowed commitment to fair employment practices, there was no possibility of mollifying the committee's die-hard opposition. "Those who object to the policy laid down in Executive Order 8802," he observed, "will oppose with more or less vigor in proportion to its effectiveness any agency created to enforce the policy. These forces cannot be appeased. I can suggest nothing which might satisfy them which will not run counter to our Constitutional principles."

Cramer readily acknowledged that the policy the president's order embodied was likely to remain a source of political controversy and bureaucratic contention no matter how the administration might seek to reformulate it. He nevertheless proposed a plan of reorganization designed both to strengthen the FEPC and to allay the concerns of those "who agree in principle with the policy" but found fault with the "two methods used by the Committee to carry out its responsibilities: its public hearings and its directive-orders to employers."

"As a first element of a possible solution, and as a means of carrying conviction to the minority groups and their supporters," Cramer proposed the creation of a full-time, paid committee of either three or five members that would operate within the White House's Office for Emergency Management and be directly responsible to the president "through a designated Executive Assistant." Furthermore, he argued, the reconstituted committee should have a combined headquarters and field staff of "at least 120 persons."

While convinced that the committee could not function effectively if its authority either to conduct public hearings or to issue directive orders was revoked, Cramer was amenable to "a solution which established controls over these methods." As a means of "allaying disquiet on the part of those within and without the Government who accept the policy of Executive Order 8802 but object to the particular means employed to execute it," he suggested an approach to future enforcement that required the FEPC to defer the convening of public hearings or the issuance of directive orders until other interested federal agencies had been afforded a "reasonable opportunity" to correct violations necessitating action by the committee. Where disputes arose between the committee and other governmental agencies over the propriety of proceeding with either type of enforcement action, Cramer recommended that they "be referred to a designated presidential Executive Assistant for final decision."

For all of its seeming innovation, the plan of reorganization Cramer submitted for White House consideration did not contemplate significant increases in the committee's enforcement authority. Indeed, his proposal that the committee's freedom of action should be subject to the express approval of a designated presidential assistant, while it reflected a pragmatic sensitivity to the administration's political concerns, did nothing to ensure that pressures of the type that had resulted in the cancellation of earlier hearings would not impede future hearings. Similarly, Cramer's proposal failed to outline what steps the committee should be authorized to take when an employer, as some already had, simply ignored its orders or directives, including those approved by White House and other interested federal agencies.

Cramer's failure to emphasize the need for expanded enforcement powers apparently reflected a conviction, as one committee staffer expressed it, "that there was nothing wrong with the FEPC that strong White House backing could not have cured."[9] Ultimately, Cramer believed, the committee's weakness was less a function of structural or administrative deficiencies than of the White House's unwillingness to place the full weight of its prestige and authority behind an unambiguous fair employment practices policy. As long as the administration's vacillation continued to provide "outward evidences of inner disagreement," he contended, the FEPC would remain vulnerable to crippling attacks from "extremists" on both sides of the issue.

Since the problems that had immobilized the committee were unlikely to be resolved until a consensus supporting its effective operation existed at the highest levels of government, Cramer argued that the time had come for "a frank discussion between the President and party leaders in Congress with the purpose of preventing the policy of Executive Order 8802 from becoming a party issue." Such a meeting, he suggested, would afford an opportunity both to discuss "the possibility of introducing and enacting legislation" in furtherance of fair employment practices and to explore "the limits to which Congress might go in supporting or enforcing the policy." Plainly, he admitted, such an undertaking did "carry with it the danger that a highly emotional issue may be subjected to public debate at a time when further exacerbation of feeling would be unfortunate, both from a domestic and from an international point of view." Still, he insisted, "A full and thorough canvass of the issue with the leaders of both political parties, without giving the appearance of attempting to throw this controversial matter into open debate, would be highly desirable."

Yet whatever course of action the administration might ultimately choose to follow, he advised McIntyre, it was "of first importance that any plan which may be finally adopted should, before its adoption, be fully discussed with the present membership of the Committee on Fair Employment Practice and with the leaders of minority and civic groups who have a vital interest in whichever decision is made."[10]

While Cramer's memorandum betrayed the frustration and disappointment that the cancellation of the railroad hearings had engendered among the membership and staff of the FEPC, it was deferential in tone and necessarily devoid of recrimination. In contrast, the reactions forwarded to the White House from representatives of the various minority, liberal, labor, civic, and church organizations that had coalesced in support of a vigorous fair employment policy were blunt and accusatory. Walter White expressed the resentment and chagrin of the committee's most ardent supporters in a caustic message to Roosevelt on behalf of the NAACP. "The summary and arbitrary action of the Administration . . . in postponing indefinitely public hearings on discrimination in the railroad industry," White sternly declared, ". . . calls for more than condemnation. It necessitates an appraisal of the fundamental attitude of the Administration to the problem involved, an analysis of Executive Order 8802, and the re-examination of the techniques employed by the Committee."

From the beginning, White noted, the FEPC's backers had anticipated that it would enjoy independent status and a "direct relationship" with the White House. Instead, he charged, the committee had been "shifted . . . from one agency to another" and routinely disregarded by the White House. "The practice," he complained, "has been to decide important matters relating to the Committee in 'off the record' conferences involving the President's Executive Assistant, other high-ranking government officials not connected with the Committee and, on occasion, some one or more of the white members of the Committee. When Mr. McNutt ordered the postponement of the railroad hearings without prior conference or consultation with the Committee, he simply followed and reflected the mode of the Administration in dealing with the Committee."

Given that the FEPC was "set up to deal with a fundamental, long-neglected problem," White observed, it followed that the administration, if its "purpose was a serious one," was obliged to provide support adequate to the task. "Yet, at no time," he charged, "has the committee had an operating staff, budget, or status commensurate with the immensity and complexity of the problem assigned to it. The militant support which the Administration has given such agencies as the National Labor Relations Board and the Securities and Exchange Commission when they were under violent attack by reactionary forces has been conspicuously absent in its dealings with the Committee on Fair Employment Practice." If the administration truly wanted the FEPC to be effective, White insisted, it was apparent that it would have to do far more than it had in the past to ensure that result.

Any effort to rehabilitate the FEPC so that it might alleviate the "national scandal" of iniquitous job discrimination, he asserted, had to begin with a frank admission that the committee's enforcement authority was woefully inadequate. In its eighteen months of operation, White observed, the FEPC's only effective means of enforcement had been the actual or threatened sanction of public hearings, and any further effort "to deprive the Committee of its right to hold public hearings . . . would be a very real tragedy" unless even stronger sanctions were substituted. "No tampering with the sanction of public hearings or with any other procedure of the Committee should even be considered," he argued, "unless the President is ready to undertake a drastic revision of Executive Order 8802 to provide positive sanctions covering every field to which the Committee has been assigned. In lieu of public hearings, it is entirely possible that the President may desire to implement the authority of the Committee by authorizing it to require a contractor receiving government contracts to make, under oath or affirmation, a statement that he has not been guilty of discriminatory employment practices."

Should the committee find subsequently that an employer had violated his oath, White noted, he could be prosecuted under "applicable provisions" of existing federal criminal statutes. The president could further strengthen the FEPC's enforcement authority, he added, by requiring "that war contracts provide money penalties for proven acts of discrimination." To ensure that unions adhered to an equally demanding standard of fairness in their policies and actions, White suggested that "the President might order the War Labor Board or the National Labor Relations Board, or other appropriate agency or agencies before which labor organizations have occasion to appear, to allow the Fair Employment Practice Committee to intervene in their proceedings involving labor organizations guilty of proven acts of discrimination."

"In short," he concluded, "the whole approach must be constructive to strengthen the hand of the Committee and not destructive to appease the most reactionary elements in the nation."[11]

In light of its action in the matter, the White House obviously believed that going ahead with the FEPC's proposed railroad hearings was likely to pose a larger political problem for the administration than was a decision to cancel them. Yet, if its course of action was commended by a close reading of the political balance sheet, the administration was soon forced to acknowledge that its decision had hardly been cost-free. With its credibility among blacks and other minorities seriously impaired and the remaining membership and staff of the FEPC demoralized to the point of near paralysis, the administration recognized that it could not ignore the increasingly insistent demands of its critics without confirming their charge that the president's order had been rendered meaningless. The responsibility for recommending an appropriate response to those demanding a clarification of the FEPC's status was delegated to attorney general Francis Biddle, whose personal views on the issue of minority rights marked him as a liberal, and to Jonathan Daniels, a pragmatic North Carolinian who served as the White House's resident authority on southern politics and the "race question."

In keeping with his particular expertise, Daniels viewed the controversy surrounding the FEPC as a problem that was political rather than organizational in nature. His advice reflected a greater concern with how Roosevelt might balance himself on the political tightrope stretched between the issue's distant poles than with loftier considerations of moral province or social justice. "My feeling," he reported to Marvin McIntyre, "is that this question is becoming one of the sorest places in the whole business of the home front. Involved in it are important aspects of both successful dealings with Southern Democrats in the present Congress and the success of the war administration at the polls in 1944. At present the President is being sharply criticized on this question by both white Southerners who think he has gone too far and by Negroes who feel that he is retreating from positions he has taken."

It was plain, he observed, that Roosevelt could not "retract the non-discrimination policy re-iterated in Executive Order 8802"; nor could he reasonably expect that a "plan of governmental reorganization involving the place of the committee in the government will solve the question." Since anything the president might do or fail to do regarding the FEPC would "involve some continuance of agitation and friction," Daniels noted, "a policy of postponement of action now will increase rather than minimize the emotions already aroused."

However devoutly his supporters might wish that it was not so, Daniels reluctantly concluded, the president had arrived at a point "where he must make his position clearer than it seems to many people now. He must re-iterate his opposition to discrimination, his rejection of any theories of racial superiority." Daniels insisted that "this position is grounded in his own views, in Federal law and in the central issues of this war. Whether the South likes it or not, it cannot be altered." Still, he added, the war imposed an obligation of patriotism on whites and blacks alike, and the president would be fully justified in insisting "that no home agitation by either threaten the full support of all in the war effort. No group can expect to use the war effort for the furtherance of its own desires. . . . Negroes cannot expect a nation trying to move forward in war toward a goal in justice for all, to solve in immediacy old questions of discriminations. On the other hand, no group can insist upon the luxury of maintaining its prejudices where those prejudices prevent the use of America's full strength in this war."

Moreover, Daniels argued, the successful implementation of a policy as inherently controversial as that embodied in Executive Order 8802 required an agency whose members were sensitive to the primacy of the war effort. To ensure that result, he suggested, the president should appoint a committee whose members, while possessing "a strong sense of justice for all people," were "more representative" than those serving on the existing FEPC. "I would like to see one member," he explained, "who represents the best type of Southern conservatism. Indeed, I think that it is important that the board not be composed of members most of whom, in a real sense, represent forces of agitation."

Once properly constituted, Daniels declared, "The committee, as one concerned with employment, must carefully avoid even the suggestion that it has responsibilities in other fields of discrimination such as housing, restaurants, etc." The committee was, he reasoned, an adjunct of the administration's "war policy," and therefore it followed that fair employment practices "must be 'sold' to the country as primarily designed to prevent limitations of the use of all manpower rather than as a present basis for the general advance of the Negro race." Thus, while it might be proper for the committee to call upon other federal agencies to help discourage discriminatory employment practices that actually threatened to impede the war effort, he noted, it should resist the temptation "to force the introduction of Negroes into industries which have never used them, while white labor is still available and where the introduction is forced to serve a cause rather than the war effort."

The administration was right, Daniels conceded, to heed the FEPC's warning that the brewing battle over its status was "'a moral issue' with minority groups." Yet it was no less important to remember, he added, that, "even if mistaken, Southerners feel that they fight for a 'moral issue,' too." Plainly, it was a problem of the sort that would not go away, which required the personal involvement of the president if it was to be successfully resolved. "There is no more explosive, no more emotional question on the American home front," he concluded. "I wish I thought it could be patched up. I don't. I wish it could be handled by subordinates. I am sure it no longer can be. This needs and deserves the thought and the courage of the President himself."[12]

Beyond suggesting the political difficulty that was likely to attend any plan the administration might adopt to clarify its nondiscrimination policy, Daniels offered little that was useful to the White House in charting a specific course of action. In his assessment of the controversy, Francis Biddle also emphasized the seemingly insoluble political dilemma it posed. The South was in "a state of emotional alarm" over the federal government's "supposed intention" to reform race relations in the country, Biddle observed, while the "widespread discontent" among blacks in the wake of the administration's cancellation of the railroad hearings placed the president in genuine danger of "losing the support of the Negro population."

Yet, unlike Daniels, Biddle was willing to recommend a concrete plan of action. "The Fair Employment Practice Committee," he advised Roosevelt, "should be reorganized and strengthened. . . . In its place should be substituted a Committee of five full-time members appointed by you, men of national standing, attached to the War Manpower Commission and using the latter's field staff, but with very broad powers." Once reconstituted, Biddle continued, the committee should direct its activity toward "preventing discrimination against workers as a problem of manpower, presenting it as a national need for full employment in the war." If properly circumspect in its means the committee could achieve its ends, he believed, without exciting undue apprehension among those who opposed a broader civil rights policy. "Public pressures arousing race emotions should be avoided," he told Roosevelt. "Results should be achieved by negotiation and persuasion locally, through men of local standing, with only occasional use of public hearings or application of sanctions."

Regarding the new committee's composition, Biddle recommended that it include a nationally prominent black who was "independent of any group"; an "outstanding industrialist," whose selection "would greatly strengthen its prestige, especially in the South"; a "labor man (to be chosen by the A.F. of L., C.I.O. and Railroad Brotherhoods, by majority vote)"; a "prominent Catholic"; and, lastly, a chairman with a proven record of effective public service. "Frank Graham would be first-rate as Chairman, if he could be spared from the War Labor Board," Biddle noted. "He feels, however, that his first obligation is to the Board."

In order to set in motion a process that would eventuate in the FEPC's restoration, Biddle suggested that Roosevelt make a public announcement of his intention to call a conference at which WMC chairman McNutt and "leaders in the field" could "discuss the immediate reorganization and strengthening of the Fair Employment Practice Committee." Because he believed it was "essential to show that the government intends to act in good faith," Biddle also urged the president to include in his announcement a pledge that "the railroad hearings will be continued as soon as the Committee is reorganized."[13]

While enthusiasm for the FEPC within the White House remained distinctly tepid, the administration's desire to quell the divisive public protest fueled by the cancellation of the railroad hearings apparently ensured its amenability to Biddle's recommendations. On February 3 the White House issued a press release announcing that the president had asked McNutt to confer with "leaders of those groups opposing discrimination in war employment to consider a revision and strengthening of the [FEPC's] scope and powers." Although the president believed that the FEPC had "done an excellent piece of work," the statement continued, he nevertheless felt that it had "been handicapped by the fact that the members of the Committee were working on a part-time voluntary basis; and did not have powers or personnel commensurate with their responsibilities." Once the necessary reforms were completed, the statement concluded, "the hearings in the railroad case and in any other cases which may have been temporarily postponed will be continued."[14]

In response to Roosevelt's directive, McNutt convened a meeting on February 19 at which he and Biddle discussed the FEPC's precarious status with representatives of nineteen groups that had been active in behalf of a vigorous fair employment policy. For the policy to be effective, its advocates argued, the FEPC needed, among other things, to have its independent status within the executive branch restored, to have a budget large enough to support a staff commensurate with its responsibilities, and to have sufficient enforcement authority to ensure compliance by private employers and government agencies alike. Other than assuring those in attendance that the administration would consider their views in deciding the FEPC's future, McNutt was unwilling to forecast the president's likely course of action in the matter.[15] The administration was no more forthcoming when the FEPC, which was limping along under the informal chairmanship of Earl Dickerson, pressed its own case in February to win White House support for the reforms that Lawrence Cramer had proposed to Marvin McIntyre a month earlier.[16]

In agreeing that a reorganization of the FEPC was in order, the Roosevelt administration was responding to the political uproar caused by its cancellation of the railroad hearings. Had it been motivated by a sincere conviction that its fair employment policy required more effective implementation and enforcement, the administration would almost certainly have approached the problem with a greater sense of urgency. Instead, the president and his aides were determined, despite increasingly impatient appeals by the FEPC and its supporters, to delay action until they were confident that the plan of reorganization ultimately adopted kept political risks to a minimum.

Although the FEPC had endured a tenuous existence even before the cancellation of the railroad hearings, the administration's studied inertia left it in what one scholar later described as "a state of suspended animation."[17] For the millions of minority workers who had entrusted their hopes for fair treatment on the job to the committee's vigilance, the early months of 1943 were a period of growing confusion and disillusionment. Yet for Chicano copper workers in the Southwest, whose persistent complaints of discrimination forced the committee to continue efforts it might otherwise have abandoned to secure compliance with the president's order by the region's dominant copper companies, the FEPC's incapacitation occurred at a particularly critical time.

The rather nebulous promises of future compliance with Executive Order 8802 that it finally coaxed from the Phelps Dodge, Miami, and Inspiration copper companies at the end of 1942, though grudging and conditional, were regarded as victories by the committee. Yet the companies' initial hostility toward FEPC investigators, as well as their persistent denials of past discrimination against Chicano workers despite overwhelming evidence to the contrary, made it apparent that the committee would have to monitor their performance closely to ensure both that the president's order was observed and that past complaints of discrimination were disposed of satisfactorily. In his personal negotiations with representatives of the companies at the conclusion of the committee's southwestern investigation, Ernest Trimble had found them either reluctant or unwilling to provide the information required to process existing complaints of discrimination and to assess prevailing wage and personnel policies in the light of the president's order. With the closing of its temporary office in El Paso and Trimble's return to Washington, the committee's capacity to determine whether or not the companies were honoring their pledges was rendered virtually nonexistent.

The difficulties involved in monitoring developments in the Southwest by correspondence from Washington were apparent almost at once, though the lack of a viable alternative left the committee understandably reluctant to acknowledge publicly the inherent deficiencies of its follow-up methods. After eighteen months of having to make do with authority and resources that were unarguably inadequate to the task before it, the committee's acute sense of its own limitations had long since mitigated its aversion to compromise. What had begun as a general investigation of discrimination against Chicano workers in the Southwest had quickly become an exclusive investigation of discriminatory employment practices in the region's copper industry. By virtue of the same reductive momentum, what started as a bold effort to enforce the president's order throughout the whole of the southwestern copper industry was reduced, by the time the committee concluded its investigation in the region, to a timorous hope that three companies might be persuaded to honor grudging promises of conditional compliance. Moreover, since the committee was limited to acting on individual complaints rather than in response to systemic discrimination, the unfair employment practices that prevailed at many of the largest mining, smelting, and refining operations in the region were ultimately ignored because the Chicano victims had not complained formally. Thus, while its investigators had found that discrimination was practiced as an apparent matter of policy at Phelps Dodge operations throughout Arizona, the committee sought to hold the company accountable only at its Douglas smelter, where the Mine, Mill and Smelter Workers Union had strongly encouraged its Chicano members to file formal complaints.

In the hope of making the best of a manifestly untenable situation, Lawrence Cramer wrote to both the Miami Copper Company and the Inspiration Copper Company at the end of 1942, reminding each of its promise of future compliance with the president's order and encouraging prompt settlements of existing complaints of discrimination.[18]

In fact, the committee was apparently at a loss to do anything other than let each company proceed as it saw fit in dealing with those of its Chicano employees who had filed formal complaints of discrimination. Ernest Trimble did advise each complainant that the companies had pledged to remedy past violations of Executive Order 8802, but he also suggested that they would be on their own in prompting the corrective action the committee had been promised. "It is requested," he informed each complainant, "that you notify the Committee when a satisfactory settlement of your complaint has been achieved with the company."[19] In effect, the approach that Trimble advised meant that the initial responsibility for arranging settlements of outstanding complaints of discrimination involving the Miami and Inspiration companies rested with those individual workers who were the alleged victims of unfair employment practices.

The committee adopted a similarly circuitous approach to enforcement in dealing with the complaints of discrimination against Phelps Dodge at its Douglas smelter. Instead of relying upon individual complainants, however, the committee sought to delegate responsibility for monitoring the company's handling of existing discrimination complaints to the Mine, Mill and Smelter Workers. In part, the committee's decision to seek the union's help reflected nothing more than its recognition of the difficulties involved in trying to monitor developments in Douglas from the remote vantage point of its Washington headquarters. Yet it was also dictated by the terms of the committee's agreement with Phelps Dodge, which provided that complaints of discrimination would be resolved through the operation of existing grievance procedures rather than by a special method of settlement that defined the issue as something other than a labor relations problem.[20]

Although the MMSW had done more than any other organization to assist the FEPC's investigation in the Southwest, the committee's negotiations with Phelps Dodge were concluded without the union's knowledge or approval. Moreover, the committee's proposed approach to settling the dozens of discrimination complaints filed by Chicano smelter workers at Douglas ignored the union's earlier warning that its badly strained relations with the company had nearly immobilized the grievance process they had agreed upon.[21]

When he belatedly informed MMSW officials in Douglas of the FEPC's agreement with Phelps Dodge, Trimble assured them that the committee was determined to see all existing complaints "handled in a manner that will be entirely satisfactory to the complainants." While he did suggest that if the union insisted a committee representative might be available "to sit in with the management and grievance committee when the individual complaints are being considered," Trimble left little doubt that the FEPC hoped to minimize its future involvement. "I wish," he told union leaders, "that you would talk with the boys who filed complaints and let them know what we have done. This will avoid my having to write to each one individually."[22]

Trimble's hope that MMSW officials might be persuaded to finish the work that he had begun in Douglas was inspired by a heightened sense of the committee's beleaguered status and dissipated capacity rather than by a reasoned assessment of the union's ability to discharge the essential function his enforcement strategy contemplated. Confronted by a management whose aversion to unionism was legendary in the Southwest, the MMSW not only had its hands full in Douglas defending its initial organizational inroads against Phelps Dodge, but also had launched toward the end of 1942 a series of ambitious organizing campaigns that would occupy union officials in Arizona throughout that period during the early months of 1943 when the FEPC hoped they might devote their attention to the settlement of discrimination complaints.[23]

Even more importantly, the committee's intended reliance upon the MMSW to enforce its agreement with Phelps Dodge overlooked the union's stated conviction that discrimination against Chicano copper workers in the Southwest was so pervasive and deeply rooted that its elimination could be achieved only through direct and forceful federal action. The MMSW's insistent demands for FEPC action in the Southwest were a confession of its own inability to end discrimination in the industry's mines, mills, smelters, and refineries by exerting the conventional pressures available to trade unions. Even if it had possessed such power, however, the union's unqualified commitment to uninterrupted war production left it unwilling to press any issue, including discrimination against Chicano workers, to the point of impeding the mining or processing of copper in even the slightest degree. In reporting the efforts of southwestern locals to combat discrimination against Chicanos, the *Union,* the MMSW's official organ, left no doubt as to the union's priorities. "In spite of their long uphill fight for . . . equal rights for Spanish-speaking workers," the paper declared, "members of these local unions are aware that their biggest job today is helping win the war."[24]

In the absence of an effective means of oversight, it remained for Phelps Dodge, Miami, and Inspiration alone to decide both the form and extent of their future compliance with the president's order and to dictate the timing and method of their individual efforts to resolve existing complaints. Not surprisingly, each company exploited the committee's weakness to its own advantage. The Miami Copper Company quickly satisfied the terms of its agreement with the committee by simply asserting that the three complaints of discrimination lodged against it earlier no longer existed. Two of the three complainants had left its employ, the company reported, and the third, when confronted by the fact of his less than exemplary work record, readily acknowledged that his "failure of promotion has not been the result of any discrimination because of national origin, but has been due wholly to his lack of qualification to perform work in any classification other than that in which he is now engaged."[25]

Satisfying its agreement with the committee proved an equally painless task for the Inspiration Copper Company. Still contending, as it had from the start, that its promotion and wage policies were in no way discriminatory despite compelling evidence to the contrary, the company reported that it had disposed of the eighteen complaints of discrimination brought to its attention by the committee. According to the company, ten of the complainants were no longer in its employ. The company decided in each of the eight cases that remained that no discrimination had occurred, although it granted small wage increases to three of the complainants. In reporting his decisions to the committee, the company's general manager failed to specify the procedures he had followed or to indicate whether or not the complainants had been consulted at any stage of his deliberations.[26] The committee's failure, in turn, to question any aspect of the procedures followed or the decisions rendered by either the Inspiration Copper Company or the Miami Copper Company suggests that it was content to regard the cases as having been satisfactorily settled.

The FEPC clearly hoped that the complaints of discrimination pending against Phelps Dodge might be settled with equal dispatch, but the inability or unwillingness of MMSW officials in Douglas to pursue the method of settlement the committee proposed left them in limbo. After a further appeal for action from Trimble, a union official in Douglas finally responded toward the end of January. But while he assured Trimble that the union was attempting to assess the status of the complaints its members had filed, he also insisted that Phelps Dodge could not be trusted to keep its promises to the committee. Referring to an earlier promise that Phelps Dodge had made to the union regarding the settlement of grievances filed by Chicano workers, the official declared, "The Company lived up to their agreement about a week or ten days, then broke every agreement they had made [with] the Union."[27]

The union's belief that Phelps Dodge had no intention of abandoning its discriminatory employment policies was reinforced by the sporadic reports that the committee received from individual complainants and Chicano activists. For those workers who had risked the company's wrath by answering the FEPC's call for formal complaints of discrimination, the committee's failure to reward their courage with prompt and effective remedial action became a source first of frustration and then of despair.

The experience of Joe Chavez was, in many ways, typical. After working in the roaster department of Phelps Dodge's Copper Queen smelter in Douglas without the advancement to which he felt his six years of loyalty and experience entitled him, Chavez had gained prominence among the initial group of Chicano workers whose formal complaints of discrimination resulted in the company becoming the focus of the FEPC's investigation in the Southwest. Chavez complained:

> As for discrimination, it is one thing that is always present at the Smelter. We are given the worst jobs and we do them without any back talk and as well as we can and still we are discriminated [*sic*]. We just don't know how to please our bosses it seems.
>
> When we ask our bosses the reason we are denied promotion they tell us we are too dumb or haven't got enough education or whatever it pleases them to tell us as long as we don't get a better job.

It was only right, Chavez argued, that Phelps Dodge should "at least . . . give us a fair trial before passing judgment," and he emphasized that he was awaiting the corrective action that the FEPC had promised with mounting impatience.[28]

After waiting more than three months for the committee to act on his complaint, Chavez contacted Ernest Trimble in late November seeking a "definite answer" to his earlier plea for FEPC assistance in redressing the alleged mistreatment he had suffered at the hands of Phelps Dodge. Halfheartedly threatening a course of action that many other discouraged Chicano complainants had already taken, Chavez wrote, "I am planning on leaving the Smelter on account of the discrimination and unfair treatment, but I will wait until I hear from you."[29] In response, Trimble advised Chavez that in light of the committee's recently concluded agreement with Phelps Dodge his complaint would have to be resolved through the operation of the grievance machinery already in place at the company's Douglas smelter.[30]

Although the War Manpower Commission had sought during the early fall of 1942 to "freeze" workers in their jobs as a means of alleviating the increasingly severe labor shortages the copper industry faced, the resourcefulness of discontented workers in finding ways around the newly promulgated restrictions ensured that the manpower drain continued.[31] Even though Phelps Dodge had complained that the loss of manpower was especially acute insofar as Chicanos were concerned, the company's failure to implement its nondiscrimination agreement with the FEPC meant that frustrated workers like Joe Chavez would continue to seek employment opportunities elsewhere.[32]

Indeed, in his final plea to the FEPC, Chavez warned that unless the committee could assure him that it intended to do something about the continuing problem of discrimination against Chicano smeltermen at Douglas he would be forced to quit his job. "I would like for you to tell me my chances about a better job," he advised Trimble in mid-January, "or else I would like to have my release so that I can look for work someplace else."[33] Yet with the committee's already dubious authority rendered still more uncertain by the forced cancellation of its proposed railroad hearings only days earlier, Trimble was unable to offer Chavez anything more than rehearsed assurances. "The Committee on Fair Employment Practice wants these complaints settled satisfactorily to the men who made them," he perfunctorily declared. "If that is not done, Phelps Dodge Corporation will not have lived up to its understanding with us and we shall take whatever further action is considered necessary." But as he once again explained to Chavez, any such "further action" by the committee was contingent upon the demonstrated failure of the MMSW to achieve a satisfactory disposition of his complaint through the grievance process available to it at Douglas. "It is impossible for me to tell you what your chances are for a better job," Trimble replied, "unless I can get a report from your union officials about your case and whether or not the company has refused to satisfactorily adjust your case." Suggesting to Chavez that the matter was, at least for the time being, out of the committee's hands, he concluded, "Suppose you see what you can do toward getting [the union] to report to me at once."[34]

It is perhaps understandable that in light of its imperiled condition the committee should have elected to place greater faith in the professed intentions of Phelps Dodge than was warranted by the company's previous record in regard to the treatment of Chicano workers. Among Chicano complainants and their supporters, however, whose confidence in the government's fair employment policy depended upon the FEPC's effectiveness in combating discrimination in the copper industry, the committee's seeming appeasement of Phelps Dodge was a source of increasing consternation and suspicion.

Theodore Provencio, a Chicano community leader in Morenci, Arizona, repeatedly implored the committee from the late fall of 1942 through the early spring of 1943 to fulfill its promise of forceful action to eliminate the discriminatory employment policies in effect at

Phelps Dodge's huge open pit mine and ore-reduction works. Although Provencio's charges had already been confirmed by FEPC field investigator Daniel Donovan, who reported following his investigation in August that discrimination against Chicano workers was "an established policy of the Phelps Dodge Corporation in the Morenci area,"[35] the committee took the position that it was powerless to act until such time as individual victims of the company's unfair practices forwarded specific complaints.[36] Suggesting that it was Provencio's responsibility to supply the committee with such information, Lawrence Cramer patronizingly observed, "You will understand how important it is for the President's Committee on Fair Employment Practice to have very definite information before it proceeds against the Phelps-Dodge Corporation or any other company."[37]

Protesting that Donovan had earlier assured local activists in Morenci that the committee had more than enough evidence of discrimination to justify action against Phelps Dodge, Provencio disputed the view that more information was required and rejected Cramer's contention that those seeking to realize the promise of Executive Order 8802 were responsible for its enforcement. "If Mr. Donovan did not take to you enough valid information for you to proceed against said Corporation," Provencio indignantly declared, "we must say there is something mysterious about that. It is up to you, who are authorized to carry on such duties, to send an investigator or investigators who in turn will take actual facts to [the] Committee of our . . . situation here. In order to comply with your duty . . . you must take immediate action in correcting the unpatriotic deeds of the Phelps Dodge Corporation."[38] In response, Cramer merely renewed his invitation to Provencio to produce any evidence he had that Phelps Dodge was not living up to its nondiscrimination agreement with the FEPC and reiterated his earlier assurance "that the Committee is interested in seeing that the Mexican workers of your section are given a fair and equal chance with other employees."[39]

There is no reason to doubt that the FEPC, had it been free and able to do so, would have acted more forcefully and forthrightly in combating discrimination by Phelps Dodge, and other copper companies in the Southwest, against workers of Mexican descent. No matter how real and inescapable its constraints, however, the committee, by failing to honor the promises it made in the Southwest, had largely forfeited its positive image among Chicanos by the spring of 1943. Despite Ernest Trimble's comment to one union leader in Douglas that the committee "[did] not want the Mexican boys . . . to feel that we are 'letting them down,'" its palpably ineffectual efforts to alleviate the discrimination faced by Chicano copper workers inspired just such a conclusion.[40]

The committee's reputation suffered an equally precipitous decline among officials of the Mine, Mill and Smelter Workers in the Southwest. The union harbored a deep and abiding distrust of the region's leading copper companies, particularly Phelps Dodge, and its initial skepticism toward Trimble's efforts to negotiate voluntary compliance with Executive Order 8802 quickly gave way to an outspoken conviction that the committee was evading its responsibility to Chicano workers. Disputing Trimble's view that the committee's agreement with Phelps Dodge afforded a reasonable basis for resolving the problem of discrimination, George Knott, an MMSW official, bluntly observed, "It is my belief that the management of Phelps Dodge is dealing with you as they deal with us . . . with their fingers crossed. I have discussed this matter at some length with the balance of the staff and our conclusions are that unless the Government itself steps in to demonstrate that we're going to have democracy for all the people then a state of anarchy is going to exist which will be extremely detrimental to the production of Copper and other strategic metals." "Our feeling," Knott concluded, "is that a hearing must definitely be held in the Southwest if we ever expect to break the stranglehold that these copper barons have over the lives of the workers. My personal reaction is that words mean little or nothing to such firms as Phelps Dodge . . . you can't do business with Hitler."[41]

The president of the MMSW local at Douglas also complained to the committee more than four months after its agreement with Phelps Dodge went into effect that, except for a few token promotions granted to confuse the issue, discrimination against Chicano workers remained a central feature of the company's employment policy. It was evident from the company's cynical behavior, he suggested, that it never intended to live up to its agreement with the committee.[42]

In the end, however, the harshest and most embittered criticism of the committee by the MMSW came from Orville Larson, one of its top officials in Arizona. Explaining to Trimble why he had ignored the committee's earlier requests for information regarding the status of discrimination complaints pending against Phelps Dodge, Larson angrily wrote:

> I am sorry that I haven't answered these communications, but when I received word that the Committee . . . had reached an agreement with the Phelps Dodge Corporation relative to their discriminatory practices without even consulting the labor groups that had originally filed complaints against this corporation, it was my opinion that your Committee had no

> intention of enforcing Executive Order #8802 against the Phelps Dodge Corporation or any other mining company in the Southwest. I am still of that opinion and unless the Committee demonstrates to the International Union of Mine, Mill and Smelter Workers Locals in the Southwest that you intend to seek enforcement of the order it is useless for us to continue to co-operate with the Committee and waste our time and yours too in meaningless gestures.

"Discrimination against the Latin-American worker," Larson bitterly insisted, "has not been eliminated in the Southwest, regardless of how many understandings your Committee has reached with the various mining companies. We are spending valuable time that we could well devote to increasing the production of copper in fighting alone to force all companies to discontinue their discriminatory practices. I again want to remind you that 75% of the Nation's copper is being produced in this area, and 60% of the workers here are of Latin-American origin."

"We are ready and willing," he advised Trimble, "to co-operate with the President's Committee to enforce Executive Order 8802, but unless the Committee itself is ready to do the job it was set up to do the Union is apparently going to have to do the job by itself." Arguing that the committee should confront intransigent employers rather than accommodate them, Larson declared, "We again demand a complete investigation of discriminatory employment practices in the Southwest, particularly . . . Phelps Dodge, Nevada Con[solidated], Inspiration [and] Miami Copper, and this time we hope the Committee will go through with the job."[43]

Although Trimble was clearly stung by Larson's criticism, the committee was long past the point of believing that it could do anything more to alleviate discrimination against Chicano copper workers in the Southwest than their employers were willing to permit. By May 1943 the skeleton staff that remained in the committee's service was merely going through the motions of enforcing a threadbare mandate that was even then in the process of being superseded by a new presidential order whose scope and content was still shrouded in secrecy.

Beyond restating the committee's good intentions, and pleading once again for the union's indulgence, Trimble was at a loss to defend the FEPC's record in the Southwest.[44] Because the committee lacked the means to determine for itself what, if any, progress had been made in effectuating its agreement with Phelps Dodge, he was not in a position to question the company's belated claim that, except for two cases destined for arbitration, each of the more than forty complaints of discrimination filed against it by Chicano employees at the Douglas smelter had been settled.[45] Indeed, of the twenty-two complaints that resulted in what it characterized as a promotion or upgrading, the company insisted that in fifteen cases, or nearly 70 percent of those in question, settlements were effected even before the committee had closed its temporary field office in El Paso.[46]

Without the assistance of MMSW officials, who had reluctantly concluded that the committee was neither willing nor able to fight discrimination by Phelps Dodge with the vigor and resolve the task required, Trimble was powerless to determine the accuracy and validity of the company's claim that the complaints of Chicano smelter workers at Douglas had been satisfactorily settled. While he explained in his final appeal to the union that the committee was anxious "to clear the record on Phelps Dodge as soon as possible," the lack of a response eloquently confirmed the MMSW's ultimate loss of confidence in the FEPC's good offices.[47] So far had the committee's reputation declined among once hopeful MMSW officials in the Southwest that at least one, Verne Curtis, sought to promote effective federal action against job discrimination in the copper industry by exercising what served from the dawn of the New Deal as the final appeal of the powerless and the disillusioned: he wrote to Eleanor Roosevelt, asking her for the help that the FEPC had failed to provide.[48] Since such special pleadings were routinely forwarded to the appropriate federal agency, in this case the FEPC, Curtis's initiative was unrewarded. That he was reduced to seeking the First Lady's intercession, however, is indicative of the frustration and despair to which at least some union officials had succumbed by the spring of 1943 as a consequence of the FEPC's manifest failure to eliminate discrimination against Chicano copper workers.

The odds against the committee's success in the Southwest were, from the beginning, overwhelming. Although always careful to emphasize that its efforts in behalf of fair employment practices were inspired by a pragmatic commitment to the fullest possible utilization of manpower rather than by an ideological devotion to egalitarian principles, the committee necessarily remained an enemy of tradition. To the extent that the establishment of fair employment practices in the Southwest was likely to promote the equality of Chicano copper workers, it threatened to sabotage the industrial culture of hardrock mining, which had long rested on the twin inequities of employer hegemony and Anglo superiority.

The possibility of the committee's success in contending against the copper companies' united opposition to Executive Order 8802 had been remote under any circumstances. But once its already limited freedom of action and jurisdictional authority were reduced still further by the forced cancellation of its proposed hearings in the Southwest and by the president's decision to place it under the control of the War Manpower Commission, any remaining possibility that the committee could force the companies to abandon their discriminatory employment practices was effectively eliminated.

Throughout the fall of 1942 the committee's deepening sense of its own weakness informed the strategy it followed in the Southwest. Once it became apparent that it could neither force nor persuade the leading copper companies in the region to comply fully with the provisions of Executive Order 8802, the committee grew increasingly willing to settle for the illusion of compliance. Yet the committee's determination to have something to show for its otherwise unavailing exertions in the Southwest, while reflecting an understandable desire to salvage a badly tattered public image, produced a legacy of increasing distrust and alienation among Chicano copper workers and their supporters during the spring of 1943 as its sanguine claims of progress proved unfounded.

By fostering the impression that its agreements with the Phelps Dodge, Miami, and Inspiration copper companies constituted a significant advance in the cause of equal rights for Chicano workers, the committee also squandered whatever opportunity it might have had to ensure that federal efforts to satisfy the industry's continuing demands for the importation of Mexican labor would be made contingent upon real progress toward fair employment practices in the Southwest. Despite growing concern toward the end of 1942 over the critical manpower shortages faced by copper companies in the Southwest, federal officials remained unwilling to support the industry's proposal to import Mexican labor as long as discrimination against Chicano workers continued. Even after the War Manpower Commission agreed in late November to press the industry's case for importing Mexican workers, other interested federal agencies refused to endorse the idea because of their common concern "about the discrimination to which these Mexican miners might be subjected and the general effect it might have on the existing friendly relations between our country and Mexico, as well as our effort to strengthen and implement the good-neighbor policy."[49]

In early December the industry's hopes were suddenly revived, however, when Lawrence Cramer reported to an interagency conference on the status of Chicanos that, due to the FEPC's success in negotiating compliance agreements with three of the Southwest's leading copper companies, the problem of discrimination against Chicano workers in the region was well on the way to being solved.[50] Given the character of the agreements, which actually reflected the committee's weakness rather than its strength, Cramer's optimistic assertion that the force of the president's order was being exerted in the region fostered a grossly misleading impression. Yet because it was the federal agency directly responsible for certifying compliance with the government's nondiscrimination policy, the FEPC's claim that it was prevailing in the Southwest removed what had been the major impediment to the copper industry's stalled campaign to import Mexican workers.[51] The War Manpower Commission, which immediately seized upon Cramer's report of progress in the copper industry, was assuring other federal agencies by mid-January that "the racial discrimination problem in Arizona and New Mexico had, in large measure, been solved."[52]

There is little evidence to suggest that the timing of its agreements with the Phelps Dodge, Miami, and Inspiration companies was influenced by a desire on the part of the committee to assist the copper industry's efforts to recruit Mexican labor. Yet the FEPC's announcement that discrimination against Chicano copper workers was being overcome cleared the way for federal action on the industry's proposal. Negotiations with the Mexican government were begun soon thereafter and proceeded without significant opposition. Even the Mine, Mill and Smelter Workers Union refrained from public criticism of the industry's campaign. Less than a year before, the union had bitterly objected to "the growing pressure to import Mexican workers to relieve the alleged labor shortage in the Southwest" and had warned federal officials that it would "oppose any steps which will aggravate the widespread discrimination against Mexican workers that already exists in this country—or will create a new army of underpaid, underprivileged workers."[53] By the spring of 1943 the MMSW, torn between its desire to help alleviate the industry's manpower shortage and its determination to ensure fair treatment of Chicano copper workers, was apparently willing to accept private federal assurances that imported Mexican workers would not be subject to discrimination.[54] Although those union officials who were closest to the situation in the Southwest continued to complain that discrimination was still rampant, the MMSW made no effort to use the information as a basis for opposing the industry's plan.[55]

Although negotiations with the Mexican government were successfully concluded in June, and plans were made to import the first group of contract workers the following month,[56] the agreement was never implemented. Apparently concerned about the domestic political uproar that the arrangement was likely to excite, the Mexican government abruptly announced on the day the first contingent of laborers was scheduled to cross the border that it was voiding the deal because of the copper industry's continuing discrimination against workers of Mexican ancestry.[57]

There is, of course, no way of knowing what, if any, gains the FEPC might have realized had it attempted to link the copper industry's keen desire to import Mexican labor to concrete improvements in the treatment of Chicano workers. As it turned out, however, the committee's eagerness to claim progress where little or none had been achieved made it an unwitting accomplice to the industry's efforts to satisfy its manpower needs without abandoning the discriminatory employment practices that had helped to create the problem in the first place.

In fairness to the FEPC, whose members and staff stoutly persisted in their devotion to the ideal of workplace equality even as their efforts to realize it faltered, reducing or eliminating discrimination against Chicano copper workers in the Southwest, as well as against millions of other minority workers throughout the country, was an unattainable goal as long as the Roosevelt administration refused to bear the political costs of a resolute and forceful fair employment policy. That the administration remained unwilling to adopt such a policy became increasingly apparent during the spring of 1943 as the FEPC, its overvalued moral authority long since expended, dejectedly awaited the announcement that would formalize its already evident demise.

Ironically, the FEPC's formal dissolution was achieved by means of a presidential order renewing the Roosevelt administration's commitment to fair employment practices and creating a new Committee on Fair Employment Practice to accomplish its implementation and enforcement. Issued on May 27, 1943, Executive Order 9346 was the belated fulfillment of a reluctant promise the president had made three months earlier in response to angry protests that the administration had turned its back on minorities by repeatedly undermining efforts to enforce the nondiscrimination policy set forth in Executive Order 8802.

Given the singularly political motives that prompted the issuance of Executive Order 9346, it remained for the administration to prove to those who had come to doubt its sincerity in the matter of minority rights that its new policy was honestly meant to be more effective than its old policy had been. In the end, however, the real burden of proof rested with the new FEPC, whose unenviable task it was to convince disillusioned and doubtful minority workers, including thousands of Chicano copper workers in the Southwest, to reinvest their hopes for fair treatment on the job in a policy that, based on its earlier history, was more deserving of their contempt than of their confidence.

6. *Starting Over*

TO QUIET THE political clamor spawned by its decision in January 1943 to block the FEPC's proposed hearings into discrimination against black workers by the nation's railroad companies and unions, the Roosevelt administration had found it necessary to reiterate its support of a fair employment policy for which it had little or no genuine enthusiasm. Indeed, even after the president had publicly committed himself to the strengthening of the FEPC, his closest aides continued to debate in private a proposal to abolish the committee favored by some.[1] In a memorandum to Roosevelt explaining how the adoption of such a "revolutionary suggestion" might promote better relations between the administration and the Congress, one unidentified adviser declared, "I am confident that the continuation of the Committee means a continuation of agitation and provides a more fertile field for the professional trouble-makers among Negroes and some white people, as well."[2] Roosevelt apparently considered the abolition of the FEPC as a viable option until Jimmy Byrnes, one of his most influential advisers, expressed strong opposition to the idea in mid-March.[3]

While the White House appears to have attached little urgency to the problem of the FEPC's reorganization, the committee's supporters grew increasingly impatient as weeks passed without the presidential action first promised in early February. By mid-March this impatience had produced the first of a steady stream of complaints from various minority, liberal, and labor groups, who sternly warned Roosevelt that his delay in rescuing the FEPC from its deepening despair and impotence was, as NAACP secretary Walter White observed, encouraging the opponents of fair employment practices to "become more emboldened and aggressive in treating . . . Executive Order 8802 as the proverbial scrap of paper. . . ."[4] In response, the White House merely restated the president's promise to take action on the matter as promptly as circumstances permitted. All requests for personal meetings with Roosevelt, including those made by the remaining members of the FEPC, were either ignored or deflected.[5]

Given the enormous demands on the president's time, it is not surprising that the question of the FEPC's status, which never received the attention commanded by the more conspicuously momentous issues confronting a nation at war, was assigned a relatively low priority within the White House. It is also likely that the administration's slowness in addressing the problem derived, in part, from an uneasy feeling among White House advisers that the president was bound to lose politically no matter what course of action he finally chose to follow. On a more practical level, however, the FEPC's resurrection was contingent upon the selection of a new chairman and the promulgation of a new mandate, and neither was readily accomplished.

Once the president was persuaded that he could not abolish the FEPC, his advisers undertook a wide-ranging search for what one described as a "suitable Chairman."[6] Based on the candidates they considered, Roosevelt's advisers apparently agreed that the chairmanship of the FEPC required a white male who enjoyed the respect and confidence of black leaders, but whose loyalty to the president made him a reliable servant of the administration's larger purposes. Whether or not it was important that a southerner be found for the job remained a subject of mild dispute among the president's men, but they all appeared to agree with Will Alexander of the War Manpower Commission, who insisted that "the only kind of person who could really lift the Committee on Fair Employment Practice above the morass of misunderstanding and pettiness is a person of great national distinction."[7]

As White House aides soon discovered, however, finding a person of "great national distinction" who was willing to accept the appointment was not easily done. Certainly any candidate familiar with the FEPC's turbulent and trouble-plagued record during the preceding twenty months had ample reasons to regard its chairmanship as a potentially thankless and unpromising undertaking. The FEPC's task was unarguably immense, yet the administration's conspicuous reluctance to equip it with powers and resources commensurate with its daunting responsibilities made the chairmanship of the committee a distinctly unappealing and perilous assignment. Moreover, since many of the most able and best-qualified candidates for the job were already serving in posts of equal or greater importance to the war effort, the White House was understandably reluctant to strip one post of an effective administrator in order to fill another.

Francis Biddle, the attorney general, had advised Roosevelt when the issue of the FEPC's reorganization was first discussed that Frank Graham "would be a first-rate Chairman, if he could be spared from the War Labor Board." Graham, who felt that his "first obligation" was to the WLB, was finally dropped as an active candidate when Jimmy Byrnes, the director of the Office of Economic Stabilization, opposed the appointment "because the War Labor Board is just now of much greater importance than the Committee on Fair Employment Practice, and Graham is doing a good job."[8]

As it turned out, Graham was only the first of a lengthy succession of nominees who were either unable or unwilling to accept the chairmanship of a reorganized FEPC. Among the candidates considered for the job, assistant secretary of the interior Oscar Chapman appears to have had the greatest appeal to Roosevelt personally. During the course of his ultimately futile attempt to persuade interior secretary Harold Ickes that Chapman could take on the chairmanship of the FEPC without neglecting his duties at the Department of Interior, Roosevelt betrayed his continuing personal belief that the work of the committee was actually less vital than its champions maintained. Responding to Ickes's testy assertion that his department simply could not spare Chapman no matter how great the administration's need for a new FEPC chairman, Roosevelt soothingly wrote, "It is only a part-time job—a temporary job—and need not interfere with his Interior Department work."[9]

Although the FEPC and its supporters were distressed by the leisurely pace at which the administration seemed to be conducting its search for a new chairman, Roosevelt and his aides had, in fact, tried without success to promote interest in the job among a growing assemblage of prominent public figures.[10] In addition to Graham and Chapman, those individuals considered for the post included Will Alexander, deputy director of the War Manpower Commission; Harper Sibley, a former president of the United States Chamber of Commerce; Harold Swift, head of Swift and Company, the giant Chicago meatpacking firm; Edwin Day, the president of Cornell University; John Stewart Bryan, president of the College of William and Mary; and former senator George Norris, whose appointment was favored by the remaining members of the FEPC.[11]

Noting Roosevelt's difficulty in finding "someone willing to take over the red-hot driver's seat of the President's Fair Employment Practice Committee," the *New Republic* sardonically commented in May that the administration had let the committee sink into such a "miserable condition" that discouraged WMC officials were predicting that the chairmanship would have to be "palmed off on some unsuspecting winner in [a] telephone-radio lottery."[12] Yet for those who believed that the FEPC's incapacitation had helped to raise racial tensions in the country to dangerous levels, the continuing delay in naming a new chairman was hardly a source of amusement.

Francis Biddle, the member of the Roosevelt inner circle who had argued most forcefully in support of the FEPC's rehabilitation, warned the president on April 23 that a new chairman should be designated without further delay. "There has been no appointment of the Chairman of the Fair Employment Practices Committee," he reminded Roosevelt, "and the matter has now been dragging for three months since you made the announcement that it would be promptly reorganized." Implying that the administration had wasted enough time courting nominees who had little or no interest in the job, Biddle reported that he had recruited a viable candidate for the FEPC chairmanship. "I have suggested to Paul [McNutt]," he informed Roosevelt, "that he recommend Monsignor Francis Joseph Haas, who in my opinion would do the job better than anyone now available. He had great success at the old NLRB, is an outstanding Roman Catholic, a strong Liberal, entirely loyal to you, and a great admirer of the New Deal." He added, however, that Roosevelt would have to act at once if he wanted Haas for the post. "The situation is getting progressively worse," Biddle warned, "and I suggest that you may wish to make the appointment promptly . . . I talked to him [Haas] recently and believe that he would accept the appointment if he could get an adequate appropriation and a free hand under the Executive Order. I am afraid that we might lose him, however, if the appointment is delayed."[13]

Despite Biddle's urgent recommendation, Roosevelt and his aides were not willing to concede that Haas was the best available candidate for the job. Keenly aware that the FEPC chairmanship was, as presidential adviser Jonathan Daniels observed, "one of the most important positions which the administration has to fill if it is to avoid a great deal of grief," the White House still hoped to appoint someone who, by virtue of commanding stature or political acumen, could steer the committee along the course of least controversy without undermining its credibility.[14]

Biddle was not alone, however, in warning the White House that the delay in reviving the FEPC was contributing to a dangerous increase in racial friction. Citing the particularly ominous conditions that prevailed in Detroit, where only a month later federal troops would be required to quell a bloody race war that left 34 dead and more than 1,000 injured,

Lawrence Cramer echoed Biddle's concern. "The situation in Detroit and elsewhere has not been improved," Cramer insisted, "by the long delay which has taken place since the President's announcement of February 4 that it was his intention to reorganize the Committee in order to strengthen its activities." He continued, "Many minority group leaders are seriously concerned because of this delay and some have expressed the fear that the President's announced purpose to strengthen the Committee will not be carried out."[15]

As the search for a new FEPC chairman dragged into May, a sense of urgency finally began to emerge in the White House. Even presidential secretary Marvin McIntyre, who had seldom missed an opportunity to undermine the committee, advised Roosevelt on May 6 that the situation demanded a prompt resolution. Following a meeting during which the FEPC's four remaining members pressed their case for the immediate selection of former senator George Norris as the committee's new chairman, McIntyre told Roosevelt, "Frankly, I think it has reached the point where an appointment has to be made."[16]

The president apparently agreed. Bypassing WMC chairman Paul McNutt, who had taken the lead in contacting each of the earlier candidates to whom the post was offered, Roosevelt personally wrote to Senator Norris on May 8, emphasizing that his acceptance of the appointment was bound to ensure that "the Committee would have a prestige that it has not enjoyed in the past."[17] When Norris demurred, however, Roosevelt quickly acceded to Francis Biddle's earlier recommendation and prevailed upon Monsignor Francis J. Haas, dean of the School of Social Sciences at Catholic University, to accept the post.[18]

Despite their outspoken criticism of the administration for its slowness in selecting a new chairman, supporters of the FEPC were well pleased with the appointment of Father Haas.[19] They were still more pleased, however, by the prospect of the FEPC's immediate resumption of its long-suspended labors in behalf of fair employment practices. In the same telegram in which he applauded Haas's appointment, NAACP secretary Walter White also urged Roosevelt to order the immediate rescheduling of the previously canceled public hearings into discrimination against both black railroad workers and Chicano copper workers.[20]

The president's belated selection of a new person to lead the FEPC, though reassuring to many, left the larger questions of the reorganized committee's direction, agenda, and authority unanswered. Until the administration decided how far it was willing to go politically to repair its dilapidated commitment to fair employment practices, the FEPC, despite its reorganization, remained a means without a clearly prescribed end.

In deciding the FEPC's future, the administration indulged the same insular tendencies that dictated the closed process by which it searched for a new committee chairman. The FEPC and its supporters had been assured by Roosevelt that the committee would be "strengthened," but the subsequent denial of an opportunity to influence the administration's deliberations left them ignorant of the president's specific intentions.

In fashioning the executive order that would serve as the new FEPC's mandate, the president's advisers readily agreed on matters pertaining to the committee's composition (a paid chairman, who would also assume the duties of executive secretary, and six voluntary members), its organizational status (an independent agency within the Office for Emergency Management and directly responsible to the president), and its purpose (to eliminate employment discrimination by reason of race, creed, color, or national origin in war industries and federal agencies in order to promote the fullest utilization of all available manpower). Where they disagreed, and profoundly so, was over the question of the new FEPC's enforcement powers.

As he had from the first, Francis Biddle argued that the success of the FEPC was necessarily linked to its ability to compel compliance with the administration's nondiscrimination policy. The committee plainly lacked that ability under Executive Order 8802, he observed, and its increasingly conspicuous impotence had emboldened violators of the president's fair employment practices policy. Persuaded that if the administration really wanted a viable FEPC it would now have to prove it, Biddle proposed an executive order incorporating enforcement powers conducive to the new committee's success.

Detailing his proposal in a memorandum to Roosevelt on May 22, Biddle frankly asserted, "unlike the prior Fair Employment Practice Executive Order, the proposed order has teeth in it." Moral authority alone had proven a woefully inadequate substitute for genuine enforcement powers, and Biddle proposed that where persuasion was unavailing the new committee should be empowered to employ coercion as a last resort. "The proposed order," he explained,

> provides that all contracts hereafter negotiated or renegotiated by the Government shall contain a provision that the contractor or subcontractor will not discriminate because of the race, creed, color, or national origin of any employee or applicant for employment. Under this provision the Fair Em-

ployment Practice Committee is given the power to decide whether there has been discrimination in any particular case. If they should decide that there has been discrimination, their decision can be enforced in the courts by the use of mandatory injunction to prevent the continuance of discrimination or by the assessment of damages against the contractor in the form of reinstatement of the employee and the payment of back pay to him.

Biddle acknowledged that granting such powers to the new FEPC would constitute a fundamental departure from the administration's existing policy, but he argued that merely by possessing the authority required for effective enforcement of its mandate the committee could use persuasion to greater advantage than it had in the past. Referring to the enforcement authority he was proposing, Biddle wrote, "I think it should be used very sparingly. But the fact that it exists will undoubtedly make negotiation and mediation activities of the Committee far more effective than they have been in the past." To buttress his case, Biddle advised Roosevelt that he had discussed the issue with Father Haas and that the chairman-designate of the new FEPC favored the enforcement provisions his proposal incorporated.[21]

Apparently fearing that opponents of his proposal within the White House would prevail in their claim that it went too far in empowering the new FEPC, Biddle almost immediately suggested an amendment providing that the committee would be free to use its enforcement authority only when "it would not interfere with the prosecution of the war."[22] Biddle's amended proposal failed, however, to mollify those White House advisers who continued to oppose the inclusion of any enforcement authority in the new executive order contemplated by the president.

As a counter to Biddle's proposal, budget director Harold Smith drafted an alternative executive order incorporating the views of those within the White House who opposed a strong FEPC. Predictably, Smith's draft eliminated any mention of the enforcement powers included in Biddle's proposal. In transmitting both versions of the executive order to Roosevelt, Smith emphasized the clear choice they presented. "The two drafts," he commented, "differ in fundamental approach to the problem of discrimination." While noting that Biddle seemed to favor what he disparagingly described as "a strictly authoritarian approach" to the elimination of employment discrimination, Smith stressed that his proposal rested upon a conviction that the FEPC could do its job without resorting to confrontational tactics and punitive sanctions.

"The Bureau of the Budget draft," he advised Roosevelt, "is based on the belief that the discrimination problem can be handled more successfully by education, persuasion, and pressure than as a matter of law enforcement. It leaves the powers of the Committee substantially as at present. It requires anti-discrimination provisions in Government contracts and authorizes the Committee to conduct hearings and investigations, make findings of fact, and take appropriate steps for eliminating discrimination, but it does not empower the Committee to issue orders enforceable in the courts."

If "the law enforcement approach" was adopted, Smith cautioned, it would necessitate the appointment of a committee composed of objective public servants rather than of partisan advocates. "It seems to me unsound," he told Roosevelt, "to vest quasi-judicial powers in a body partly composed of representatives of the very minority groups which are interested parties to the proceedings. I would recommend a three member Committee consisting only of public members if it is to have such powers."

In the end, however, Smith and his like-minded White House colleagues opposed the creation of a strong FEPC because of the controversy its enforcement efforts were likely to foment. "I seriously question the desirability of trying to handle the discrimination problem on a law enforcement basis," he wrote. "Serious labor trouble may be expected," he warned, "if the Government attempts by quasi-judicial action to force employment of racial minorities on the same basis as whites. The major obstacle in eliminating discrimination is not employer prejudice but the attitude of workers in the plant. This attitude is a hard fact which cannot be ignored. An enforcement program would probably result in work stoppages which might substantially interfere with war production."

Merely by possessing the power to enforce its will, Smith contended, the FEPC would be obliged by its most zealous constituents to use its authority fully and without prudent regard for the potential consequences. A strong FEPC, he insisted,

> would strengthen the hands of the extremists in the minority groups and intensify the pressure for strict enforcement based on a legalistic interpretation of the Order.
>
> It would be very difficult for the Committee to follow a moderate course. Any attempt to adjust its action to the realities of the situation where racial feeling runs high would bring charges that the Committee had

> failed to perform its legal duty. The Committee would face the danger either of being discredited with minorities or of having to adhere to a uniform body of case law in all regions and situations.

Such an approach, he added, would almost certainly "be attacked in Congress as an attempt to legislate social reform by Executive Order" and would induce "southern members of Congress . . . [to] block the appropriation of funds for a Committee with mandatory powers." In light of the potential dangers that a strong FEPC posed, Smith concluded, the administration would be wise to ensure that the new committee kept to the path traveled by the old. "I believe that the best course," he advised Roosevelt, "would be to reconstitute the Committee with a carefully selected membership which avoids minority extremists and let it operate for a time under a charter that does not confer mandatory authority over private employment. I do not feel that the old Committee was afforded a fair demonstration of what can be accomplished through education and pressure. If after a reasonable effort the new Committee is convinced that a stronger Executive Order is needed, it can then be revised."[23]

Apparently unimpressed by Biddle's report that Father Haas expected to preside over a strong FEPC, Roosevelt promptly endorsed Smith's proposal for a new committee that was, in its most crucial aspect, identical to its discredited predecessor. Issued by the president on May 27, Executive Order 9346 merely reiterated the administration's policy "that there shall be no discrimination in the employment of any person in war industries or in Government by reason of race, creed, color, or national origin. . . ." For those who had hoped that Roosevelt would honor his earlier pledge to "strengthen" the FEPC, the new order was a source of keen disappointment. It did restore the committee's independence by locating it within the Office for Emergency Management. And, although the committee's freedom of action would remain an unsettled issue, the new order expressly authorized the use of hearings as an investigative device. Still, insofar as enforcement powers were concerned, Executive Order 9346 left the FEPC in the same unhappy predicament in which it had found itself under the original order. In those cases in which violators of the president's order could not be persuaded to comply with its provisions on a voluntary basis, the committee remained powerless to compel compliance. Given the president's continuing unwillingness to adopt a forceful policy, there was no reason for the new committee to expect any more assistance from the White House in disciplining violators than its predecessor had received.

Notwithstanding its carefully crafted flimsiness as a declaration of policy, Executive Order 9346 was important if for no other reason than because it symbolized the resurrection of an ideal that the nation's minorities continued to cherish despite the first FEPC's scant success. The sense of renewal fostered by the issuance of Executive Order 9346 was reinforced as well by an infusion of fresh personnel and the provision of an operating budget large enough to permit the new committee, through the eventual establishment of twelve regional offices, to project a national presence.[24]

Beyond ensuring that no "extremists" ended up on the new committee, the White House was generally willing to entrust the selection of its members to Father Haas.[25] Of the four remaining members of the old FEPC, the White House approved the reappointment of three: John Brophy, Milton Webster, and Boris Shishkin, who had replaced Frank Fenton at the end of 1942 as the AFL's representative on the committee. Only Earl Dickerson, whose thinly veiled criticisms of the administration's attitude toward the FEPC were still fresh in the minds of some White House aides, was denied reappointment.[26] The remaining members of the new committee, whose selection in each case was intended to contribute to the representative balance the White House hoped to achieve, were Samuel Zemurray, a southern Jew who headed the United Fruit Company; Sara Southall, the director of personnel for the International Harvester Company; and P. B. Young, publisher of the *Norfolk Journal and Guide,* a prominent black newspaper.[27]

When the new committee began its labors at the beginning of July it faced a daunting array of immediate challenges. Heir to an insolvent image that rendered it suspect even before it began to function, the committee was acutely conscious of the need to restore confidence in a fair employment policy that had collapsed under the weight of its apparent irrelevance. But while Father Haas undoubtedly recognized that nothing short of a highly visible campaign of enforcement was likely to satisfy skeptics, he was also made aware that the White House expected the committee to do its job without attracting undue attention or provoking controversies of the sort that had entangled its predecessor.

The White House communicated its expectations through a confidential prospectus that Marvin McIntyre sent to Haas shortly after he accepted the FEPC chairmanship. Predicated upon a belief that the original FEPC's difficulties were largely of its own making, the White House critique contemplated an approach to the enforcement of Executive Order 9346 that shunned confrontational methods in favor of quiet and patient negotiations conducted, whenever possible, on an informal basis. Too often, the White House observed, the old committee's reliance on "contentious open hearings" had succeeded only "in giving it the reputation of being a social reform unit bent on changing people's mores by Federal intervention." The purpose of the president's order, the White House insisted, was not to eliminate employment discrimination as an end in itself, but rather to combat job bias as an expedient means of promoting the fullest possible utilization of available manpower. Remembering that purpose, Haas was obliquely cautioned, would spare the new committee the unhappy fate that had befallen the old committee when it lost sight of its essential *raison d'être*.[28]

Beyond the immediate problems of reorganization that confronted him, including the establishment and staffing of regional offices in each of the War Manpower Commission's twelve administrative districts, Haas faced insistent demands that the new committee declare its intentions regarding those still unresolved issues that had figured so prominently in the piecemeal undoing of its predecessor. As the NAACP's Walter White had noted, two challenges in particular loomed before the new committee as urgent and inevitable tests of its mettle: the rescheduling of public hearings on discrimination against black railroad workers and the convening of public hearings to explore discrimination against Chicano workers in the Southwest.[29]

The railroad hearings, whose earlier cancellation had plunged the old FEPC into a crisis of confidence from which it never recovered, commanded a symbolic importance that the new committee immediately acknowledged. And at its very first meeting the committee rescheduled the railroad hearings for mid-September.[30] Charting an appropriate course of action in regard to the Southwest, however, proved a more complicated undertaking. In response to concerns expressed by Mexican consular officials in Texas, whose investigations of alleged discrimination against Chicano workers at various oil refineries in the Houston area had fostered renewed demands for federal action, Haas promised that the Southwest would be an immediate focus of the new committee's attention. "At its first meeting," Haas assured an aide to the Mexican ambassador in early July, "the situation in the Southwest relative to discrimination will be presented to the Committee for its action."[31]

Although the status of Chicano workers in the Southwest was a "pending matter" on the agenda for its first meeting, the committee discussed it only tangentially. Other than a decision to seek additional information concerning new allegations of discrimination against Chicano refinery workers in Texas, the committee ignored the subject of job bias in the Southwest.[32] In part, the committee's failure to take prompt action regarding the situation in the Southwest merely reflected its overburdened condition as pressing organizational and procedural matters competed with substantive issues for immediate attention and resolution. More to the point, however, ameliorative action in behalf of Chicano workers was contingent upon an informed assessment of prevailing conditions in the Southwest, and the information available to the new committee as it began its work was, at best, fragmentary and outdated.

The old committee's unwarranted claims of progress in combating discrimination against Chicano workers by three of the region's leading copper companies had only served to confuse the situation. When its hapless plan to monitor compliance from afar failed, the committee was left with little more than vague, and largely misleading, impressions of the extent to which Chicano copper workers had benefited from its ultimately feckless intercession.

During its first few weeks of operation the new committee's only source of up-to-date information regarding the treatment of Chicano copper workers were those few individual complainants who bothered to answer Ernest Trimble's continuing appeals for progress reports. Although hardly definitive, these sporadic reports strongly suggested that the discriminatory wage, hiring, and promotion practices documented by the committee's investigation during the previous fall remained in effect. Jesus Gutierrez, an employee of the Inspiration Copper Company in Miami, Arizona, complained to Trimble shortly after the new committee began its work that discrimination against Chicano workers was as common and virulent as ever. The company continued to maintain separate "Mexican" and "Anglo" wage rates, he claimed, and inexperienced Anglo workers were still being hired to fill highly paid skilled jobs for which experienced Chicano workers remained ineligible. Gutierrez did report that the Mine, Mill and Smelter Workers Union, which had recently won bargaining rights at Inspiration's Miami operations, was pressing the War Labor Board to eliminate the company's discriminatory wage classifications. But, he warned, Chicano workers were so angry and disheartened as a consequence of their continued mistreatment that, in the absence of immediate reforms, they were contemplating a "mass migration to other war industries where racial discrimination does not exist."[33]

Recognizing that it could not take action in the Southwest until it was better informed, the committee was unable to offer anything more than vague, perfunctory assurances of future assistance to persistent complainants like Jesus Gutierrez.[34] The committee did, however, take two important actions intended to clarify the extent to which Chicano workers remained subject to discriminatory employment practices: it ordered a candid assessment of the old committee's efforts to promote fair employment practices in the copper industry and it appointed Carlos Castañeda, a respected history professor at the University of Texas, to oversee its future field investigations of discrimination against Chicano workers in the Southwest.[35]

Conducted by Marjorie Lawson of the FEPC's newly created Division of Review and Analysis, the investigation of the old committee's efforts to combat discrimination against Chicano workers by the Southwest's leading copper companies disclosed a record almost completely devoid of enduring accomplishments. With very few exceptions, Lawson found, the discriminatory practices that the committee had hoped to eliminate through its separate compliance agreements with the Phelps Dodge, Miami, and Inspiration copper companies remained as common in the fall of 1943 as they were a year earlier. Referring to what she regarded as the fraudulent record of Phelps Dodge in living up to its agreement with the committee, Lawson wrote, "It is possible that the company's agreement with the Committee, which was implemented only at the Douglas branch and which resulted in a number of upgradings of Mexican workers, was made with the interest of confusing the issue of discrimination raised both by the CIO union and the Committee. At that time, the threat of a public hearing in the Southwest had not been lifted. A record of settlements would, therefore, have provided the company with a worthy defense."

"The real issue," Lawson observed, "appears to remain unsolved as a result of action taken to date. There is still a double wage scale and no upgradings of Mexican workers have taken place except at the Copper Queen Smelter at Douglas. Everyone interested in the problem, the workers themselves, the CIO union, the labor leadership of the Southwest and the representatives of the Mexican Government are of the opinion that conditions can be improved only by overall Government action." "Actually," she bluntly concluded, "all that has been accomplished is formal paper compliance and token upgrading of a few Mexicans."[36]

Lawson reached equally damning conclusions regarding the committee's record in eliminating unfair employment practices by other copper companies in the Southwest. In those cases where the committee's overtures were not simply ignored or brazenly rebuffed, she observed, its efforts achieved nothing more than "token" adjustments and "paper" compliance with the president's order. Although its lengthy field investigation during the fall of 1942 had "confirmed the essential truth" of the complaints of discrimination lodged by Chicano workers and their supporters, the committee abruptly abandoned its enforcement efforts in the Southwest, Lawson suggested, once it became apparent that the region's leading copper companies would not agree to anything more than conditional compliance with Executive Order 8802. In the wake of the committee's retreat, she noted, the only significant effort to continue the fight for fair employment practices in the Southwest was undertaken by "various CIO locals which almost alone have championed the cause of the Mexican worker."

Beyond failing to alleviate the problem of discrimination in the Southwest, Lawson argued, the committee compounded its difficulties in the region by alienating those who had placed their faith in its good offices. As a consequence, she cautioned, any initiatives in the region by the new committee would face the suspicion and distrust unwittingly sowed by its predecessor. "It may be said," she wrote, "that months of silence and inactivity by the Committee, after an on-the-spot investigation which had aroused the hope of the Mexican people and their friends, have affected the prestige of the Committee seriously in the Southwest. It would be unwise to reopen the cases without careful consideration of the magnitude of the problem and a determination to pursue to its conclusion whatever course of action may be necessary to carry out the policies of Executive Order 9346."

Despite her caution to the committee, however, Lawson recognized that discrimination against Chicanos in the Southwest was so pervasive and egregious that to ignore it further was to evade the FEPC's newly reconfirmed commission. "The plight of the Mexican worker," she maintained,

> is the concern of the Committee because it results in non-utilization or under-utilization of his skills in war production. But the problem has a broader significance also directly connected with the prosecution of the war, which is not the Committee's concern, but which inevitably will be affected by the settlement of the complaints [in the Southwest]. The Spanish-speaking people who live in the United States, both citizens and non-citizens, are a link between this country and Mexico and all of Latin America. If discrimination exists against them in this country, the other Americas are aware of it. The Good Neighbor policy can flourish only as we implement our pronouncements of democracy by democratic action.

"There are those," she disdainfully observed, "who advocate, as in the case of the Negro problem, a long range program of education, both for Anglo Americans and for the 'backward' Mexican. The policy of gradualism appeals to many who fear the consequences of a forthright program. However, neither war production nor the war ideology can wait for the results of gradualism, which, if successfully begun now, might find expression in the next generation."

It was plainly incumbent upon the new committee to finish the task that its predecessor had started and then abandoned in the Southwest, Lawson concluded, and she recommended the adoption of a prudent but resolute plan of action to promote that end. "In reopening the Mexican cases," she wrote, "the Committee should consider them as a group and should plan an overall strategy for their disposition. In a few instances, Committee intervention has resulted in paper compliance and a few token upgradings of Mexican workers. There is little doubt that by now the situation has degenerated and that even these gains have been modified. In other cases . . . the Committee has issued no directives and has had little contact with the Management." Also, she warned, the situation remained complicated by the continuing conflict between the CIO and AFL over bargaining rights in the copper industry; thus enforcing Executive Order 9346 meant overcoming the obstacles to full compliance created by union rivalries as well as those erected by intransigent employers.

As a first step, Lawson proposed that "a corps of . . . field investigators and 'trouble shooters' be assigned" to the Southwest in order "to determine the present situation of the individual complainants and of conditions in the [copper] industry generally which affect minority workers." She further proposed that field investigators be authorized where circumstances warranted both to issue "proper directives . . . in line with the Committee's present policies and procedures for the adjustment of cases" and to refer to the FEPC's Washington headquarters "for further action . . . all cases which cannot be settled at the regional level." Insofar as the unions in the region were concerned, Lawson urged the committee to put them on notice that its revived investigation of employment practices would include a careful analysis of "the status of all contracts between these unions and the companies involved, with particular reference to those clauses in the contracts dealing with nondiscrimination and with seniority rights."

In light of the old committee's unhappy experience in the Southwest, which ended in an unseemly, if not wholly unjustified, retreat from its announced purpose and the consequent disillusionment of its Chicano clients and their supporters, Lawson insisted that the new committee should not recommit itself to action in the region unless it was prepared to follow through to the limits of its resources and authority. Specifically, she cautioned, the committee should be prepared, if the situation demanded, to convene public hearings in the Southwest. "It is especially noted," she reported, "that the Mexican workers, the CIO unions, the liberal leaders of the Southwest, many government officials who have been consulted in Washington, and finally the Mexican Embassy itself, are of the opinion that nothing short of a public hearing will serve to correct the evils now under consideration." That being the case, she reasoned, it was essential that "the Committee decide, in advance, that is before the cases are reopened, that if developments warrant a public hearing in the Southwest or at any place on this issue, that its plans to hold such a hearing will not be thwarted by any agency or person, except by direction of the President."[37]

Between August and November 1943, the period during which Lawson was conducting her investigations, the committee purposely followed what she described as "a policy of delay" in regard to its handling of the complaints of discrimination that Chicano workers and their advocates continued to lodge.[38] Yet, as Lawson had noted in her report, which she submitted at the beginning of November, the committee was necessarily disposed to defer action until it decided how far it should or could go in seeking to redress the problem of employment discrimination in the Southwest.

Still, the committee did not entirely ignore the issue of Chicano workers while it awaited Lawson's findings. In the hope of countering claims of Anglo superiority, which remained a principal rationale for discrimination in the Southwest, the committee approved an ill-advised proposal to study "the comparative productive skills" of Chicano workers. In mid-October FEPC deputy chairman Malcolm Ross, who was shortly to succeed to the chairmanship of the committee following Father Haas's sudden elevation to the bishopric of Grand Rapids, Michigan, asked the Industrial Personnel Division of the War Department for information "pertaining to [the] physical stamina, intelligence quotients, manual dexterity, ability to learn English, qualities of leadership, personality characteristics, aptitudes and skills" of Chicano workers. This information was needed, Ross explained, for the purpose of "comparing the Spanish speaking people to other groups in the population. . . ."[39]

The controversy that such a misguided study might have provoked was ultimately avoided due to a lack of relevant data and because of the strong opposition voiced by Marjorie Lawson.[40] Such a study, Lawson warned, was "capable of being interpreted as constituting a doubt on the part of the Committee as to whether differences based on racial identification may actually exist, when, in fact, medical science, anthropology and sociology have exploded the theory of superior and inferior races." The committee should do nothing, she insisted, that might appear to legitimize employment discrimination. "If management believes that Mexican workers are inferior," she argued, "then the burden of proof rests upon management, not the Committee."[41]

As long as the committee was bogged down with questions of policy and procedure in regard to the Southwest, it was not in a position to take full advantage of the special talents of Carlos Castañeda, its newly appointed authority on Chicano workers. Yet while Castañeda spent most of his time during the summer and fall of 1943 managing the FEPC's recently established regional office in Dallas, it was the prospect of an all-out campaign to eliminate discrimination against Chicano workers that sustained his enthusiasm for the committee's work.

In Castañeda the new committee had what its predecessor had conspicuously lacked: an investigator whose expertise in the matter of the Chicano population of the Southwest was informed by intimate personal experience no less than by dispassionate inquiry. Moreover, Castañeda brought to his work as the FEPC's resident expert on Chicanos an impatience for change that led him to conclude that Executive Order 9346, despite its promulgation as a wartime expedient, ought to be wielded boldly and decisively in the battle against discrimination on the job.[42]

Castañeda's initial effort to project the new FEPC's authority in the Southwest, however, received less than enthusiastic support from his superiors. At the suggestion of the Nonferrous Metals Commission, the special subagency of the War Labor Board with jurisdiction over the copper industry, Castañeda sought the committee's approval in mid-September to undertake a joint investigation of alleged wage discrimination against Chicano workers by the American Smelting and Refining Company at its operations in Vanadium, New Mexico.[43] The potential value of a close working relationship with the WLB had long been recognized by the committee's membership and staff. The particular appeal of such a relationship in dealing with the problem of wage discrimination in the Southwest, however, was enhanced shortly after the issuance of Executive Order 9346 when the WLB, in a case involving the Southport Petroleum Company, ordered the elimination of wage differentials based on racial considerations.[44] Noting the apparent relevance of the WLB's decision to the discriminatory wage policies of southwestern copper companies, James Fleming and Daniel Donovan, two of the field investigators involved during the previous fall in the committee's ill-fated enforcement campaign in the region, urged Ernest Trimble to use it as a basis for launching a renewed effort to eliminate the industry's so-called Mexican wage. "It seems to us," Fleming wrote, "that now is a good time for you to recapitulate our experiences and findings in the Southwest in regard to wage differentials against Mexicans and persons of Spanish-American background, both citizens and aliens. The WLB decision undoubtedly gives FEPC and other agencies of the Government an opportunity for the first time to correct the unfair practices against Spanish-American workers and, particularly, gives FEPC an opportunity to reconsider the 'unfinished business' of the Southwest."[45]

While the new committee cautiously pondered an appropriate southwestern strategy during the summer and fall of 1943, discrimination against Chicano workers became a source of increasing concern to the WLB as the Mine, Mill and Smelter Workers Union, which had recently scored impressive victories over its AFL rivals in their continuing battle for jurisdictional supremacy in the copper industry, vigorously pressed the "Mexican wage" issue in contract negotiations.[46] In anticipation of having to address the issue, the WLB's Nonferrous Metals Commission began its own investigation of alleged wage discrimination against Chicano copper workers in late August.[47] When its inquiry disclosed the necessity for remedial action against specific companies, the NMC sought to enlist the FEPC's cooperation as a means of countering potential objections from employers that its jurisdiction did not extend to questions of discrimination.[48]

Although Carlos Castañeda strongly urged the committee to join forces with the NMC in combating the copper industry's discriminatory dual-wage system, his superiors feared that the broad approach to enforcement that such an alliance contemplated threatened to take the FEPC beyond the boundaries of its legitimate authority. In denying Castañeda's request to take part in the NMC's investigation of alleged wage discrimination by the American Smelting and Refining Company, Will Maslow, the FEPC's director of field operations, explained, "The Committee has for some time been considering the general question of whether regional directors should make investigations of what they believe to be discriminatory employment practices in the absence of filed complaints. The problem is a complicated one because the [War Manpower Commission] feels that such work is properly within its jurisdiction." Accordingly, Maslow declared, the committee was not prepared to authorize the course of action Castañeda proposed. Maslow did promise Castañeda that he would seek "some clarification of the entire problem."

The committee's continuing uncertainty regarding an appropriate enforcement strategy in the Southwest finally led it to conclude in early December that the NMC would have to pursue its investigation of possible wage discrimination against Chicano workers by American Smelting and Refining without the FEPC's active assistance.[49]

Despite the committee's unwillingness to endorse his initial plan of action in the Southwest, in late November Castañeda received a personal assurance from FEPC chairman Malcolm Ross that discrimination against the region's Chicano workers would shortly be accorded the attention that it had earlier been denied. Explaining why he was resisting pressures to appoint Castañeda permanent director of Region X,[50] Ross insisted that such an appointment might thwart the committee's intentions by distracting its "specialist on Spanish-American and Mexican-American problems" from his central mission. "Your special interests extend beyond regional boundaries and include the whole Southwest," Ross reminded Castañeda. "This obviously spreads very thin the good which one man can do. We need all your energy and wisdom on the one specified problem." The directorship of Region X would burden Castañeda with "administrative details" and "the problems of all the Negroes in [the] region," Ross insisted, and would therefore deny Chicano workers the full benefit of his undivided attention. Confiding to Castañeda the committee's tentative plan of action in the Southwest, Ross wrote: "I may say to you (although this must be kept in complete confidence for the time being) that the Committee may very well hold hearings in its mining cases some time in February or March, and perhaps at Phoenix. The plan is very tentative, but you can see that your duties in connection with it would be very intense. The entire issue of eliminating discrimination against Mexicans depends upon how wisely and well we conduct ourselves during the next few months." "It might be tragic to miss that opportunity," he pointedly cautioned Castañeda, "because of a need to divert your attention constantly to the administrative job and to the problems of the Negroes in your region."[51]

If the committee appeared overly cautious to Castañeda and other advocates of immediate and forceful action in the Southwest, its deliberateness was well advised. As Marjorie Lawson had emphasized in her report on the status of fair employment practices in the Southwest, successful enforcement of the president's order would ultimately depend upon the committee's willingness and ability to convene public hearings in the region as a last resort. And while the language of Executive Order 9346 appeared to grant the FEPC the authority it required to take such a step, the still vivid memory of its predecessor's ill-fated plan to conduct public hearings in El Paso a year earlier created genuine doubts regarding the new committee's actual freedom of action.

In the hope of ensuring that it would not further undermine its credibility among Chicanos in the Southwest by making promises it could not keep, the committee sought explicit White House authorization to proceed with public hearings in the region should they prove necessary to the enforcement of the president's order. In a letter to presidential aide Jonathan Daniels in early November, Malcolm Ross reported that the continuing problem of discrimination against Chicano workers in the Southwest clearly demanded forceful action by the FEPC. Yet it would be pointless for the committee to address the issue, he observed, unless it received an assurance from the White House that the Department of State would not once again prevail upon the president to prohibit the public hearings that FEPC enforcement efforts in the region would almost certainly necessitate. Recalling the unhappy consequences of the committee's earlier involvement in the Southwest, Ross declared, "The cancellation of the hearings, the withdrawal of the Committee's representatives from the Southwest and the refusal of the [copper] companies to comply with the stated non-discrimination policy of Executive Orders 8802 and 9346, have resulted in great discouragement to the Spanish-speaking people of the Southwest. In many situations, the minimum gains of the summer of 1942 have been lost." "The complainants, the labor unions which have espoused their cause, the representatives of the Mexican Government, and the liberal leadership of the Southwest," he advised Daniels, "are of the opinion that nothing but overall Government action can eliminate discrimination against these workers." To neglect the problem further, Ross asserted, was to jeopardize both the war effort and the Good Neighbor Policy. "The Committee therefore considers it expedient," he explained, "to reopen the Mexican cases, which have been quiescent since December, 1942. It would be futile, however, to raise these issues again without prior consideration of the ultimate steps which may be required for the adjustment of these grievances. The eventual necessity of a public hearing appears to be inevitable. The history of Committee action in the Mexican cases has deprived it of prestige and the confidence of the workers, who will be reluctant to cooperate without assurance that the Committee, this time, will prosecute the investigation to its logical conclusion."[52]

By requesting the Roosevelt administration's support for a plan of action that committed the FEPC to enforce Executive Order 9346 in the Southwest to the utmost limits of its authority and resources, Ross presented the White House with just the sort of political dilemma that the president and his aides hoped the new committee would avoid. As it had on previous occasions, the White House responded to the committee's request for presidential backing of a potentially controversial undertaking with the reflexive caution that was its controlling instinct when questions of the FEPC's enforcement powers arose.

Recalling the controversy generated more than a year earlier when the old committee first proposed to hold public hearings in the Southwest, Jonathan Daniels immediately sought to determine whether or not the Department of State continued to oppose the idea. What he found in place of the unalloyed opposition voiced by the Department of State in the summer of 1942 was something of a division within the ranks of its Latin American experts based on conflicting assessments of the Mexican government's probable reaction to public hearings that would almost certainly expose widespread systemic discrimination against Chicano workers in the Southwest.

While stressing that the State Department remained "convinced . . . that discrimination difficulties can be solved only by means of long-range programs embracing the education and the improvement of the standard of living of the alien population involved and the education of both aliens and citizens to a better understanding of each other," Lawrence Duggan, head of the Division of the American Republics, concluded in an internal memorandum that "public hearings on certain phases of the discrimination question, carefully planned and conducted, may be considered a good way of determining whether discrimination exists and of determining effective ameliorative measures for its correction." The State Department had "valid reasons for opposing public hearings on this question last year," he insisted, because of concerns expressed by the Mexican government. Yet now, he conceded, the "attitude of the Mexican Foreign Office has . . . apparently changed, and it has evidenced interest in public action regarding discrimination problems."

"The Department, therefore, would now be prepared to withdraw its objections to hearings by the Committee on Fair Employment Practices [*sic*]," Duggan reported, "provided there are assurances that the hearings will be carefully planned and carried out by persons thoroughly familiar with the social and economic environment and problems of the Southwest." It would be particularly helpful, he added, if in planning for such hearings the FEPC consulted with Consul General William P. Blocker, whose lengthy consular service in Ciudad Juárez afforded him an extensive knowledge of Anglo-Chicano relations in the El Paso area.

Duggan further proposed that any hearings held in Texas be "coordinated" with the state's Good Neighbor Commission, which had been established by Governor Coke Stevenson in mid-1943 largely as a public relations gambit designed to win a reversal of the Mexican government's decision barring the use of contract labor in Texas because of its especially egregious record of discrimination against Chicanos.[53]

Yet if the State Department's Washington-based Latin American specialists viewed FEPC hearings in the Southwest as a less alarming prospect than they had a year earlier, U.S. ambassador to Mexico George S. Messersmith remained staunchly opposed to the idea. Messersmith, whose rigid and often condescending views toward Latin America frequently placed him at odds with department specialists, argued forcefully that a change of policy was unwarranted.[54] "I still remain of the opinion that no useful purpose can be served by the holding of such hearings," he curtly advised Washington on November 18. If the Mexican government now appeared to be more favorably disposed to public hearings than it was in 1942, Messersmith explained, it was only because public opinion in Mexico had to be assuaged. In reality, he suggested, nothing had changed. "I believe . . . that fundamentally the attitude of our Mexican Government remains the same and that the less said about discrimination, except in the most constructive way, the better for the relations of the two countries."

The problem of discrimination against Chicanos in the Southwest was of long standing, Messersmith insisted, and not amenable to solutions other than those based on forbearance and gradualism. "Those of us who have to deal with this problem of discrimination every day," he wrote, "realize that it is one that will not be solved in a day nor in a year nor by fact finding commissions nor by holding hearings such as those planned by the President's Committee on Fair Employment Practice." Moreover, he argued, any effort to deal with the problem in a precipitate way would probably imperil the bilateral labor contracts that the State Department had, only after "the greatest difficulty," negotiated with the Mexican government. "I feel that it is necessary," Messersmith declared,

> to inject a realistic note into this discussion by stating frankly and bluntly that the holding of hearings by the Committee on Fair Employment Practice with respect to Mexican workers in the Southwest may merely lead to the raising of all sorts of questions, the repercussion of which will be such in Mexico that the Mexican Government will not be able . . . in view of public pressures within Mexico itself to continue to send . . . workers . . .

> to the United States. In other words, it remains my opinion that the holding of such hearings by the Committee may seriously prejudice the whole movement of workers from Mexico to the United States . . . during the war.

"As I see it," he insistently reiterated, "the only result that we could possibly expect to get from hearings by this Fair Employment Practice Committee would be the possibility and very grave probability of stirring up problems and discussions of which the Mexican Government would have to take note with the consequent result that questions would be raised with us which would almost certainly destroy the sending of labor under these . . . agreements."

Dismissing Malcolm Ross's claim that the FEPC's already fragile reputation in the Southwest would suffer further if public hearings were not held, Messersmith disparagingly observed, "I think what is at stake in this matter is not whether there will be hearings in order to maintain the prestige of the Committee but whether there is some useful result to be obtained. This Embassy does not see [one] and it feels that it is its duty to state that if such hearings are undertaken, it must be with the full knowledge that the results of the hearings, no matter how well conducted they may be, will be to destroy this movement of labor . . . from Mexico to the United States." "Under the circumstances," he warned, "the Committee could not possibly assume such a responsibility before public opinion and before the sections of our country which need this labor."

Finally, the ambassador suggested, enough progress was already being realized in the fight against discrimination in the Southwest to make the FEPC's inherently risky approach to reform unnecessary as well as unpropitious. "So far as the problems themselves are concerned," he argued in regard to discrimination against Chicanos, "there is no special problem in this particular respect which is not being dealt with now in an increasingly understanding and effective way. There is, therefore, nothing which the Committee could do which would be helpful and there is much which it could do which could prove very disastrous, although it carried through its activities with the best will in the world." "It is my very sincere hope," Messersmith concluded, "that the Department and Mr. Daniels will impress on Mr. Ross and his Committee the desirability of not holding any hearings until we are all in accord that a useful purpose will be served."[55]

Although there was clearly no enthusiasm within the State Department for FEPC hearings in the Southwest, prior to Ambassador Messersmith's intervention the committee remained hopeful that it could proceed with its plans for the region. Once Messersmith stated his adamant opposition to the proposed hearings, however, the possibility that the State Department might acquiesce in the FEPC's plan was quickly extinguished. Yet not until January of 1944, when Messersmith personally conveyed his objections to Malcolm Ross, did the committee learn for certain that the State Department was poised to oppose a public inquiry into discrimination in the Southwest.

Anticipating that the State Department would, as it had eighteen months earlier, seek to enlist White House support in an effort to block public hearings in the Southwest, the committee undertook its own personal appeal to the president. Already convinced that its increasingly evident inability to enforce the provisions of Executive Order 9346 made a strong show of presidential support imperative, the committee believed the proposed Southwest hearings represented one of a handful of critical challenges to its authority that could be surmounted only through the president's direct intercession. Accordingly, the full committee wrote to Roosevelt on January 31 requesting a meeting for the purpose of discussing the general problem of the FEPC's still ambiguous status and "extremely inadequate" enforcement powers; the "status" of presidential assistant Jonathan Daniels "in his relationship with the Committee and in the enforcement of . . . Executive Order 9346"; the continuing failure of most of the nation's railroad companies and unions to comply with the findings resulting from the hearings conducted by the committee six months earlier; and the necessity for forceful action to combat "discrimination against Americans of Mexican blood in the Southwest mining region."[56] To emphasize further the special importance it attached to the last issue, the committee appended to its request a memorandum defending the need for public hearings in the Southwest and rebutting Ambassador Messersmith's arguments opposing them.

"In a recent discussion between Ambassador Messersmith and our Chairman," the committee advised Roosevelt,

> it developed that Ambassador Messersmith has reservations regarding the hearings the Fair Employment Practice Committee proposes to hold on complaints of discrimination filed by American born copper miners of Mexican blood.
>
> A study of the . . . mining regions convinces the Committee that action upon these complaints is a duty already too long deferred, and that an objectively held hearing on the barriers to the full use of Mexican-American labor would increase production and have a heartening effect on these unjustly treated American workers.

> Ambassador Messersmith fears possible implications within Mexico. The Committee finds that these fears are not shared by other officials of the State Department intimately acquainted with the problem.

"The withholding of the benefits of Executive Order 9346 from American citizens of Mexican blood is so serious a matter," the committee declared, "that we respectfully request you to defer final decision with regard to a Committee hearing in the Southwest until the Committee has an opportunity to present to you its views."[57]

To its chagrin and disappointment, the committee found that Roosevelt was no more inclined to place the prestige of his office behind its enforcement initiatives in the Southwest in 1944 than he had been in 1942. Deflecting the committee's request for a meeting on the ground that it would be "more profitable" to meet at a later date, Roosevelt claimed that he had "heard nothing about the proposed hearings in the Southwest with regard to the full use of Mexican-American labor from either the Department of State or Ambassador Messersmith." Leaving little doubt, however, as to his likely position on the issue should his intervention become necessary, the president added, "The Department of State does, of course, have a proper concern in this matter and I am sure will be able to give a clear statement of its views."[58]

Yet if Roosevelt's evident unwillingness to endorse its enforcement strategy in the Southwest deflated the committee's hopes, it did not extinguish them. While the committee intended, as it again reassured the president, to pursue its task "with the utmost discretion," it still felt obliged to act "without compromising the non-discrimination objective" of Executive Order 9346. And although it did not specify when, the committee resolved only a week after Roosevelt's rebuff to place the State Department on notice that it still intended "to hold a hearing in the Southwest."[59]

Whether or not the committee truly believed that it was possible to overcome the barriers that might be placed in the way of its plans for public hearings in the Southwest is not clear. That the president had stopped short of stating his outright opposition to the idea may well have persuaded the committee to persist in its intentions even if his seemingly deferential attitude toward State Department opinion discouraged optimism. As a practical matter, however, the committee had little choice except to sustain its intention to hold hearings in the region, since to have done otherwise would have been to concede that the problem of discrimination against Chicano workers was somehow outside the purview of the president's order.

The committee had authorized Carlos Castañeda to undertake a preliminary survey of existing complaints of discrimination filed by Chicano workers in the Southwest even before it broached the subject of public hearings with the president. Following his formal appointment by Malcolm Ross at the end of 1943 as "special assistant to the chairman on Latin American problems," Castañeda eagerly addressed the issue of discrimination against Chicano workers in anticipation of eventual public hearings in the region. In keeping with the FEPC's existing policy, Castañeda's initial efforts were directed toward dealing with the problem only to the extent that individual Chicano workers were bold enough, and retained sufficient confidence in the FEPC's good offices, to lodge formal complaints against their employers. From the outset, however, Castañeda's acute conviction that employment discrimination in the Southwest was a problem affecting Chicanos as a class rather than as individuals led him to champion a less passive approach to enforcement, one that permitted him to seek out violations of Executive Order 9346 instead of merely docketing and processing complaints referred to his attention. "I feel confident," he told Will Maslow in late January, "that there are many instances of discrimination in [the Southwest] which a field trip would reveal. A personal visit to the various regions in which . . . Latin Americans make up the bulk of the population should be undertaken at as early a date as possible, if the discrimination against Latin-Americans is to be remedied."[60]

Although it was nearly six weeks before he was authorized to undertake a preliminary tour of a few of Arizona's principal mining regions in preparation for a more comprehensive investigation later on, Castañeda found ample evidence that in matters of wages, job assignments, and promotion, as well as in the more general realms of social and economic interaction with Anglos, Chicano copper workers continued to face "rank discrimination." In a few locations, he noted, militant locals of the Mine, Mill and Smelter Workers Union had succeeded in mitigating some of the more conspicuous forms of employment discrimination affecting their Chicano members. For the most part, however, Castañeda found that the major copper companies in the region, frequently abetted by AFL unions and local officials of the U.S. Employment Service, had successfully preserved their discriminatory wage and employment policies while making nothing more than token gestures of compliance with the president's order.

The distressingly familiar picture that emerged from Castañeda's hurried investigations in Arizona confirmed the inefficacy of the first FEPC's equivocal efforts to combat discrimination against Chicano copper workers in the Southwest during the latter half of 1942. In the course of documenting the old committee's failure Castañeda noted in particular the challenge its successor faced in overcoming the residual cynicism and suspicion that flourished within the ranks of Chicano workers and MMSW officials alike. He was hopeful, however, that the confidence of both could be restored if the committee was willing to make the effort. It was especially important, he argued, that the committee employ Spanish-speaking field investigators sufficiently well acquainted with the history and culture of the Southwest to facilitate a rapport with Chicano copper workers. "In securing information as to conditions, and in interviewing the individual workmen," Castañeda insisted, "the ability to speak Spanish fluently is of the greatest importance. It is true that more than one-half of the Latin-American workers speak English, [but] most of them speak very brokenly. They know the terminology of the mines, they understand instructions and orders in connection with their work, but they are unable to explain in English the condition against which they wish to complain." Moreover, he stated, his contacts with Chicano copper workers had revealed "that they tell their troubles much more freely to me because I am of their own race than they do to an Anglo examiner. They feel innate distrust because they have been betrayed so frequently by men who have posed as their friends, and who have sold them out stock and barrel."

Convincing MMSW officials in the Southwest to cooperate with a new investigation would also require a special effort, Castañeda observed, since they were "still resentful, and have little confidence in the Committee." Explaining the skepticism that his visit evoked among union leaders in the region, Castañeda wrote, "they cannot forget how about 18 months ago they attempted to cooperate with representatives of the Committee as created under Executive Order 8802, before it was reorganized, and how they were let down." Even so, he reported, they appeared willing to give the new committee a chance to prove itself once it was "made . . . clear to them that we really mean business this time, and that we are not going to let them down."[61]

Since the committee had already decided that it could no longer ignore evidence of widespread discrimination against Chicano copper workers in the Southwest, and had even gone so far as to notify the administration of its intention to take action in the region, following Castañeda's proposal that it authorize a comprehensive field investigation in preparation for public hearings was commended by a sequential logic too compelling to resist. Accordingly, the committee decided in late

March to undertake "a thorough investigation of complaints involving Mexicans in the copper industry in the Southwest."[62] The timing of the public hearings that were to follow remained in doubt, but the committee appeared determined to press ahead with them even at the risk of conflicts that it devoutly hoped to avoid.

Yet despite the committee's apparent resolve and Carlos Castañeda's personal ardor, the likelihood that Chicano copper workers would at last realize the promise of fair treatment embodied in the president's nondiscrimination order was no greater in the spring of 1944 than it had been in the fall of 1942. The vehemence with which the region's leading copper companies denied any and every complaint of discrimination lodged by Chicano workers had not diminished, nor had their determination to resist whatever efforts the committee might undertake to correct alleged violations of Executive Order 9346. Moreover, their earlier confrontations with the FEPC had left distinct impressions of its ultimate impotence insofar as effective enforcement authority was concerned. Finally, the companies had learned from their earlier experiences that outright defiance of the FEPC was avoidable as long as token compliance in response to individual complaints of discrimination served to complicate and undermine the committee's efforts to address the more fundamental issue of bias against Chicano workers as a class.

The heated jurisdictional battles that continued to divide the ranks of organized labor in the copper industry also threatened to complicate and impede the committee's work in the Southwest during the spring of 1944 in the same way that they had eighteen months before. As the MMSW continued to use the discrimination issue as a principal component of its aggressive organizing drives among Chicano copper workers, its AFL rivals became even more emphatic in their defense of the special occupational privileges afforded Anglo workers through the maintenance of traditional wage and employment policies. Thus while the committee could reasonably expect the MMSW to assist its renewed effort to institute fair employment practices in the region, it could also expect that AFL unions would not readily abandon those policies, including collusive understandings with many of the copper industry's biggest companies, that helped to perpetuate discrimination against Chicano workers.

As it had during the fall of 1942, the committee's credibility in the Southwest ultimately depended upon its success in translating the easy promise of fair treatment on the job into routine practice. Yet notwithstanding the hopeful expectations of greater strength and elevated stature occasioned by its resurrection, the FEPC was as ill-equipped to enforce its will under the terms of Executive Order 9346 as it had been under Executive Order 8802. Still lacking the authority required to compel compliance with its orders and directives, the FEPC remained hostage to an intentionally unavailing scheme of enforcement that subordinated fair employment practices to the Roosevelt administration's desire for political equanimity. And in light of the president's already evident inclination, the committee had little hope of winning White House backing for its proposed southwestern hearings in the face of determined opposition from the State Department.

To an important degree, the administration's never more than lukewarm support for the FEPC reflected the continuing ambivalence of the nation toward a policy of nondiscrimination commended by wartime necessity rather than moral compunction. If the committee was tempted to think that its actual or imagined contributions to the war effort during nearly three years of operation had earned it a grudging tolerance among those who initially opposed its creation, it was rudely disabused of any such tendency in the spring of 1944 when unreconstructed southern opponents of fair employment practices led a determined, and almost successful, effort in Congress to kill the FEPC by blocking its budget appropriation.[63] In the face of such bitter and unyielding opposition to its continued existence, the committee, though perpetually beleaguered, was made acutely aware that undertaking a vigorous, and thus inevitably contentious, enforcement campaign in the Southwest was likely to expose it to further attack from those both inside and outside the administration who sought its demise.

Finally, the committee's prospects for success in the Southwest were further diminished by its own reluctant, but still faithful, obeisance to a restrictive interpretation of its authority that discouraged any attempt to deal with the problem of discrimination against Chicano copper workers on a basis that conceded its generic nature. To persist in an approach to the enforcement of Executive Order 9346 in the Southwest that treated wage and employment discrimination as a problem affecting individual workers rather than Chicano labor as a class was to ignore the unarguable influence of race and ethnicity in both the allocation of job opportunities and the determination of wages in the copper industry. As long as offending employers were called to account by the committee only insofar as individual workers were bold enough to register formal complaints, they were free to substitute token concessions for full compliance with the president's order.

The collective status of Chicano workers in the copper industry bore the deep and burdensome imprint of discriminatory practices that were rooted in the history and traditions of the Southwest, and any approach to reform that remedied effects but neglected causes was destined to fall short of achieving enduring progress.

7. *Divided Counsel*

IT IS MORE than a little ironic that of the several federal agencies, offices, and departments that had occasion to deal with the problem of employment discrimination during the war, the one bearing the greatest burden of direct and continuing responsibility, the FEPC, was also the one least able to summon the authority and resources necessary to effective remedial action.

From the beginning, the disparity between its daunting responsibility and puny authority was the FEPC's central dilemma and foremost complaint. On those rare occasions when other federal agencies only tangentially concerned with the issue of employment discrimination brought to bear the full weight of their superior authority and greater prestige in redressing a particular problem of bias in the workplace, the committee was afforded a tantalizing glimpse of what might have been accomplished in behalf of minority workers in general had the Roosevelt administration been courageous enough to grant it enforcement powers commensurate with its responsibilities.

The new committee was made keenly aware of the possibilities of effective federal authority while it was taking its first halting steps early in 1944 to resume the enforcement efforts in the Southwest that its predecessor had abandoned a year earlier. This demonstration of forceful action in behalf of fair employment practices was authored by the Nonferrous Metals Commission, which was forced to address the issue of discrimination against Chicano workers when contract negotiations between the Mine, Mill and Smelter Workers Union and three copper companies in the vicinity of Miami, Arizona, broke down in August 1943 over the union's attempt to eliminate what it claimed were unfair wage differentials and promotion policies affecting employees of Mexican ancestry. Backed by the formidable authority of the War Labor Board, the NMC sought to determine the extent of such discrimination through a comprehensive analysis of the wage and occupational patterns disclosed by the companies' personnel files rather than by scrutinizing the employment histories of individual Chicano employees. Based on its conclusion that the stark disparities that existed between Anglo and non-Anglo employees could only be explained as a function of discriminatory practices that violated Executive Order 9346, the NMC issued an order on February 5, 1944, requiring wage and job reclassifications designed to remedy the companies' systematic discrimination against Chicano workers.[1]

At the core of the NMC's otherwise dispassionate analysis was an assumption that the discrimination to which Chicano copper workers had been subject in matters of pay and promotion was a manifestation of the pervasive bias that had long defined and governed the essential relations between Anglos and Chicanos in the Southwest. When the empirical evidence it adduced during the course of its inquiry appeared to confirm that assumption, the NMC devised an appropriately inclusive remedy, one that treated discrimination as an injustice inflicted upon Chicanos collectively rather than individually.

Yet as forceful and effective as the NMC was in redressing the problem of discrimination against Chicano copper workers when it became a subject of collective bargaining—the MMSW lavishly praised its decision as "a magnificent contribution to the literature of labor law"[2]—the commission had enforced Executive Order 9346 more by inadvertence than by design. While the FEPC briefly considered the possibility that the NMC might be persuaded to function as its surrogate in the Southwest, the committee was quickly obliged to acknowledge that enforcing the president's order in the region was its responsibility alone.[3]

That the FEPC approached its reinvestigation of discrimination against Chicano copper workers in the spring of 1944 with as much trepidation as confidence is not surprising. Despite an apparently sincere determination to redeem the promises that its predecessor had failed to keep, the new committee was captive to a course of action whose inherent limitations had become discouragingly apparent when the old committee followed it to a futile end in 1942. Lacking the enforcement powers of the NMC, and still reluctant to expose itself to new attacks by assuming authority under the president's order to combat employment discrimination on the basis of statistical evidence as well as in response to individual complaints, the committee proceeded toward its ultimate goal of public hearings in the Southwest with utmost caution. As a result, the plodding and time-consuming field investigation it finally authorized centered around specific cases of alleged unfairness while merely noting the broader patterns of racial and ethnic bias that disclosed the general occupational subordination of Chicanos to Anglos in the copper industry. Denials of equal treatment to Chicano copper workers were "general and can be proved beyond a doubt," Carlos Castañeda confidently assured his superiors, yet he sought to gather evidence of the chronic discrimination in the industry, including that adduced by the NMC, largely for the purpose of corroborating the testimony of individual complainants.[4]

Assisted at the outset by two field investigators, neither of whom had what he regarded as the requisite credentials for truly effective work among Chicanos, including fluency in Spanish, Castañeda finally launched his inquiry in mid-April. The scale of the new committee's investigation—Castañeda and his assistants would visit every important mining, milling, smelting, and refining operation in the Southwest during the spring of 1944—was substantially greater than that conducted by its predecessor eighteen months before. The method and purpose of the second investigation, however, were identical to those of the first. At each stop on their itinerary committee investigators, often aided by local union and community activists, explained the provisions of Executive Order 9346 and invited formal complaints from Chicano workers who believed that they had been denied fair treatment on the job as a consequence of their Hispanic ancestry.[5]

While Castañeda had initially expected to complete his field survey in time for public hearings to be held in Phoenix sometime in early May,[6] that timetable was promptly scrapped when, over his strong objection, his superiors instructed him to combine his investigations of individual complaints with immediate efforts to resolve them through conferences with the appropriate representatives of management at each site. What appeared on the surface to be nothing more than a mild disagreement between Castañeda and his superiors over a question of tactics was, in fact, symptomatic of a fundamental conceptual conflict that was destined to become increasingly apparent in the weeks and months ahead.

Castañeda's objection to holding conferences with management was rooted in a deeper concern that attempts to settle complaints of discrimination on a case-by-case basis were likely to afford the region's leading copper companies an opportunity to blunt the committee's larger effort to enforce Executive Order 9346. By encouraging strategic, but still only token, concessions that left the companies' discriminatory wage and employment policies toward Chicano workers largely undisturbed, the committee was, he feared, reducing the likelihood of public hearings that would frame the issue in a way that enhanced the prospects for general, industry-wide reform. Explaining his concern to Malcolm Ross, Castañeda wrote:

> If such conferences are held by me, and I take up with the companies the individual cases already docketed, the companies will either correct the individual grievance or explain it away. I seriously doubt that in a private conference we will be able to obtain from the companies a correction of their discriminatory practices. The individual cases docketed are symptomatic. Like the pulse and temperature of a patient they merely indicate a serious organic disorder. Specific drugs can lower the heartbeat and the temperature without curing the patient or permanently removing the cause for the symptoms observed.

"The settlement of individual cases," he warned, "may be made to give the appearance of a correction of discriminatory practices without in fact curing the illness."[7]

Beyond raising serious doubts regarding just how much it was likely to accomplish in the Southwest, the committee's insistence upon management conferences eliminated any possibility of timely public hearings in the region. Of the one hundred formal complaints of discrimination filed by Chicano workers during the course of Castañeda's investigation, eighty had been lodged as of the beginning of May. Yet due to the delays occasioned by time-consuming, and generally unavailing, efforts to negotiate settlements of individual complaints, Castañeda's field investigations were not completed until the end of June.[8]

To no one's surprise, the evidence gathered by Castañeda and his assistants during their ten-week investigation confirmed the continuing existence of widespread, systemic discrimination against Chicano copper workers in the Southwest. Just as FEPC investigators had in 1942, Castañeda and his aides found that Chicano workers were denied equal opportunities for promotion and upgrading, were concentrated as a result of arbitrary and capricious work classifications in the least desirable and lowest-paying jobs, and were, as a consequence of routine misclassifications, subject to discriminatory wage differentials. Each type of discrimination, he concluded, was based on considerations of race and national origin and thus plainly violated Executive Order 9346.[9]

While the general patterns of discrimination in the industry remained unchanged, Castañeda did note during the course of his inquiry a subtle shift toward somewhat less rigid employment practices than those observed by committee investigators in 1942. The slightly greater number of Chicano workers employed in skilled capacities, though still constituting no more than token representation within Anglo-dominated job categories, was, he reported, an encouraging sign. Although he attributed the change for the most part to growing union pressures and the effects of continuing manpower shortages, he also noted that it appeared to reflect a belief among employers that token integration of skilled job categories previously reserved for Anglos only would reduce their vulnerability to charges of discrimination. Accounting for the modest gains achieved by a handful of Chicano copper workers in El Paso, Castañeda commented, "Both the American Smelting and Phelps-Dodge Companies have been aware for the last two or three months of the need of avoiding all appearance of discrimination. They have, consequently, given employment to Latin Americans in departments where they were never employed before, but in restricted numbers, just sufficient to avoid an open charge of discrimination. Likewise, they have upgraded Latin-Americans to semi-skilled and skilled positions in limited numbers for the same purpose. Nevertheless, it is evident from the complaints that there is still much discrimination."[10]

On rare occasions, Castañeda encountered evidence of what appeared to be a genuine commitment to reduce discrimination against Chicano workers. When Anglo employees of the Miami Copper Company protested "because equal opportunities are given to others regardless of race, creed, color or national origin," he reported, "they are told frankly that if they do not care to work on an equal basis with all other workers, they are free to seek employment elsewhere." "There is no doubt in my mind," he declared, "as to the sincerity of the company's representatives in their earnest desire to live up to the provisions of Executive Order 9346."[11]

Castañeda also noted that, while bitter jurisdictional battles between the MMSW and its Anglo-dominated AFL rivals continued to impede the advancement of Chicano workers in a few mining centers, throughout most of the region labor's internecine conflicts were no longer fueling discrimination. "The CIO locals are still living up to their promise and they are securing higher wages and new avenues of promotion for Latin-Americans," he reported. And the AFL, "impelled by necessity," had "become much more liberal in its attitude toward Latin-Americans . . ." since "to maintain their membership they must give assurances to the Latin-Americans that they will defend them in their rights for promotion in accord with their ability and seniority." Only the Brotherhood of Railway Trainmen, whose contract with the Kennecott Copper Company at Silver City, New Mexico, covered a substantial number of Chicano workers, continued to pursue what he described as "frankly discriminatory" policies intended to perpetuate the exclusive occupational privileges of its Anglo membership.[12]

In assessing the influences exerted by other federal agencies in the Southwest, Castañeda found that, except for the Nonferrous Metals Commission, which had addressed the issue of discrimination against Chicano copper workers only when it arose as a subject of collective bargaining, neither the ideal of equal opportunity in the workplace nor the practical goal of maximum manpower utilization inspired a desire on their parts to assist the FEPC's efforts. The War Manpower Commission, whose regional representatives continued during 1944 to advocate the importation of Mexican workers to meet the still critical manpower shortages plaguing the copper industry, remained curiously uninterested in solving the problem of discrimination against Chicano workers even though it promised a means of augmenting the supply of labor available to the industry from the Southwest's existing pool.[13] Much more troubling and detrimental than the WMC's studied neglect of the problem, however, was the U.S. Employment Service's continuing abetment of discrimination. Castañeda reported that in some locations USES officials openly undermined Executive Order 9346 by filling the blatantly discriminatory labor requests submitted by various copper companies.[14]

Before completing his investigation Castañeda also encountered clear evidence of at least one new expression of the copper industry's generally undeterred commitment to discrimination as usual. In response to critical labor shortages, the copper industry in the Southwest finally, and reluctantly, followed the lead of other major defense industries in the country in 1943 by recruiting female workers for production work previously reserved to males only. Almost without exception, however, the employment of women in the mills, smelters, and refineries of the Southwest occurred on a basis that extended and reinforced existing patterns of racial and ethnic discrimination in the industry. In most cases, Castañeda reported, Chicano women were either denied employment entirely or, as in the case of the Phelps Dodge refinery at El Paso, hired on an exclusive basis due to "the fact that Latin-American women work for less money."[15]

In summarizing the results of his investigation, Castañeda emphasized that the one hundred formal complaints of discrimination he had received from Chicano workers as he methodically crisscrossed the region failed to reveal the actual scope and inherent nature of the problem. They were merely "indicative of a discriminatory condition," he cautioned. "They do not represent the actual number of men affected by the discriminatory practices . . . in the mining industry." Chicanos constituted between 40 and 50 percent—8,000 to 9,000 workers—of the copper industry's workforce in the Southwest, he noted, and few, if any, were exempted from the unfair treatment on the job to which their ancestry alone exposed them. That more workers had not filed complaints, he suggested, was due to a chronic and pervasive fear, as well as a well-conditioned cynicism, that doing so would expose them to various forms of employer retribution against which neither the committee nor their unions could guarantee certain protection.[16]

Castañeda's insistence upon an emphatic distinction between the problem of discrimination, which was generic and encompassing, and the complaints of individual victims, which were intrinsic and singular, derived from a concern that the committee not allow its functional preoccupation with the latter to obscure its transcending obligation to confront the former. Yet by the time his field investigations were completed, concurrent efforts to negotiate settlements of individual cases had already fostered a subtle shift in the rationale for public hearings in the Southwest. Originally valued as an indispensable forum for exploring and exposing the general character and scope of employment discrimination in the copper industry, public hearings were soon being discussed in tactical terms as a threat from which the committee would willingly retreat if the companies agreed to settle the individual complaints against them on a basis consistent with the requirements of Executive Order 9346.[17] Although the committee had earlier reached a confidential "understanding" with the Department of State that had effectively placed Texas off limits to any public efforts it might undertake to combat discrimination, its apparent amenability to the idea of dropping public hearings entirely in return for satisfactory settlements of individual complaints raised the possibility that an attempt to resolve the larger problem of discrimination against Chicano copper workers in the Southwest might be abandoned.[18]

To Castañeda's surprise and gratification, however, the committee's seeming drift toward expedient solutions was abruptly halted in mid-July when Stanley Metzger, a senior member of its headquarters staff, was instructed to review the findings of the Southwest investigations for the purpose of recommending an appropriate course of action. Metzger, who had personally assisted Castañeda during the initial phase of his investigations in the region, proved to be an especially valuable and timely ally in the cause for FEPC action that emphasized the organic and structural character of discrimination in the copper industry.

Persuaded on the basis of his review that "the entire pattern of discrimination in the industry [was] intimately tied up" with the complaints Castañeda had docketed, Metzger strongly endorsed the view that in order to derive the greatest potential benefit from public hearings in the Southwest the committee should shift its focus from the settlement of individual cases to the reform of industry-wide practices. "I am very doubtful," he wrote,

> whether this case by case system will be effective either in eliminating discrimination informally or in the presentation of a hearing. Rather, I believe that any hearing should be keyed to expert testimony . . . with individual cases thrown in as illustrative material. . . . I do not believe that a hearing should be keyed to individual grievances and their redress. . . . Each individual case can be made into a lawsuit of its own at a hearing, and such a hearing can easily be bogged down in a morass of detail. Further, the individual complaints we have are both too few and not colorful enough to pitch the problem in the key which is necessary. In addition, with the exception of a very few cases . . . , the companies would undoubtedly adjust the few individual cases which are outstanding in advance of a hearing in order to forestall it.

He concluded, "The adjustment of these cases . . . would certainly do nothing to eliminate the widespread discrimination in the industry. It would, however, serve to tie up the FEPC if it proceeds on the individual case method of handling such a hearing."[19]

Although the casual tone of the response left the committee's ultimate course of action in doubt, Metzger's superiors responded sympathetically to his recommendation. Commenting that he could "see no objection to varying our procedure and building a hearing around expert testimony," FEPC deputy chairman George Johnson even suggested that the committee "might consider using some of the experts who were used in connection with the [Nonferrous Metals] Commission's investigation" of discriminatory wage differentials in the copper industry.[20]

Still, the committee remained wary of overly bold initiatives. When Castañeda pressed Washington in late July for specific instructions regarding his future course in the Southwest, he was directed by Will Maslow, the director of field operations, both to continue his efforts to negotiate satisfactory settlements of individual complaints with the copper companies in question and to develop plans for public hearings that would employ expert testimony to expose "the broader issues of discrimination in the mining industry."[21] Yet whatever its supposed merits, the committee's cautious strategy to seek enforcement of Executive Order 9346 on a case-by-case basis at the same time that it prepared to combat industry-wide discrimination against Chicano copper workers through public hearings ignored Castañeda's, and Metzger's, contention that individual settlements would impede the committee's progress toward more general reforms.

The inability or unwillingness of the committee to take decisive action even though Castañeda's investigation had reconfirmed the existence of chronic discrimination against Chicano copper workers indicated that the sense of urgency attending the issue in the Southwest was conspicuously absent in Washington. As Castañeda dutifully continued his sporadic efforts to persuade recalcitrant copper companies in the region to settle individual complaints of discrimination that had already been pending against them for up to four months, his still embryonic plan for a more general assault on the problem languished. In early September the committee finally authorized public hearings in the Southwest, but refused to specify when they might take place.[22]

Given that the copper industry had, for all intents and purposes, become the exclusive focus of the FEPC's interest in the problem of discrimination against Chicano workers—it was the only industry in the country "in which the Negro worker was not the main source of complaints"[23]—the committee's effectiveness in combating unfair employment practices in the mines, mills, smelters, and refineries of the Southwest was bound to serve as the ultimate measure of its commitment to them. By its own reckoning, the committee could claim little progress in ensuring that Chicano workers in the Southwest benefited from the federal government's nondiscrimination policy.

Based on official reports in September 1944 from Region X and Region XII, which together included most of the approximately three million Chicanos in the United States, the exceedingly modest gains realized by workers of Mexican ancestry resulted from manpower shortages rather than from FEPC enforcement activities. In southern California, where Chicanos constituted roughly 20 percent of the population, barely 6 percent had found employment in the region's sprawling defense industries. And even though they outnumbered blacks in the region by at least four to one, Chicano workers remained only barely visible in the statistical record of the FEPC's enforcement activities.[24] According to the reports of the committee's regional suboffice in Los Angeles, blacks outnumbered Chicanos by nearly four to one (230 to 60) in the number of discrimination cases docketed between September 1943 and September 1944. Moreover, while 60 percent (139) of the cases involving blacks had been closed, only 20 percent (12) of the cases involving Chicano complainants were similarly resolved during the same period.[25] Commenting on the committee's meager efforts in behalf of Chicano workers in Region XII, regional director Harry Kingman wrote, "The Mexicans do not readily bring in their complaints. But they are, nevertheless, not unaware of the employment discrimination to which they are subjected. . . . A more continuous and comprehensive attempt to win fair employment opportunity for this large minority should, however, be provided for."[26]

A simultaneous report on the committee's activities in behalf of Chicano workers in Region X, which included Texas and New Mexico, disclosed an equally barren record. In part, regional director W. D. Ellinger noted, the lack of progress in Region X was due to chronic understaffing, which made timely investigations of complaints impossible. Yet it was the committee's failure to proceed with promised public hearings, he insisted, that denied it the credibility required to inspire confidence in its resolve among Chicano workers and to foster respect for its authority among employers. "The fact that no hearings have been held in this region," Ellinger complained, "has weakened the effectiveness of this weapon here. Hearings which were requested nine months ago have not been held, and the parties who might have modified their discriminatory practice in face of a public hearing are disposed now to think that the threat of such hearings is empty and that the committee fears to publicize the objectives of the program." Referring specifically to the committee's evident faintheartedness in challenging the pervasive discrimination against Chicano workers in the copper industry of the Southwest, Ellinger added, "It is essential to this region's work that well selected and carefully handled public hearings be held in order that other industries realize that public inquiry will be made into the charges of discrimination."[27]

In testimony during early September before a Senate subcommittee considering the creation of a permanent FEPC, Carlos Castañeda, the committee's resident expert on what he termed "the largest underprivileged minority group in the Southwest," confirmed that more than three years after equal opportunity on the job was declared the public policy of the United States Chicano workers remained subject to systematic discrimination.[28]

From the moment that it reluctantly launched its reinvestigation of discrimination in the mining industry, the committee had tenaciously indulged the hope that if enough progress could be achieved in settling individual complaints it might avoid the risks inherent in convening public hearings. As long as most of the copper companies in the region conveyed even a remote willingness either to negotiate or to contemplate voluntary settlements of the complaints lodged against them, the committee had resisted the view that the general nature of discrimination in the industry made public hearings necessary regardless of any progress made in resolving individual cases.

At the beginning of September, however, Castañeda advised Washington that his initial doubts regarding the efficacy of conciliation as a means of combating discrimination in the mining industry had been confirmed. Pointedly reminding the committee of his earlier assertion that the case-by-case approach it favored "would not correct the discriminatory conditions found to exist, as the companies would either agree to correct the individual cases presented, or explain them away, without relaxing their general discriminatory policies," Castañeda reported:

> This opinion has been borne out in the conferences held. The companies have uniformly denied a discriminatory policy. Out of 100 cases discussed in detail in conferences with management, only 27 were satisfactorily adjusted, but even had the 100 complaints been satisfactorily adjusted, it would not have corrected the discriminatory policies of the companies involved, who employ a total of over 20,000 men in their plants in Western Texas, New Mexico and Arizona, of which over 40%, taking the industry as a whole, are Spanish-speaking citizens of Mexican extraction. It is evident that the upgrading or reclassification of 100 men is no proof of the elimination of the discrimination which exists. . . . The 100 cases filed and docketed reveal the general pattern of discrimination and, as already stated, are symptomatic or symbolic.

Under the circumstances, he concluded, the committee's only viable recourse was to proceed with public hearings, which he recommended be held in Phoenix "at as early a date as possible." Castañeda further proposed, as he had earlier, that the hearings should rely on expert testimony confirming the generic character of discrimination against Chicano copper workers and that the individual complaints in the committee's files should be "used as evidence of the general policy prevalent in the industry."[29]

Although its belated decision on September 7 authorizing public hearings in the Southwest appeared to endorse Castañeda's view, the committee's failure both to specify when they would be held and to order necessary preparations betrayed its continuing ambivalence toward so forceful and potentially precarious a plan of action.[30] Castañeda's mounting frustration with the committee's laggardly and irresolute conduct finally led him to press Washington in late September for a statement of intent that would permit him "to know concretely" when and where the hearings would be held and whether they would focus on individual complaints or employ expert testimony in a broader assault against industry-wide discrimination.[31]

In apparent response to Castañeda's appeal, the committee agreed on October 11 to set a "definite date," possibly during the first week of December, for its long-delayed public hearings in the Southwest.[32] It also instructed the legal division of the FEPC to review Castañeda's earlier recommendations regarding the location and essential focus of the hearings. Although it was not immediately evident, the legal division's assumption of a central role in deciding the basis on which the proposed public hearings would proceed was destined to have a profound, and perhaps controlling, influence on the FEPC's ultimate response to the problem of discrimination against Chicano copper workers in the Southwest.

To the task of assessing Castañeda's recommendations, which had earlier won the backing of field operations director Will Maslow, FEPC attorneys brought a ready predisposition to view the issue of public hearings within a narrow, technical context that betrayed the singular influences of their legal training. Frank Reeves, the attorney initially called upon to evaluate Castañeda's proposed approach to the hearings, was emphatic in recommending against an overly broad focus. Without contradicting Castañeda's argument that "little good would be accomplished by presenting only the individual cases," Reeves nevertheless insisted that no other approach was feasible.

"While I appreciate the arguments advanced in favor of proceeding on a broad policy basis," he wrote,

> . . . consideration must be given the question of whether the committee has, or can obtain, the expert testimony and detailed technical information necessary to support findings on this basis. For instance, where, as is alleged in certain of the complaints, Spanish-Americans are precluded from opportunities for upgrading into certain job classifications, it would seem necessary that we be able to present evidence based on exhaustive job and qualification analysis, indicating that Anglos working in those classifications were advanced thereto, or hired therein, in preference to Spanish-Americans having equal or better qualifications.

"Although circumstantial evidence of this might exist in the case where we can show that a particular Spanish-American . . . was discriminated against," Reeves continued, "it is questionable whether such circumstances . . . would be sufficient to justify a finding of discrimination on a policy basis."

Consistent with his preference for a narrow frame of reference, Reeves found little merit in Castañeda's recommendation that the proposed hearings should be "keyed" to expert testimony relating to "the general pattern of discrimination against Spanish speaking Latin-Americans of Mexican extraction in community life." While acknowledging that some information and assistance from such agencies as the War Manpower Commission and the Nonferrous Metals Commission might facilitate the hearings, he remained convinced that it was essential "to limit consideration to those issues over which the Committee is to assume jurisdiction." In light of his analysis, Reeves informed Bruce Hunt, the fellow attorney in charge of preparations for the hearings, that he intended to proceed with his review "on an individual party charged basis."[33]

As long as the committee remained in doubt regarding its authority under Executive Order 9346 to act except in response to individual complaints of discrimination, its evident reluctance to pursue the broad approach to enforcement that Castañeda's assessment of conditions in the Southwest prescribed was understandable. That concern ought to have abated, however, once assistant solicitor general Hugh Cox gave FEPC chairman Malcolm Ross "informal" assurances on October 13 that the committee did, in fact, have authority under the president's order to act in the Southwest on the basis that Castañeda had proposed. According to Evelyn Cooper, a committee lawyer who had accompanied Ross to the meeting, it was Cox's opinion that "investigations and hearings under . . . Executive Order 9346 can properly be based upon either the complaint or complaints of a person or persons aggrieved by discriminatory practices, or the complaint of an organization on behalf of such person or persons, or a general complaint from an organization relating to a particular employer or . . . several employers. . . ." In addition, Cox reportedly advised, "Complaints may also take the form of evidence of discrimination (specific or general) referred or reported by other Government agencies."

Furthermore, the language of the president's order, according to Cox, granted the committee broad authority in deciding the appropriate form and scope of its response to a complaint of discrimination. He told Ross and Cooper:

> Investigations and hearings instituted on the basis of complaints need not be limited in scope by the complaints but may be as broad or as narrow as the Committee deems appropriate under the circumstances. Thus, if specific complaints against a single employer . . . or investigation of such complaints indicates that the employment practices of the employer . . . are generally discriminatory, investigation and hearing could properly cover all incidents of discrimination. . . . Similarly, investigation and hearing could cover an entire industry . . . where it appears that the practices of the single employer . . . complained against are representative of the practices of the industry.

Finally, the FEPC was authorized, in Cox's view, to seek remedies that were commensurate in scope with the unfair practices it found to exist. "Directives of the Committee," he reportedly concluded, "can properly include proposals for specific remedial action in the case of any person or persons found, on the basis of the record of the hearing, to have been discriminated against, regardless of whether such persons filed complaints or whether complaints were filed on their behalf. . . . In addition, directives of the Committee can properly propose general remedial action for the elimination and correction of discriminatory practices."[34]

To the extent that Cox's opinion appeared to relieve much of the doubt that the committee had harbored regarding its freedom of action, it should have enhanced the likelihood of broadly focused hearings in the Southwest. The fact that the committee made no effort to exercise the wider investigatory authority that Cox's findings seemed to sanction strongly suggests that its unwillingness to take bold, broad-based action against discrimination in the copper industry resulted from a habitual fear of fueling further accusations by its ever vigilant critics that the FEPC's true purpose was social engineering rather than efficient manpower utilization. Yet, for whatever reasons, the committee did nothing to resolve the confusion that continued to cloud its intentions in the Southwest.[35]

In the weeks following the committee's decision to proceed with public hearings in the Southwest, those staff members involved in planning them worked at cross-purposes. The lawyers, Reeves and Hunt, undertook detailed analyses of individual complaints to determine the intrinsic merit of each case, while Castañeda endeavored to line up expert witnesses in anticipation of hearings attuned to the general problem of employment discrimination in the copper industry. Castañeda was instructed in late October to curtail his efforts while the legal review of individual complaints was still proceeding, but he clearly continued to believe that when the hearings finally took place they would be broadly focused.[36]

By emphasizing general patterns of discrimination against Chicano workers in the copper industry, the proposed hearings might, Castañeda believed, relieve the heavy burden of proof the committee would otherwise have to bear in prosecuting individual complaints against specific companies. When considered in the light of compelling statistical evidence and expert testimony supporting the contention that discrimination against Chicano workers was woven into the fabric of the copper industry's wage and employment policies, the individual complaints would, Castañeda implied, have a presumptive credibility that the companies would be forced to refute. Thus, by employing such a strategy, the committee might shift the burden of proof to an extent that was not possible, he feared, if the hearings addressed each individual complaint of discrimination on the basis of its own merits alone.

As the process of judging the merits of individual complaints proceeded under the auspices of committee lawyers, the concern Castañeda had earlier expressed was soon borne out. Based on his narrowly focused reviews of individual complaints and the rebuttals offered by the six copper companies against which they were directed, and in disregard of industry-wide patterns that tended to confirm the existence of systematic discrimination against Chicanos, Frank Reeves reported in early November that most of the cases appeared to lack sufficient merit to warrant presentation at a public hearing. In a few cases, he noted, further investigation, including extensive analyses of job qualifications, work assignments, seniority rights, promotion patterns, and the personal attributes of individual complainants, was necessary before issues of merit could finally be decided.

In some cases, Reeves's tendency to give the companies the benefit of the doubt where conflicts of interpretation existed, and to accept token promotions as "some evidence of the non-existence of a policy to exclude Mexicans" from skilled job classifications, suggested a nearly total insensitivity to the discriminatory traditions that had long dictated relations between Anglos and Chicanos in the Southwest.[37] Yet such seeming insensitivity was more probably only a studied matter-of-factness that derived from his perception of public hearings as quasi-judicial proceedings bound by strict rules of evidence and exacting standards of proof. Still, proving discrimination in individual cases on the basis of detailed examinations of wage and employment records that the companies were unlikely to divulge voluntarily—which the committee lacked authority to subpoena—held little promise as an effective approach to solving the problems affecting Chicano copper workers either individually or as a class.

Whatever the deficiencies of his approach, however, Reeves's assessment had an immediate impact. Indeed, even before Reeves had completed his case reviews, Bruce Hunt persuaded the committee that the public hearings tentatively scheduled to begin in Phoenix on December 4 would have to be postponed because most of the individual complaints pending against copper companies in the Southwest were simply too weak or unconvincing as they currently stood to sustain charges of discrimination.[38] Although the committee seemed intent upon rescheduling the hearings as soon as further investigations of individual complaints established a foundation of evidence strong enough to support them, the lingering conceptual and strategic discrepancies in the thinking of those responsible for carrying out the FEPC's mission in the Southwest quietly militated against concerted and effective action.

Not until mid-December did Bruce Hunt, the staff lawyer who controlled the ultimate fate of the proposed hearings, finally embark upon his own field investigation in the Southwest. On the eve of his fact-finding venture in the region, Hunt advised Castañeda that his personal review of the files relating to discrimination against Chicano copper workers placed him "in full accord with those persons who say that the problem should not be handled on a case-by-case basis at the hearing. To try the matter in such a way would surely result in a very lengthy hearing, involving such discussion of technical operations and 'dry' facts. Too, as has been said, it is questionable whether much good would flow therefrom."[39] At once surprised and gratified to learn that planning for the hearings was apparently "progressing satisfactorily," Castañeda was sufficiently encouraged by Hunt's statement to suggest a number of experts who might be called upon to offer testimony confirming the general and pervasive character of discrimination against Chicanos throughout the Southwest.[40]

Yet if Hunt's stated preference was for hearings that focused on chronic, industry-wide violations of Executive Order 9346, his lawyerly instinct was to decide the committee's ultimate course of action in the Southwest on the basis of the narrow considerations that informed his personal reinvestigations of individual complaints that had already languished for up to nine months in many cases.[41] Hunt's professed commitment to broadly focused public hearings was further contradicted by his view of the relationship of expert testimony on the general character of discrimination against Chicano workers to the individual complaints that occupied his attention. Unlike Castañeda, who had repeatedly emphasized that individual complaints were chiefly important as illustrations of the broad patterns of discrimination to be delineated by expert witnesses, Hunt insisted upon treating the individual cases as primary. At nearly every stop on his southwestern tour he reached the same arbitrary conclusion: the individual complaints "will not support available expert testimony and do not warrant a hearing."[42]

For Castañeda, who was powerless to influence the committee's approach to enforcement in the Southwest once the legal division took charge, Hunt's determination to decide the future of public hearings on the basis of narrow, legalistic assessments of individual complaints was a source of deepening aggravation and despair. Still convinced that the individual complaints were merely representative of industry-wide discrimination against Chicano copper workers in the Southwest, Castañeda was nevertheless at a loss to do anything more than dissent from Hunt's conclusion that public hearings were unwarranted since the individual cases expected to sustain them had, for the most part, been judged to be without merit.

From the first, Castañeda had emphasized that the formal complaints filed with the committee failed to disclose the actual extent of employment discrimination in the copper industry, especially given the evident unwillingness of most Chicano workers to risk possible employer retaliation by formally complaining to the FEPC. His conviction was buttressed by officials of the Mine, Mill and Smelter Workers Union, who frankly informed Bruce Hunt during his Arizona tour that the complaints in the committee's files barely scratched the surface of the discrimination problem in the Southwest. According to Castañeda, who reported the encounter to field operations director Will Maslow, union officials had advised Hunt that they were "not convinced yet that the Committee is serious as regards a hearing; that there is doubt in their minds as to how much the committee can do for their workers; and that they have other cases much stronger which they would furnish us when we can convince them we are in earnest." One leading MMSW official, when told that the committee was considering public hearings in the Southwest, reportedly replied, "I'll believe it when I see it."[43]

In a subsequent report to FEPC deputy chairman George Johnson, who was also Hunt's immediate superior, Castañeda noted that another prominent MMSW official in Texas and New Mexico and expressed an equally distrustful opinion of the committee's commitment to fair employment practices in the Southwest. Castañeda solemnly informed Johnson:

> He frankly stated to me that the mine workers in northwestern Texas and southern New Mexico are completely disillusioned with the Committee; that the members . . . in recent meetings have questioned the Committee's efficiency to help them in any way to eliminate the deep-rooted discrimination which they have suffered for years. He stated that the men praised the stand which the Non-ferrous Metals Commission in Denver had taken on the question of discrimination as being much more positive than that exhibited at any time by the various representatives of the FEPC who had visited the mining areas to investigate complaints.[44]

As long as the possibility remained that the committee, despite its vacillatory tendencies, might still proceed with public hearings that addressed the general problem of discrimination against Chicano copper workers in the Southwest, Castañeda stifled his increasingly keen desire to protest the narrowly focused approach to enforcement encouraged by Hunt's seeming preoccupation with individual complaints. Not until mid-January, when he assisted Hunt and Frank Reeves in their reinvestigations of individual complaints at Silver City and Santa Rita, New Mexico, did Castañeda observe firsthand how subversive of the FEPC's essential purpose their legalistic, case-by-case approach to enforcement could be. He used the experience to frame a final, bitter protest against what he regarded as the incongruous and self-defeating method the committee had adopted to combat discrimination in the Southwest.

No longer willing to repress his mounting frustration and disappointment, and convinced that the committee's efforts in the Southwest were so hopelessly misguided that their failure was assured, Castañeda forwarded to Washington on January 23 a scathing critique of the legal division's approach to enforcement. It was increasingly apparent, he complained to Will Maslow, that if Hunt and Reeves continued to find fault with the individual complaints they were reinvestigating "the Southwestern Hearing would have to be postponed indefinitely." Yet whatever they decided in assessing the merit of individual complaints, Castañeda insisted, the general problem of discrimination against Chicano copper workers as a class would remain neglected. "Not being a lawyer," he wrote, "I cannot speak with authority on the legal merits of the cases dismissed as not meritorious. But regardless of the merit or lack of merit of the complaints reinvestigated, the fact remains that discrimination is evident on every hand; that the men have grown increasingly dissatisfied with our efforts in their behalf and seriously doubt our sincerity; and that the union itself looks with askance [*sic*] upon the supercilious approach of our legal representatives."

"When all but two of the seventeen cases in the Silver City–Santa Rita region were declared as without merit," he informed Maslow,

> Mr. Curtis and his assistant, Mr. Anchondo, of the CIO, presented for our consideration [a] case . . . not previously docketed, as one which they considered had merit. . . . Both Mr. Curtis and Mr. Anchondo of the CIO felt this was a clearcut case of discrimination, but Mr. Hunt and Mr. Reeves were of the opinion that it would be very difficult to prove. Not being a lawyer, I cannot express an opinion as to the legal merits of the case, but the attitude of Mr. Hunt and Mr. Reeves did not leave a very good impression either with the complainant or with the representatives of the CIO.

Given that Hunt and Reeves were unlikely to alter their approach, Castañeda observed, there was little reason to believe that the individual cases still to be reviewed would be judged any more worthy of presentation at a public hearing than those already considered. "I am convinced," he told Maslow,

> that the reinvestigation of the remaining cases . . . when judged according to the rigid standards set in the Silver City–Santa Rita area, will not hold and that the hearing will have to be indefinitely postponed.
>
> I agree that if from a legal point of view such cases as may be found to have some merit, are in fact weak, it would be a serious mistake to hold a hearing in which the trial attorneys may lose them. Such a failure would be fatal. In other words I am in full accord with the opinion of Mr. Hunt and Mr. Reeves that it is far better not to go to a hearing unless we have cases which we feel reasonably certain can be sustained.

Yet the predicament in which the committee now found itself, Castañeda vehemently maintained, was a direct, and perhaps inevitable, result of the legal division's ill-informed decision to make individual complaints the central focus of its efforts in the first place. Recalling the arguments that both he and Stanley Metzger had made against such an approach when the committee originally contemplated an appropriate enforcement strategy in the Southwest during the summer of 1944, Castañeda insisted that their "misgivings" had been fully validated by subsequent events. It had been his and Metzger's view, he reminded Maslow, that "the type of hearing that should be held to remedy the widespread policy of discrimination in the mining industry throughout the Southwest" was one "keyed to expert testimony on general conditions, . . . with individual cases thrown in as illustrative material." Castañeda further recalled that both he and Metzger had expressly warned the committee that little would be gained in the end if the proposed hearings were "keyed to individual grievances and their redress."

Despite the strong case that he and Metzger had presented in support of broadly based hearings, Castañeda complained, their notion of what the situation in the Southwest demanded was simply ignored by the legal division. "It seems to me," he sullenly told Maslow, "that this idea was not in the minds of Mr. Hunt or Mr. Reeves. It seems that their idea was a limited case by case hearing and that it is due to this misconception that our efforts have proved fruitless." Had Hunt and Reeves done their homework, he suggested, they might have recognized the compelling necessity for a wide-ranging effort against discrimination in the copper industry. "As early as May 4, 1944, in a report made to Chairman Ross," Castañeda declared, "this idea was clearly expressed and it was restated with clearness and force in the report of Mr. Metzger. It is unfortunate that the representatives of the legal division assigned to the mining cases did not acquaint themselves thoroughly with the background of this investigation; that they did not give sufficient time to this matter before getting out in the field; and that they did not have a clear conception of what had gone before and what was their real task."

Instead, he noted, Hunt and Reeves had permitted their preference for a rigid, legalistic review of individual complaints to dictate a course of action that virtually eliminated any possibility that the committee's promise of public hearings in the Southwest would be kept. "After the discussion held with Mr. Hunt and Mr. Reeves in Silver City on . . . January 13, 1945," Castañeda reported, "I became convinced that under the standards adopted for the determination of the validity of the various complaints, it would be impossible to carry the matter to a hearing." He was equally convinced, moreover, that as a consequence of its failure to keep its word the committee could expect a further depreciation of its already sharply devalued reputation in the Southwest. "The indefinite postponement of the hearing," Castañeda ruefully predicted, "is going to be a severe blow to the prestige of the Committee in the Southwest. Both the unions and the companies, as well as the working men themselves, know that since 1942, when [it] first investigated discrimination in the mining industry, the Committee has periodically promised to eliminate discrimination, has sent from time to time representatives supposedly to bring the matter to a head, and that each time it has turned out to be a fizzle."

"Men who have in good faith presented their complaints to members of the Committee at various times," he dejectedly observed, "have suffered the consequences of their daring. The companies and such unions as share the same views, have gloried in the inability of the complainants to have their lot improved. They have gone further and victimized those who have protested against the age-old and honored practices of discrimination. The faith of the minority groups in the mining industry, particularly the Latin-Americans, will certainly not be strengthened by another failure to help them."

For all of his avowed pessimism, however, Castañeda was in the end loath to conclude that all hope was lost for Executive Order 9346 in the Southwest. "It may be too late," he confessed to Maslow. "The Southwest Hearing may be beyond resurrection." But, he added, "I still feel that it can be salvaged and prestige restored to the Committee in the Southwest if Mr. Metzger's memorandum . . . and my Summary Report . . . are restudied and if the recommendations as outlined therein are faithfully carried out, a hearing that would not fizzle can still be held."[45]

In fact, the committee had no apparent desire to salvage its commitment to public hearings in the Southwest. Responding to Hunt's discouraging assessment of its prospects in the region, the committee quietly decided on February 12 to abandon the idea of public hearings in the region. To the extent that any further effort would be made to redress complaints of discrimination from Chicano copper workers, the committee nebulously concluded, it would be through "Examiner-type hearings."[46] As its subsequent neglect of the issue made plain, however, the committee's abandonment of public hearings ended any remaining possibility that Chicano workers in the Southwest would realize the promise of fair treatment embodied in Executive Order 9346. As the FEPC increasingly turned its attention during the spring of 1945 to an ultimately futile campaign to persuade a sharply divided Congress to preserve it as a permanent champion of fair employment practices in postwar America,[47] those Chicano copper workers who had trusted in the committee even in the face of repeated disappointments were at last fully disabused of its endlessly professed good intentions.

8. *Promises to Keep*

GIVEN THAT CHICANO workers remained distantly situated from the mainstream of majority consciousness and concern during the war, it is curiously fitting that assessments of the benefits they derived from the activities of the FEPC were largely based on vague impressions. In its final report, the FEPC insisted that Chicano workers had realized significant gains in the workplace during the war, but was at a loss to document the progress it alleged or to claim that it resulted from committee enforcement efforts. "In the mining industry," the committee reported, "great wartime improvement was made in the proper use of Mexican-Americans." Yet it refrained from any suggestion of an instrumental role for its own efforts. "The exodus of white miners to better-paid jobs on the west coast," the committee explained, "left places open for Mexican-Americans. They were also aided by the efforts of the War Labor Board to end discriminatory wage rates and by the cooperation of the unions concerned."[1] The committee's final reckoning of the progress realized in southern California, where it noted that tens of thousands of Chicano workers were employed in aircraft factories and shipyards by war's end, was also oddly devoid of references to its own influence and conspicuously passive in addressing the postwar debate over just how much improvement had actually occurred. "Opinion is divided regarding the Mexican-American," the committee wanly observed in regard to the wartime gains of Chicano workers in the Los Angeles area. "One source," it rather disinterestedly commented, "states that these minority workers did not make as great advances during the war as Negroes, chiefly because they did not protest against discrimination as vigorously and lacked leadership. Their wartime advances are said . . . to have resulted from their filling the vacuum created by the Japanese. Actually, thousands did obtain war work in aircraft, oil refineries, shipbuilding and other industries. Another source states that Mexican-Americans have achieved 'occupational acceptance,' which means, of course, that they are often frozen at levels below their training, experience and ambition."[2]

That the committee relied upon the casual impressions of third parties to summarize the collective experience of Chicano workers during the war reflected a long-evident tendency within the FEPC to let its understandable preoccupation with the larger problem of discrimination against black workers obscure the equally iniquitous, if not always equally visible, mistreatment of other minorities in the workplace. In summing up the committee's feeble efforts in behalf of Chicanos, Malcolm Ross readily acknowledged that "prejudice against Mexican-Americans is more widespread than the number of complaints filed with the FEPC would indicate." Still, he suggested, more might have been accomplished if Chicanos had endeavored to liberate themselves from those confining patterns of thought and behavior that facilitated their mistreatment by obscuring it from public view. "Mexican-Americans are a diffident people, largely keeping (or being kept) to themselves," Ross concluded. "Only the top few have the sophistication to demand civil rights from Anglos."[3] Yet while it may well have been the case that a lack of solidarity and organization within their communities, as well as a tradition of wariness in confronting their Anglo oppressors, contributed to the relative neglect that Chicanos suffered during the war, the committee's own grossly ineffectual response to the entreaties that were repeatedly articulated by Chicano workers and their supporters in various copper-producing districts of the Southwest hardly served to encourage and reward those who did protest discriminatory employment practices.

Yet whatever the particular deficiencies that might be alleged in regard to its performance in the Southwest, the FEPC ultimately failed to combat discrimination against Chicano workers for the same reasons that it was unable to secure the full promise of Executive Orders 8802 and 9346 for every other eligible minority group. Denied both the resources and the authority required to contend successfully against one of the most daunting and intractable domestic problems facing the nation, and routinely undermined by an administration whose attitude toward its mission oscillated between grudging tolerance and a thinly veiled contempt, the FEPC was bound to disappoint.

Throughout its brief and troubled career the FEPC was, as friends and foes alike ultimately came to understand, little more than a gesture. "FEPC was never armed with the authority to do a proper job," Malcolm Ross succinctly explained. "It was a wartime makeshift."[4] Indeed, given that the Roosevelt administration never intended that the committee should be anything more than a bone tossed among civil rights activists to distract them from their incessant nipping at the president's heels, it is remarkable that the FEPC was taken as seriously as it was. Both unable and unwilling to agree with advocates of equal rights that the time was uniquely propitious to dismantle at home those barriers to freedom and equality the nation was sworn to demolish overseas, Roosevelt resorted to the artful dodges for which he was justly renowned.

Hoping for a federal antidiscrimination policy of genuine substance, supporters of fair employment practices were forced to settle instead for the decorative trappings and sophistical illusions of change. What might have been an opportunity for profound and enduring reform was thus reduced to cynically crafted episodes of political theater. When circumstances demanded ritual highmindedness Roosevelt and his spokesmen unhesitatingly served up generous portions of meaty rhetoric intended to suppress, if never to satisfy, the appetites of those hungering for equal rights. That it was a perverse ritual, one that all but the most naive celebrants knew from past experience to be empty of real meaning and sincere commitment, was somehow never reason enough to abandon it. Seemingly, for those Americans whose race, color, creed, or national origin served as grounds for continuing denials of equal rights, even these otherwise empty endorsements of the nation's egalitarian ideals were valued if only because they confirmed the justness of their hopes and validated the righteousness of their anger.

Beyond the crippling debilities for which Roosevelt was ultimately accountable, the FEPC was also subject to the singular constraints imposed by the paradoxical circumstances confronting a democratic nation at war. For while wartime conditions created a political atmosphere that rendered the Roosevelt administration susceptible to the activist pressures from which the FEPC germinated, those same conditions severely limited the committee's capacity for effective operation. The war necessarily dictated federal priorities; when the committee's activities in behalf of fair employment practices brought it into conflict with other agencies and departments of government, its moral errand proved no match for the temporal exigencies they claimed to serve. Had the frustrations it suffered and the impediments it faced because of the actions or inactions of other federal agencies resulted from motives that betrayed only the racist malice to which some disappointed proponents of equal opportunity too readily attributed its every setback, the FEPC might at least have deduced a simple explanation for its many defeats. Yet for the most part, when the committee was impeded by the Department of State, the War Manpower Commission, the War Labor Board, or any other of the several federal agencies whose jurisdiction abutted or overlapped its own, the explanation was less likely to be found in malevolent obstructionism than in a well-conditioned unwillingness within a fractious federal bureaucracy made even more territorial by wartime conditions to defer to any rival unable to compel such a dénouement. In short, when other federal agencies blocked the FEPC's efforts to enforce equal employment opportunity they were, notwithstanding the insensitivity and indifference their singlemindedness sometimes implied, neither acting in bad faith nor necessarily pandering to racist sentiment.

That other federal agencies could have used their superior authority to facilitate the success of the FEPC is undeniable. If the Roosevelt administration had not been so conspicuously fainthearted and disingenuous in its commitment to fair employment practices, those within the federal bureaucracy who could have assisted the committee might have been emboldened to do so. "The wartime FEPC was of course an extreme example of the necessity to appear to dominate," Malcolm Ross later wrote. "Having no real powers, it had to shop around for other government arms which might be kind enough to give it support."[5] Even when these other "government arms" were kindly disposed, however, there was never any realistic likelihood that they would routinely compromise or subordinate their own equally legitimate wartime functions in order to enhance the FEPC's effectiveness.

This compelling dynamic of war—that victory must be America's foremost objective—operated with equal force and irresistibility among the intended beneficiaries of the president's nondiscrimination orders. Throughout the war minority workers, out of both simple patriotism and an acute appreciation of the majority's limited forbearance, subordinated their hopes for fair treatment on the job to demands for unimpeded war production and a seemingly irrefutable necessity for national consensus. Thus despite the periodic gusts of threatening rhetoric provoked by the FEPC's inability to enforce their new rights to fair treatment in the workplace, Chicano copper workers in the Southwest, like disappointed minority workers elsewhere, continued to sacrifice self-interest to the primacy of the war effort.[6]

In the end, however, the FEPC's inability to guarantee equal employment opportunity to the nation's minorities was a function of the majority's unwillingness to honor at home the democratic and egalitarian ideals for which Americans of every race, color, creed, and national origin were dying abroad. Simply put, it was the FEPC's unhappy fate to champion an idea whose time was yet to come in America. Still, even as it fell far short of fulfilling the hopes that it inspired among millions of minority workers, the FEPC forced the American people to glimpse, if not to comprehend and accept, the wrenching future that lay before them.

Notes

Preface

1. Among the best of these recent studies are Mario T. García, *Desert Immigrants: The Mexicans of El Paso, 1880–1920;* Albert Camarillo, *Chicanos in a Changing Society: From Mexican Pueblos to American Barrios in Santa Barbara and Southern California, 1848–1930;* Richard Griswold del Castillo, *The Los Angeles Barrio, 1850–1890;* Thomas E. Sheridan, *Los Tucsonenses: The Mexican Community in Tucson, 1854–1941;* Richard A. García, "The Making of the Mexican-American Mind, San Antonio, Texas, 1929–1941"; Douglas G. Monroy, "Mexicans in Los Angeles, 1930–1941: An Ethnic Group in Relation to Class Forces"; and David Montejano, "A Journey through Mexican Texas, 1900–1930: The Making of a Segregated Society."

2. Mario T. García, *Mexican Americans: Leadership, Ideology, and Identity, 1930–1960,* p. 19.

3. Ibid., p. 15.

4. Ibid., pp. 15–16.

1. *A People in the Distance*

1. Because it ignored discrimination on the basis of gender, Executive Order 8802, and later Executive Order 9346, did not establish a federal policy that was comprehensive in addressing fair employment practices during the war.

2. For accounts of the genesis of Executive Order 8802, see Herbert Garfinkel, *When Negroes March: The March on Washington Movement in the Organizational Politics for FEPC;* Louis C. Kesselman, *The Social Politics of FEPC,* pp. 3–15; Louis Ruchames, *Race, Jobs, and Politics: The Story of the FEPC,* pp. 3–21; Jervis Anderson, *A. Philip Randolph: A Biographical Portrait,* pp. 241–261; Lerone Bennett, Jr., *Confrontation: Black and White,* pp. 143–168; Walter White, *A Man Called White,* pp. 186–193; William H. Harris, "A. Philip Randolph as a Charismatic Leader," *Journal of Negro History* 64 (Fall 1979): 301–315.

3. Malcolm Ross, *All Manner of Men,* p. 21.

4. Committee on Fair Employment Practice, *First Report, July 1943–December 1944,* p. 37; Ross, *All Manner of Men,* pp. 24–25.

5. FEPC, *First Report,* p. 37; Ross, *All Manner of Men,* pp. 24–30; *Progress Report of the President's Committee on Fair Employment Practice* (War Manpower Commission, December 1, 1942), pp. 7–8, in Records of the President's Committee on Fair Employment Practice, Headquarters Files, Microfilm Reel 48, National Archives and Records Service (hereafter cited as FEPC Records).

6. Because of the inadequacy and awkwardness of other common forms of ethnic, cultural, and national designation—(Mexican, Mexican American, Spanish-speaking, Hispanic, Latin American, etc.) the term "Chicano," though anachronistic, is used throughout to describe workers of Mexican heritage in the United States. To the extent that "Spanish Americans" in New Mexico and Colorado were employed in the copper industry of the Southwest, they are, despite their long tradition of differentiating themselves from those of Mexican heritage, included in the term "Chicano." On this issue, see Richard L. Nostrand, "'Mexican American' and 'Chicano': Emerging Terms for a People Coming of Age," in *The Chicano,* ed. Norris Hundley, Jr., pp. 143–160.

7. Leo Grebler et al., *The Mexican American People,* p. 10.

8. Ibid., p. 111.

9. For a brief but informative assessment of the collective status of Chicanos in the early 1940s, see Carey McWilliams, "The Forgotten Mexican," *Common Ground* 3 (Spring 1943): 65–78. A fuller treatment can be found in Carey McWilliams, *North from Mexico: The Spanish-speaking People of the United States.* Additional useful studies are W. Rex Crawford, "The Latin American in Wartime United States," *Annals of the American Academy of Political and Social Science* 222 (September 1942): 123–131; Will W. Alexander, "Aliens in War Industries," ibid., pp. 138–143; Harold F. Gosnell, "Symbols of National Solidarity," ibid., pp. 157–161; Peter N. Kirstein, *Anglo over Bracero: A History of the Mexican Worker in the United States from Roosevelt to Nixon;* Manuel P. Servin, *The Mexican Americans: An Awakening Majority;* Ruth S. Lamb, *Mexican Americans: Sons of the Southwest;* Ernesto Galarza, *Merchants of Labor: The Mexican Bracero Story;* Matt S. Meier and Feliciano Rivera, *The Chicanos: A History of Mexican Americans,* pp. 185–216; John H. Burma, *Spanish-speaking Groups in the United States,* pp. 35–137; Beatrice W. Griffith, *American Me;* Ruth D. Tuck, *Not with the Fist;* William D. Altus, "The American Mexican: The Survival of a Culture," *Journal of Social Psychology* 29 (May 1949): 211–220; Leonard Broom and Eshref Shevsky, "Mexicans in the United States: A Problem of Social Differentiation," *Sociology and Social Research* 36 (January–February 1952): 150–158; Hugh Carter and Bernice Doster, "Social Characteristics of Aliens from the Southwest Registered for Selective Service during World War II," *Immigration and Naturalization Service Monthly Review* 8 (1951): 88–94; Pauline R. Kibbee, *Latin Americans in Texas;* Edward C. McDonogh, "Status Levels of Mexicans," *Sociology and Social Research* 32 (July–August 1948): 944–953; George I. Sanchez, *Forgotten People;* National Catholic Welfare Council, *The Spanish-speaking of the Southwest and West;* Barron B. Beshoar, "Report from the Mountain States," *Common Ground* 4 (Spring 1944): 23–30; Rodolfo Acuña, *Occupied America: The Chicano's Struggle toward Liberation,* especially pp. 198–208; Emory S. Bogardus,

"Current Problems of Mexican Immigrants," *Sociology and Social Research* 25 (November 1940): 166–174; James Burnhill, "The Mexican People in the Southwest," *Political Affairs* 32 (September 1953): 43–52; Manuel P. Servin, "The Pre-World War II Mexican American: An Interpretation," *California Historical Society Quarterly* 45 (1966): 325–338; Brian F. Grattan, Arturo Rosales, and Hans DeBano, "A Sample of the Mexican-American Population in 1940," *Historical Methods* 21 (Spring 1988): 80–87; and a fictional account: Guy Nunn, *White Shadows*. For the best recent study, see Mario T. García, *Mexican Americans: Leadership, Ideology, and Identity, 1930–1960*.

10. M. C. Gonzales to Sidney Hillman, November 17, 1941, Reel 28, HQ Files, FEPC Records.

11. Ernesto Galarza to Mark Ethridge, September 25, 1941, Reel 28, HQ Files, FEPC Records.

12. Ibid.

13. Gonzales to Hillman, November 17, 1941.

14. U.S. Department of Commerce, Bureau of the Census, *Sixteenth Census of the United States: 1940, Population*, vol. II, part 1, table 4, p. 516, table 21, p. 541.

15. Fair Employment Practice Committee, *Public Hearings in the Matter of Complaints of Discrimination in Employment in Defense Industries Because of Race, Creed, Color or National Origin*, October 20–21, 1941, Los Angeles, California, p. 99, Reel 18, HQ Files, FEPC Records (hereafter cited as FEPC, *Los Angeles Hearings*).

16. Carey McWilliams, *Brothers under the Skin*, pp. 113–121; "Spanish-Americans in the Southwest and the War Effort," August 18, 1942, Report No. 24, Special Services Division, Bureau of Intelligence, Office of War Information, pp. 1, 12–15, in Reel 48, HQ Files, FEPC Records. See also Juan Gomez-Quiñones, *Development of the Mexican Working Class North of the Rio Bravo*, pp. 44–45; McWilliams, *North from Mexico*, pp. 7–8, 209–214; Grebler et al., *The Mexican American People*, pp. 378–399, 542–555; Robin F. Scott, "The Mexican-American in the Los Angeles Area, 1920–1950: From Acquiescence to Activity"; Octavio Romano, "The Anthropology and Sociology of the Mexican-Americans: The Distortion of Mexican-American History," *El Grito* (Fall 1968): 13–26.

17. On the origins, policies, and activities of El Congreso, see García, *Mexican Americans*, pp. 146–174.

18. Testimony of Manuel Ruiz, FEPC, *Los Angeles Hearings*, pp. 99–102.

19. Ibid., pp. 101–104. Ruiz informed FEPC field representatives prior to the Los Angeles hearings that most Chicano victims of job discrimination in southern California were unwilling to appear before the committee because "the idea of a Federal Hearing frightened them." See Manuel Ruiz to Guy Nunn, October 18, 1941, Reel 77, HQ Files, FEPC Papers.

20. Testimony of Dr. Victor M. Egas, FEPC, *Los Angeles Hearings*, pp. 105–106.

21. Ibid., pp. 106–107.

22. FEPC, *Los Angeles Hearings*, p. 658; Lawrence W. Cramer to James G. Bryant, October 9, 1941, Reel 77, HQ Files, FEPC Records.

23. Testimony of Manuel Ruiz, FEPC, *Los Angeles Hearings*, pp. 103–105; testimony of Dr. Victor Egas, ibid., p. 107. See also Manuel Ruiz, Jr., to Guy Nunn, October 18, 1941; and "Suggested Representatives of Minority Groups to Appear be-

fore the FEPC" [n.d.], both in Reel 77, HQ Files, FEPC Records.

24. Testimony of Phillip M. Connelly, FEPC, *Los Angeles Hearings,* p. 120. In his report to the FEPC following the Los Angeles hearings, Eugene Davidson, the field representative responsible for their preparation, recommended that "no hearings of this size and importance be undertaken without preparation in the territory of at least one month." See Eugene Davidson, "Report on First Public Hearings, Committee on Fair Employment Practice of the President of the United States, Los Angeles, California, October 20 and 21, 1941," Reel 77, HQ Files, FEPC Records.

25. A study conducted by the Office of War Information during the spring of 1942 confirmed that discrimination against Chicanos was widespread throughout the defense industries of southern California in general and in the military aircraft industry in particular. As the OWI study noted, "The aircraft industry of Southern California has been consistent in asserting that it does not discriminate, but payrolls show almost no Mexicans employed. One plant personnel man stated that his company would employ them if they were not 'too racial'—'too dark.' American-born girls of Mexican ancestry in San Diego have taken training courses, have come out at the top of their class, only to find that employers have passed them up to take less competent white girls, or have gone as far north as Los Angeles and San Bernardino to recruit white help." See "Spanish-Americans in the Southwest and the War Effort," p. 11.

26. *Progress Report of the President's Committee on Fair Employment Practice,* part II, pp. 4–5.

27. Ibid., part I, p. 4.

28. Stephen Early to Mark Ethridge, July 9, 1941, in President's Official File No. 4245G, Box 3, Franklin D. Roosevelt Papers, Franklin D. Roosevelt Library (hereafter cited as OF, FDR Papers).

29. Mark Ethridge to Stephen Early, August 20, 1941, OF 4245G, Box 3, FDR Papers.

30. Ibid. In addition to Ethridge, Dickerson, Webster, and Sarnoff, the original appointees to the FEPC included William Green, president of the American Federation of Labor, and Philip Murray, president of the Congress of Industrial Organizations. Because neither Green nor Murray could attend FEPC meetings on a regular basis, Roosevelt appointed Frank Fenton, the AFL's director of organization, and John Brophy, chairman of the CIO's industrial union councils, as permanent alternates. See "Important Dates in FEPC History" [n.d.], Reel 69, HQ Files, FEPC Records. See also *Amsterdam News,* July 26, 1941.

31. Mark Ethridge to Stephen Early, December 23, 1941, OF 4245G, FDR Papers.

32. John Beecher, "8802 Blues," *New Republic* 108 (February 22, 1943): 248.

33. Garfinkel, *When Negroes March,* pp. 76–77; Ruchames, *Race, Jobs, and Politics,* p. 45; Beecher, "8802 Blues," pp. 248–249. On the distinctly secondary importance of the "race problem" during the war, see John M. Blum, *V Was for Victory: Politics and American Culture during World War II,* pp. 182–220.

34. Lawrence W. Cramer to M. C. Gonzales, November 26, 1941, Reel 77, HQ Files, FEPC Records. Cramer, who had just completed a lengthy term as governor of the Virgin Islands, directed the day-to-day operations of the FEPC until the commit-

tee was reorganized in mid-1943. On Cramer's credentials, see *Amsterdam News,* July 26, 1941.

35. McWilliams, *North from Mexico,* pp. 275–276.

36. Ibid., p. 276.

37. W. G. Carnahan to Will Alexander, December 9, 1941, Reel 77, HQ Files, FEPC Records.

38. Will Alexander to W. G. Carnahan, December 16, 1941, Reel 77, HQ Files, FEPC Records.

39. McWilliams, *North from Mexico,* p. 276.

40. David J. Saposs, "Report on Rapid Survey of Resident Latin American Problems and Recommended Program," Office of the Coordinator of Inter-American Affairs (April 3, 1942), p. 1, in Reel 28, HQ Files, FEPC Records.

41. "Spanish-Americans in the Southwest and the War Effort," p. i. Although this confidential report was officially released in August 1942, it was completed and made available to the FEPC in the spring of 1942. See Lawrence W. Cramer to Wilma L. Shannon, June 1, 1942, Reel 48, HQ Files, FEPC Records.

42. "Report on the Spanish-speaking Peoples in the Southwest, Field Survey March 14 to April 7, 1942," p. 13, in Reel 70, HQ Files, FEPC Records.

43. Saposs, "Report on Rapid Survey of Resident Latin American Problems and Recommended Program," p. 1.

44. "Spanish-Americans in the Southwest and the War Effort," pp. i, 3, 5, 17.

45. "Report on the Spanish-speaking Peoples in the Southwest," pp. 2–3.

46. "Spanish-Americans in the Southwest and the War Effort," p. i. Federal fear of subversion in the Chicano barrios and *colonias* of the Southwest centered on the potential influences of *sinarquismo,* a virulently nationalistic movement active in the northern states of Mexico that borrowed heavily from the fascist tenets of both German National Socialism and Spanish Falangism. See "Union Nacional Sinarquista de Mexico (Sinarquismo)," pp. 1–13, appended to "Report on the Spanish-speaking Peoples in the Southwest"; "Spanish-Americans in the Southwest and the War Effort," pp. 12–13; Heinz H. F. Eulau, "Sinarquismo in the United States," *Inter-American* 3 (March 1944): 25–27, 48; Meier and Rivera, *The Chicanos,* pp. 195–197; García, *Mexican Americans,* pp. 168–170.

47. Saposs, "Report on Rapid Survey of Resident Latin American Problems and Recommended Program," p. 3; McWilliams, *North from Mexico,* p. 276.

48. "Spanish-Americans in the Southwest and the War Effort," pp. i, 13.

49. Malcolm S. MacLean to Marvin H. McIntyre, February 6, 1942, OF 4245G, Box 3, FDR Papers. At Ethridge's suggestion, Roosevelt enlarged the size of the FEPC by one member so that its former chairman could continue on the expanded committee as one of its seven members. See Mark Ethridge to Stephen Early, December 23, 1941; and Sidney Hillman to the President, January 27, 1942, both in OF 4245G, Box 3, FDR Papers.

50. Malcolm S. MacLean to Marvin H. McIntyre, February 24, 1942, OF 93, Box 4, FDR Papers.

51. "Minutes of the Meeting of the President's Committee on Fair Employment Practices," January 18, 1942, Reel 1, HQ Files, FEPC Records.

52. Frances Anne Hardin, "The Role of Presidential Advisors: Roosevelt Aides and the FEPC, 1941–1943, p. 133.

53. Malcolm S. MacLean to Marvin H. McIntyre, February 6, 1942, OF 4245G, Box 3, FDR Papers.

54. Sidney Hillman to Marvin H. McIntyre, February 4, 1942, OF 4245G, Box 3, FDR Papers. Hillman reported that committee members David Sarnoff and Milton Webster remained opposed to the transfer despite his recommendation.

55. Ibid.

56. Malcolm S. MacLean to Marvin H. McIntyre, May 12, 1942, OF 4245G, Box 3, FDR Papers.

57. Malcolm S. MacLean to the President, March 18, 1942, OF 4245G, Box 3, FDR Papers.

58. MHM [Marvin H. McIntyre] to the president, March 20, 1942, OF 4245G, Box 3, FDR Papers.

59. FDR to the Director of the Budget, March 21, 1942; and Harold Smith to the President, March 28, 1942, both in OF 4245G, Box 3, FDR Papers.

60. Franklin D. Roosevelt to Malcolm S. MacLean, March 28, 1942, OF 4245G, Box 3, FDR Papers.

61. Malcolm S. MacLean to Marvin H. McIntyre, April 2, 1942, OF 4245G, Box 3, FDR Papers. For correspondence relating to MacLean's futile efforts to enlist White House support for the FEPC, see in the same file Lawrence W. Cramer to Malcolm S. MacLean, March 31, 1942; MHM [Marvin H. McIntyre] to the President, March 31, 1942; Marvin H. McIntyre to Malcolm S. MacLean, March 31, 1942; Malcolm S. MacLean to Franklin D. Roosevelt, May 12, 1942; Malcolm S. MacLean to Marvin H. McIntyre, May 12, 1942; "Mac" [Marvin H. McIntyre] to the President, May 13, 1942; and "Draft of Letter to President of CIO, President of American Federation of Labor and Presidents of Railway Brotherhoods" [n.d.; marked "not sent"].

2. *Last among Equals*

1. Victor S. Clark, *Mexican Labor in the United States,* p. 485. On the general status of Chicano labor in Arizona and the Southwest during this period, see Joseph Park, "The History of Mexican Labor in Arizona during the Territorial Period." Also useful are Mario Barrera, *Race and Class in the Southwest,* pp. 34–103; Mark Reisler, *By the Sweat of Their Brow: Mexican Immigrant Labor in the United States, 1900–1940,* pp. 3–48; Manuel P. Servin and Robert L. Spude, "Historical Conditions of Early Mexican Labor in the United States: Arizona—a Neglected Story," *Journal of Mexican American History* 5 (1975): 43–56; Carey McWilliams, *North from Mexico,* pp. 142–144, 196–197; Arthur F. Corwin, "Early Mexican Labor Migration: A Frontier Sketch, 1848–1900," in *Immigrants—and Immigrants: Perspectives on Mexican Labor Migration to the United States,* ed. Arthur F. Corwin, pp. 25–37; Mario T. García, "Racial Dualism in the El Paso Labor Market," *Aztlán* 6 (Summer 1975): 197–217.

2. Clark, *Mexican Labor in the United States,* pp. 485–486.

3. Ibid., p. 486. In addition, see *Arizona's Hispanic Perspective,* pp. 10, 76, 81, 85; Acuña, *Occupied America,* p. 89; *Arizona: A State Guide,* p. 96; McWilliams, *North from Mexico,* p. 196; Meier and Rivera, *The Chicanos,* p. 108; Park, "The History of Mexican Labor in Arizona during the Territorial Period," pp. 151–207.

4. Clark, *Mexican Labor in the United States,* p. 486. See also *Arizona: A State Guide,* p. 96.

5. Acuña, *Occupied America,* pp. 88–92; Park, "The History of Mexican Labor in Arizona during the Territorial Period," p. viii; McWilliams, *North from Mexico,* pp. 196–197, 212–217; Barrera, *Race and Class in the Southwest,* pp. 40–46, 50–53, 83–84; *Arizona's Hispanic Perspective,* pp. 79–82; Ralph C. Guzman, *The Political Socialization of the Mexican American People,* pp. 61–65. See also Douglas Monroy, "An Essay on Understanding the Work Experience of Mexicans in Southern California, 1908–1939," *Aztlán* 12 (Spring 1981): 59–74, and Andres Jimenez, *Political Domination in the Labor Market: Racial Division in the Arizona Copper Industry.*

6. *Arizona: A State Guide,* p. 97.

7. Clark, *Mexican Labor in the United States,* pp. 492–493; Park, "The History of Mexican Labor in Arizona during the Territorial Period," pp. 263–279; McWilliams, *North from Mexico,* p. 196; Rufus Kay Wyllys, *Arizona: The History of a Frontier State,* pp. 290–291.

8. *Arizona: A State Guide,* pp. 97–99; *Arizona's Hispanic Perspective,* pp. 86–88; McWilliams, *North from Mexico,* pp. 196–197; Park, "The History of Mexican Labor in Arizona during the Territorial Period," pp. 261–279; Wyllys, *Arizona,* pp. 291, 307; James W. Byrkit, *Forging the Copper Collar: Arizona's Labor-Management War of 1901–1921,* pp. 28–29.

9. Reflecting the attitudes expressed by employers in the Southwest, Victor Clark concluded, "The Mexican laborer is unambitious, listless, physically weak, irregular, and indolent. On the other hand, he is docile, patient, usually orderly in camp, fairly intelligent under competent supervision, obedient, and cheap. If he were active and ambitious, he would be less tractable and would cost more. His strongest point is his willingness to work for a low wage." Clark further noted, however, that Chicano workers were "very tenacious of their rights," and that their "suspicions of the fairness of their employer seem easily aroused, and they will quit a job at once if they think they are being cheated" (Clark, *Mexican Labor in the United States,* p. 496).

10. Vernon H. Jensen, *Heritage of Conflict: Labor Relations in the Nonferrous Metals Industry up to 1930,* p. 356; Acuña, *Occupied America,* pp. 95–96; Park, "The History of Mexican Labor in Arizona during the Territorial Period," pp. 256–257; *Arizona's Hispanic Perspective,* pp. 86–87; *Arizona: A State Guide,* p. 97.

11. James R. Kluger, *The Clifton-Morenci Strike: Labor Difficulty in Arizona, 1915–1916;* Jensen, *Heritage of Conflict,* pp. 364–368; Acuña, *Occupied America,* pp. 96–97; *Arizona: A State Guide,* p. 99; McWilliams, *North from Mexico,* p. 197; Byrkit, *Forging the Copper Collar,* pp. 55–62; John A. Fitch, "Arizona's Embargo on Strike-Breakers," *Survey* 36 (May 6, 1916): 143–144; Meier and Rivera, *The Chicanos,* pp. 172–173.

12. Jensen, *Heritage of Conflict,* pp. 354–380; Melvyn Dubofsky, *We shall Be All: A History of the Industrial Workers of the World,* pp. 369–371; Byrkit, *Forging the Copper Collar,* pp. 97–143.

13. The Bisbee deportation has spawned a voluminous literature. In particular, see Dubofsky, *We Shall Be All,* pp. 385–391; Byrkit, *Forging the Copper Collar,* pp. 1–9, 97–328; Jensen, *Heritage of Conflict,* pp. 400–407; *Report on Bisbee Deportations Made by the President's Mediation Commission to President of United States, November 6, 1917;* Philip Taft, "The Bisbee Deportation," *Labor History* 13 (Winter 1972): 3–40; and John H. Linquist and James Fraser, "A Sociological Interpretation of the Bisbee Deportation," *Pacific Historical Review* 38 (November 1968): 401–422.

14. Vernon H. Jensen, *Nonferrous Metals Industry Unionism, 1932–1954,* p. 2. See also Jensen, *Heritage of Conflict,* pp. 411–429, 452–466; *Arizona: A State Guide,* pp. 99–100; and Byrkit, *Forging the Copper Collar,* pp. 297–328.

15. National Labor Relations Board, *Decisions and Orders,* Case No. C-1193, Vol. 15, September 27, 1939, pp. 732–756. See also ibid., vol. 6, pp. 624–641; vol. 7, pp. 862–866; vol. 19, pp. 552–605; and Jensen, *Nonferrous Metals Industry Unionism,* p. 43.

16. National Labor Relations Board, *Decisions and Orders,* Case No. C-500, Vol. 19, January 16, 1940, pp. 547–605.

17. Jensen, *Nonferrous Metals Industry Unionism,* pp. 42–43, 48–49; National Labor Relations Board, *Decisions and Orders,* Case Nos. R-3643 to R-3651, R-3681, vol. 41, May 20, 1942, pp. 140–153.

18. Jensen, *Nonferrous Metals Industry Unionism,* p. 43. For an example of the NLRB's application of the globe doctrine in the copper industry of the Southwest, see National Labor Relations Board, *Decisions and Orders,* Case Nos. R-2732 to R-2736, vol. 34, August 23, 1941, pp. 846–857.

19. As a result of their work in behalf of the CIO's Committee on Latin America, which John L. Lewis created in 1939, MMSW leaders had already acknowledged that winning the allegiance of Chicano workers was crucial to the union's fortunes in the Southwest. See James Robinson to Kathryn Lewis, January 19, 1940; Kathryn Lewis to John L. Lewis, March 11, 1940; and Reid Robinson to Kathryn Lewis, March 18, 1940, all in CIO files of John L. Lewis, Part II: General Files on the CIO and AFL, 1929–1955, Reel 5, Microfilm Edition (University Publications of America). See also Congress of Industrial Organizations, "Daily Proceedings of the Second Constitutional Convention, October 12, 1939" (San Francisco), p. 37; and CIO, "Daily Proceedings of the Third Constitutional Convention, November 18–22, 1940" (Atlantic City), pp. 105, 119.

20. Lawrence W. Cramer to Franklin D. Roosevelt, July 10, 1942, OF 4245G, Box 4, FDR Papers. See also John Brophy to Lawrence Cramer, December 22, 1941; Lawrence W. Cramer to John Brophy, December 31, 1941; and Barron B. Beshoar, "Complainants Interviewed in Region XI," May 6, 1942, all in Reel 28, HQ Files, FEPC Records.

21. Cramer to Brophy, December 31, 1941, Reel 28, HQ Files, FEPC Records.

22. "Problems of Resident Latin Americans: Conference with Dr. Will W. Alexander, Chief Minorities Section, Labor Division War Production Board, 1/31/42," February 3, 1942, in Records of the Office of the Coordinator of Inter-American

Affairs, Box 1717, Record Group No. 229, Federal Records Center, Suitland, Maryland (hereafter cited as OCIAA Records, RG 229). See also Nelson A. Rockefeller to Secretary of War [n.d.; draft]; Joseph F. McGurk to Secretary of State, February 4, 1942, both in OCIAA Records, Box 1717, RG 229.

23. Cramer to Roosevelt, July 10, 1942, OF 4245G, FDR Papers. MMSW president Reid Robinson had reiterated his demand that the FEPC hold hearings in the Southwest only a few days before the committee announced its intentions. See Beshoar, "Complainants Interviewed in Region XI," May 6, 1942, Reel 28, HQ Files, FEPC Records.

24. President's Committee on Fair Employment Practices, "Press Release," May 12, 1942, OCIAA Records, Box 1717, RG 229.

25. See chapter 1. See also Lawrence W. Cramer to Wilma L. Shannon, June 1, 1942, Reel 48, HQ Files, FEPC Records.

26. For a brief commentary on Maverick's liberal credentials, see Arthur M. Schlesinger, Jr., *The Age of Roosevelt: The Politics of Upheaval,* pp. 142–144. See also Judith Kaaz Doyle, "Maury Maverick and Racial Politics in San Antonio, Texas, 1938–1941," *Journal of Southern History* 53 (May 1987): 194–224.

27. Maury Maverick to Lawrence W. Cramer, June 10, 1942, Reel 28, HQ Files, FEPC Records.

28. Lawrence W. Cramer to Ernest G. Trimble, July 21, 1942, Reel 28, HQ Files, FEPC Records.

29. Dennis Chavez to Lawrence Cramer, July 6, 1942; Lawrence W. Cramer to Honorable Dennis Chavez, July 15, 1942, both in Reel 77, HQ Files, FEPC Records.

30. Sumner Welles to the President, June 20, 1942, OF 4245G, Box 4, FDR Papers.

31. On the origins of the wartime importation of Mexican workers, see Robert C. Jones, *Mexican War Workers in the United States: The Mexico–United States Manpower Recruiting Program and Operation;* Wayne D. Rasmussen, *A History of the Emergency Farm Labor Supply Program, 1943–1947;* Peter N. Kirstein, *Anglo over Bracero: A History of the Mexican Worker in the United States from Roosevelt to Nixon;* Ernesto Galarza, *Merchants of Labor: The Mexican Bracero Story;* Manuel García y Griego, *The Importation of Mexican Contract Laborers to the United States, 1942–1964: Antecedents, Operation and Legacy;* Otey M. Scruggs, "The Evolution of the Farm Labor Agreement of 1942," *Agricultural History* 341 (July 1960): 140–149.

32. Jones, *Mexican War Workers in the United States,* pp. 2–3; Scruggs, "The Evolution of the Farm Labor Agreement of 1942," pp. 143–144.

33. FDR to "Mac," June 23, 1942, OF 4245G, Box 3, FDR Papers.

34. Lawrence W. Cramer to Franklin D. Roosevelt, July 10, 1942, OF 4245G, Box 3, FDR papers.

35. This episode is briefly described in Barron B. Beshoar, "Report from the Mountain States," *Common Ground* 4 (Spring 1944): 24–25.

36. Cramer to Roosevelt, July 10, 1942, OF 4245G, Box 3, FDR Papers.

37. Marvin McIntyre to Department of State, July 11, 1942, OF 4245G, Box 3, FDR Papers.

38. Sumner Welles to Marvin H. McIntyre, July 24, 1942, OF 4245G, Box 3, FDR Papers.

39. "M.H.M." [Marvin H. McIntyre] to the President, July 30, 1942, OF 4245G, Box 3, FDR Papers; David J. Saposs, "Weekly Progress Report, July 2 to July 30, 1942," OCIAA, Box 1717, RG 229.

40. War Manpower Commission, *Progress Report of the President's Committee on Fair Employment Practice* ("First Draft"), December 1, 1942, part I, pp. 1–4, Reel 48, HQ Files, FEPC Records.

41. Only committee member Earl Dickerson openly objected to Ethridge's defense of segregation, but he waited until well after the hearings had ended before registering his dissent. The committee ultimately adopted a policy providing that segregation was contrary to the letter of Executive Order 8802 only when it resulted in employment discrimination. See Louis Ruchames, *Race, Jobs, and Politics: The Story of the FEPC,* pp. 40–41. Presidential assistant Marvin McIntyre, a southerner who seldom missed an opportunity to oppose the FEPC, warmly endorsed Ethridge's defense of segregation. "Personally," he told War Manpower Commission boss Paul McNutt, "I am very strong for Mark Ethridge's remarks." See M. H. McIntyre to Paul V. McNutt, August 19, 1942, OF 4245G, Box 3, FDR Papers.

42. Lawrence W. Cramer to the President, July 3, 1942; Robert P. Patterson to the President, July 14, 1942; FDR to "Mac," July 17, 1942; "Summary of the Hearing of the President's Committee on Fair Employment Practice on Discrimination in Defense Training with Findings and Directions Held April 13, 1942," all in OF 4245G, Box 3, FDR Papers.

43. Beecher, "8802 Blues," *New Republic* 108 (February 22, 1943): 249–250; *New York Times,* July 2, 1942, p. 44; Lawrence W. Cramer to Marvin McIntyre, June 22, 1942, OF 4245G, Box 3, FDR Papers.

44. Beecher, "8802 Blues," p. 250; Malcolm S. MacLean to Marvin McIntyre, August 3, 1942, OF 4245G, Box 3, FDR Papers.

45. Franklin D. Roosevelt to Malcolm S. MacLean, July 30, 1942, OF 4245G, Box 3, FDR Papers.

46. Malcolm S. MacLean to Marvin McIntyre, August 3, 1942, OF 4245G, Box 3, FDR Papers.

47. White House press release, April 14, 1942, OF 4905, Box 1, FDR Papers.

48. Malcolm S. MacLean to Marvin McIntyre, May 12, 1942, Reel 41, HQ Files, FEPC Records.

49. Paul V. McNutt to the President, May 29, 1942, OF 4905, Box 1, FDR Papers.

50. Harold Smith to the President, June 18, 1942, OF 4245G, Box 3, FDR Papers.

51. Malcolm S. MacLean to Marvin McIntyre, August 3, 1942, OF 4245G, Box 3, FDR Papers; Beecher, "8802 Blues," p. 250; *Chicago Defender,* July 11, 1942, p. 1.

52. Minutes of the Staff Meeting of the Office of the Director of Operations, War Manpower Commission, July 20, 1942, in Records of the War Manpower Commission, Record Group 211, National Archives (hereafter cited as ODO Records, WMC, RG 211); Lawrence W. Cramer to Dr. [Robert] Weaver and Dr. [Will] Alexander, July 16, 1942; and "Relationship between President's Committee on Fair Employment Practice and the War Manpower Commission in the Field" [n.d.], both in Reel 41, HQ Files, FEPC Records; *New York Times,* June 21, 1942, p. 38.

53. Malcolm Ross, *All Manner of Men,* pp. 21–22; Herbert Garfinkel, *When*

Negroes March, pp. 104–105; Beecher, "8802 Blues," p. 250; *New Republic,* February 22, 1943, p. 240; *New York Times,* July 24, 1942, p. 7; ibid., July 2, 1942, p. 44.

54. Malcolm S. MacLean to Marvin McIntyre, August 3, 1942, OF 4245G, Box 3, FDR Papers.

55. Walter White to Hon. Franklin D. Roosevelt, August 7, 1942, OF 4245G, Box 9, FDR Papers.

56. F. H. LaGuardia to Hon. Franklin D. Roosevelt, August 10, 1942; A. Philip Randolph to Mayor Fiorello LaGuardia, August 6, 1942, both in OF 4245G, Box 9, FDR Papers.

57. Malcolm S. MacLean to Marvin McIntyre, August 13, 1942, OF 4245G, Box 9, FDR Papers.

58. M. H. McIntyre to Hon. F. H. LaGuardia, August 14, 1942, OF 4245G, Box 9, FDR Papers.

59. Malcolm S. MacLean to Marvin McIntyre, August 3, 1942, OF 4245G, Box 3, FDR Papers.

60. FDR to "Mac," August 8, 1942, OF 4245G, Box 3, FDR Papers.

61. "Memorandum for Mr. Hassett," August 15, 1942, OF 4245G, Box 9, FDR Papers.

62. Walter White to Hon. Franklin D. Roosevelt, August 19, 1942; Walter White to Hon. Paul V. McNutt, October 13, 1942; and Lester A. Walton to Franklin D. Roosevelt, October 22, 1942, all in OF 4245G, Box 3, FDR Papers; Walter White to Hon. Franklin D. Roosevelt, December 8, 1942; and Walter White to Hon. Franklin D. Roosevelt, December 18, 1942, both in OF 93, Box 5, FDR Papers.

63. M. H. McIntyre to Walter White, December 14, 1942, OF 93, Box 5, FDR Papers; Franklin D. Roosevelt to Hon. Lester A. Walton, November 11, 1942, OF 4245G, Box 3, FDR Papers.

64. Walter White to Hon. Franklin D. Roosevelt, December 18, 1942, OF 93, Box 5, FDR Papers; Garfinkel, *When Negroes March,* pp. 104–11.

3. *No Small Task*

1. G. James Fleming to Lawrence W. Cramer, July 22, 1942, Reel 77, HQ Files, FEPC Records.

2. Lawrence W. Cramer to Ernest G. Trimble, July 21, 1949, Reel 28, HQ Files, FEPC Records; E. G. Trimble to Lawrence W. Cramer, July 31, 1942, Reel 48, HQ Files, FEPC Records.

3. E. G. Trimble to Lawrence W. Cramer, July 31, 1942, Reel 48, HQ Files, FEPC Records.

4. Lawrence W. Cramer to Ernest G. Trimble, July 21, 1942, Reel 28, HQ Files, FEPC Records.

5. Lawrence W. Cramer to M. C. Gonzales, July 27, 1942, Reel 77, HQ Files, FEPC Records.

6. E. G. Trimble to Lawrence W. Cramer, July 31, 1942, Reel 48, HQ Files, FEPC Records.

7. *Union,* April 13, 1942, p. 2; ibid., May 25, 1942, p. 10 (The *Union* was the official publication of the MMSW.)

8. E. G. Trimble to Lawrence W. Cramer, July 31, 1942, Reel 48, HQ Files, FEPC Records.

9. Ibid.; *Union,* May 25, 1942, p. 10.

10. Because employers did not distinguish between workers of Spanish and Mexican descent, the term "Mexicans," which was the most common contemporary designation of these workers, is inclusive. On this point, see "Spanish-Americans in the Southwest and the War Effort," August 18, 1942, Report No. 24, Special Services Division, Bureau of Intelligence, Office of War Information, pp. 1–4, in Reel 48, HQ Files, FEPC Records.

11. Statement of Harry Hafner and Leo Ortiz to Dr. Ernest G. Trimble, et al., July 30, 1942, pp. 1–2, Reel 77, HQ Files, FEPC Records.

12. Ibid., pp. 2–7. The Shattuck-Denn Company, founded in 1906 by Lemuel Shattuck, a former miner who enjoyed a reputation for tolerance and liberal-mindedness among workers in the Bisbee region, was frequently at odds with the labor policies of Phelps Dodge and the other leading copper companies in the Southwest. See James Byrkit, *Forging the Copper Collar,* pp. 17, 190, 244.

13. Hafner-Ortiz Statement, pp. 1–3; "Spanish-Americans in the Southwest and the War Effort," p. 5.

14. Hafner-Ortiz Statement, pp. 6–7; For an independent expression of the same point of view regarding AFL unions in the region, see "Spanish-Americans in the Southwest and the War Effort," pp. 15–16.

15. Lawrence W. Cramer to Ernest G. Trimble, July 21, 1942, Reel 28, HQ Files, FEPC Records.

16. A small number of complaints filed by Chicano employees of the Phelps-Dodge Corporation in the Clifton-Morenci district of eastern Arizona were received by the committee in late May. Senator Dennis Chavez of New Mexico forwarded a few complaints to the committee in early July and the MMSW turned over additional information relating to individual cases of alleged discrimination when FEPC investigators arrived in El Paso. Copies of these complaints are in Reels 28 and 77, HQ Files, FEPC Records. See also M. C. Gonzales to Ernest G. Trimble, August 10, 1942, Reel 77, HQ Files, FEPC Records.

17. E. G. Trimble to Barron Beshoar, August 3, 1942, Reel 48, HQ Files, FEPC Records.

18. E. G. Trimble to Lawrence W. Cramer, July 31, 1942, Reel 48, HQ Files, FEPC Records.

19. "Investigation of Employment Practices in the Southwest: Nevada Consolidated Copper Company," August 10–13, 1942, Reel 48, HQ Files, FEPC Records.

20. National Labor Relations Board, *Decisions and Orders,* Case Nos. R-3004 to 3014 inclusive, April 29, 1942, vol. 40, pp. 986–1007; ibid., vol. 42, pp. 35–44.

21. "Investigation of Employment Practices in the Southwest: Nevada Consolidated Copper Company," pp. 3–10.

22. Ibid., pp. 3–4.

23. Louis Ruchames, *Race, Jobs, and Politics: The Story of the FEPC,* pp. 47–48; Herbert Garfinkel, *When Negroes March,* p. 106; Louis C. Kesselman, *The Social*

Politics of FEPC, pp. 20–21; John Beecher, "8802 Blues," *New Republic* 108 (February 22, 1943): 250; Lawrence W. Cramer to Mrs. Franklin D. Roosevelt, September 26, 1942, Reel 25, HQ Files, FEPC Records.

24. "Investigation of Employment Practices in the Southwest: Nevada Consolidated Copper Company," pp. 5–6.

25. Although the MMSW had earlier proposed the creation of a labor-management committee that would function to ease or eliminate labor relations problems that threatened to impede the war effort by limiting copper production, Nevada Consolidated rejected the proposal. See *Engineering and Mining Journal* 143 (January 1942): 33; "Investigation of Employment Practices in the Southwest: Nevada Consolidated," pp. 5–6.

26. "Investigation of Employment Practices in the Southwest: Nevada Consolidated," pp. 6–8.

27. T. H. Miller, "Copper in 1941," *Mining Congress Journal* 28 (February 1942): 45–47.

28. Barron B. Beshoar, "Report to the President's Committee on Fair Employment Practice," August 13, 1942, pp. 4–5, Reel 48, HQ Files, FEPC Records (hereafter cited as Beshoar Report).

29. Ibid., pp. 7–11. Also see the chapter on Miami, Arizona, in *Arizona: A State Guide,* pp. 202–207.

30. Beshoar Report, pp. 7–8.

31. Ibid., pp. 10–11. In its earlier independent analysis of the discrimination faced by Chicano and Spanish American workers in the Southwest, the Office of War Information concluded that the U.S. Employment Service regularly "cooperated with employers in continuing . . . practices of discrimination." See "Spanish-Americans in the Southwest and the War Effort," August 18, 1942, Report No. 24, Special Services Division, Bureau of Intelligence, Office of War Information, p. 11, in Reel 48, HQ Files, FEPC Records. See also Barron B. Beshoar, "Report from the Mountain States," *Common Ground* (Spring 1944): 27.

32. Prior to 1932, when severely depressed market conditions forced the Miami Copper Company to shut down its facilities in the Globe-Miami district, Chicanos constituted approximately 70 percent of the company's total workforce. When the company reopened its mine and mill in 1938, it limited employment to American citizens only. As a result, Chicanos made up less than 5 percent of the company's total labor force of 1,353 in mid-1942. Whatever its official hiring policy, however, Beshoar found that in practice the company hired Chicanos only as a last resort, when Anglo labor was unavailable. Had the company followed its stated policy of hiring American citizens only, it is likely that it would have employed a larger number of Chicanos, since most were either native-born or naturalized citizens. Of the 456 Chicanos employed at the nearby Inspiration Consolidated Copper Company, for example, more than 75 percent were American citizens. See Beshoar Report, pp. 19–21; and Hafner-Ortiz Statement, p. 4. See also A. S. Winther to E. G. Trimble, August 26, 1942; and "Inspiration Consolidated Copper Company Reply to Questionnaire Submitted by the President's Committee on Fair Employment Practice dated August 20, 1942," August 25, 1942, both in Reel 77, HQ Files, FEPC Records.

33. Beshoar Report, pp. 26–32; Hafner-Ortiz Statement, pp. 5–6.

34. Robert Glass Cleland, *A History of Phelps Dodge, 1934–1950,* p. 240.

35. Ibid., pp. 239–241.

36. Beshoar Report, p. 33.

37. Ibid., pp. 33–35; Cleland, *A History of Phelps Dodge,* pp. 280, 284.

38. Daniel R. Donovan, "Report on Complaints of Discrimination against Spanish-Americans (Mexicans) by Phelps Dodge Corporation: Morenci-Clifton Area" n.d.; mid-August 1942], pp. 1–3, Reel 48, HQ Files, FEPC Records. Manuel Gonzales, executive secretary of the League of United Latin American Citizens, complained to Ernest Trimble while the committee's investigation was in progress that draft boards in the Southwest were using the threat of military induction as a means of dissuading Chicano workers from protesting job discrimination. Gonzales also suggested that the concentration of Chicano workers in unskilled and semiskilled jobs made them disproportionately vulnerable to the draft. In its study, "Spanish-Americans in the Southwest and the War Effort," the Office of War Information partially confirmed Gonzales's allegations, declaring, "There is evidence that Anglo-dominated draft boards in the Southwest have been conscripting Spanish-Americans in higher ratios than Anglos. When protests were made, some draft officials stated that this was necessary in order to preserve the more valuable manpower." See M. C. Gonzales to Ernest G. Trimble, August 10, 1942; M. C. Gonzales to Lawrence W. Cramer, August 18, 1942, both in Reel 77, HQ Files, FEPC Records, and "Spanish-Americans in the Southwest and the War Effort," p. 3.

39. Donovan, "Report on Phelps Dodge: Morenci-Clifton Area," p. 2. On the dominant position of Louis Cates within the Phelps Dodge Corporation, including his role in developing the company's operations in the Clifton-Morenci district, see Cleland, *A History of Phelps Dodge,* pp. 216–260. The belief among many local residents of Morenci that Phelps Dodge had greatly increased the degree and scope of discrimination against Chicano workers was confirmed by an independent investigation conducted by the Office of the Coordinator of Inter-American Affairs early in 1943. See Joseph E. Weckler to Victor Borella, "Discrimination against Spanish-speaking People in Morenci, Arizona," February 25, 1943, OCIAA Records, Box 1717, RG 229.

40. Donovan, "Report on Phelps Dodge: Morenci-Clifton Area," p. 3.

41. Daniel R. Donovan and Barron B. Beshoar, "Report to President's Committee on Fair Employment Practice on Phelps Dodge Corporation Operations at Bisbee, Arizona and Douglas, Arizona," August 19, 1942, Reel 77, HQ Files, FEPC Records, pp. 2–3.

42. Ibid., p. 3; *Arizona: A State Guide,* p. 175; Cleland, *A History of Phelps Dodge,* pp. 165–192.

43. Donovan and Beshoar, "Report on Phelps Dodge: Bisbee and Douglas," pp. 3–4.

44. National Labor Relations Board, *Decisions and Orders,* Case Nos. R-3643 to R-3651 and R-3681, vol. 42, July 10, 1942, pp. 288–298; ibid., Case Nos. R-3643 and R-3681, vol. 43, September 3, 1942, pp. 943–945.

45. Donovan and Beshoar, "Report on Phelps Dodge: Bisbee and Douglas," pp. 1–2, 4; E. G. Trimble to Lawrence W. Cramer, August 20, 1942, Reel 77, HQ Files, FEPC Records.

46. Donovan and Beshoar, "Report on Phelps Dodge: Bisbee and Douglas," p. 5.

47. "Complaint of Jose P. Chavez," August 17, 1942, Reel 28, HQ Files, FEPC Records.

48. "Complaint of Jose Estrada," August 17, 1942, Reel 28, HQ Files, FEPC Papers.

49. "Complaint of Carlos B. Rivera," August 17, 1942, Reel 28, HQ Files, FEPC Records.

50. "Statement of R. C. Carter," August 17, 1942, Reel 28, HQ Files, FEPC Records.

51. "Statement of William Bates," August 17, 1942, Reel 28, HQ Files, FEPC Records.

52. Donovan and Beshoar, "Report on Phelps Dodge: Bisbee and Douglas," p. 5.

53. Daniel R. Donovan and Barron B. Beshoar to Dr. Ernest G. Trimble [n.d.; August 1942], Reel 28, HQ Files, FEPC Records.

54. E. G. Trimble to Lawrence W. Cramer, August 15, 1942, Reel 77, HQ Files, FEPC Records.

55. E. G. Trimble to Lawrence W. Cramer, August 20, 1942, Reel 77, HQ Files, FEPC Records.

56. Ibid.

57. E. G. Trimble to Lawrence W. Cramer, August 15, 1942; and E. G. Trimble to Lawrence W. Cramer, August 6, 1942, both in Reel 77, HQ Files, FEPC Records.

58. E. G. Trimble to Lawrence W. Cramer, August 15, 1942, Reel 77, HQ Files, FEPC Records.

4. *Retreat from Fairness*

1. "Labor Market Developments in the Mining and Refining of Copper, Lead and Zinc, May, 1942," in Records of the Office of the Director of Operations, War Manpower Commission, Record Group 211, National Archives (hereafter cited as ODO Records, WMC, RG 211).

2. "Minutes of the Staff Meeting," July 6, 1942, ODO Records, WMC, RG 211.

3. "Manpower Shortages in Western Copper Mines and in Other Western Metal Mines," June 23, 1943, Labor Production Division, War Production Board, p. 5, in Box 2379, Records of the Nonferrous Metals Commission, National War Labor Board, Record Group 202, National Archives (hereafter cited as NMC Records, NWLB, RG 202).

4. "Metal Mining's Manpower Problem," *Mining Congress Journal* 28 (September 1942): 23–24; "Who's Blocking the Labor Supply," *Mining Congress Journal* 28 (October 1942): 15; *Engineering and Mining Journal* 143 (September 1942): 42; "Minutes of the Staff Meeting," July 6, 1942, and "Minutes of the Staff Meeting," September 12, 1942, both in ODO Records, WMC, RG 211.

5. "Minutes of the Staff Meeting," September 12, 1942, ODO Records, WMC, RG 211; Clinton S. Golden, "Recommendations on Manpower Problem in Non-Ferrous Metals," June 23, 1943, War Production Board, Box 2379, NMC Records, NWLB, RG 202.

6. "Who's Blocking the Labor Supply," *Mining Congress Journal* 28 (October 1942): 15.

7. Jessica Rhine to Reid Robinson, "Importation of Mexican Workers," December 14, 1942, Box 2379, NMC Records, NWLB, RG 202.

8. "Mexicans to Help Relieve Shortage," *Union,* October 23, 1942, p. 12.

9. E. G. Trimble to Lawrence W. Cramer, August 20, 1942, Reel 77, HQ Files, FEPC Records.

10. E. G. Trimble to Lawrence W. Cramer, August 6, 1942; Lawrence W. Cramer to Ernest G. Trimble, August 14, 1942; E. G. Trimble to Lawrence W. Cramer, August 20, 1942; E. G. Trimble to Lawrence W. Cramer, August 22, 1942, all in Reel 77, HQ Files, FEPC Records. See also Lawrence W. Cramer to Ernest G. Trimble, August 27, 1942, Reel 41, HQ Files, FEPC Records.

11. E. G. Trimble to Lawrence W. Cramer, August 20, 1942, Reel 77, HQ Files, FEPC Records.

12. Daniel R. Donovan, "Report on Inspiration Copper and Phelps Dodge Properties: Miami-Globe and Jerome-Clarksdale Area," August 26–29, 1942, Reel 28, HQ Files, FEPC Records.

13. E. G. Trimble to Lawrence W. Cramer, August 20, 1942, Reel 77, HQ Files, FEPC Records.

14. Dan R. Donovan to Frank Fenton, August 20, 1942, Reel 77, HQ Files, FEPC Records.

15. The "labor unity" program established with the help of FEPC field investigators at the facilities of the Nevada Consolidated Copper Company in Hurley and Sant Rita, New Mexico, collapsed under the weight of enmity and distrust before it ever went into effect. See R. P. Erbachen to President's Committee on Fair Labor Standards [*sic*], October 16, 1942, Reel 25, HQ Files, FEPC Records.

16. O. A. Dever to Daniel Donovan, September 3, 1942, Reel 77, HQ Files, FEPC Records.

17. On the contribution of Chicano workers to the building of the MMSW in the Southwest, see Mario T. García, *Mexican Americans: Leadership, Ideology, and Identity, 1930–1960,* pp. 175–190.

18. Ibid., pp. 29–64. See also Theodore Provencio to President's Committee on Fair Employment Practice, March 16, 1943, Reel 28, HQ Files, FEPC Records.

19. E. G. Trimble to Lawrence W. Cramer, August 22, 1942, Reel 77, HQ Files, FEPC Records.

20. E. G. Trimble to Lawrence W. Cramer, August 20, 1942, Reel 77, HQ Files, FEPC Records.

21. Lawrence W. Cramer to Ernest G. Trimble, August 27, 1942, Reel 41, HQ Files, FEPC Records.

22. In rendering its decision the National War Labor Board ordered that all arbitrations of discrimination complaints arising from the operation of Phelps Dodge's promotion policies at the Douglas smelter "should be guided by the spirit and language of the President's Executive Order on Fair Labor Practice. . ." See National War Labor Board, "In re Phelps Dodge Corporation [Douglas, Arizona] and International Union of Mine, Mill and Smelter Workers, Local No. 470 (CIO), No. 5, February 19, 1942," *War Labor Reports:* 29–35; and "In re Phelps Dodge Corpora-

tion [Douglas, Arizona] and International Union of Mine, Mill and Smelter Workers, Local 470 (CIO), Nos. 5 and 114, June 24, 1942," *War Labor Reports:* 52–68.

23. E. G. Trimble to Lawrence W. Cramer, August 29, 1942, Reel 77, HQ Files, FEPC Records.

24. On the FEPC's beleaguered condition following its transfer to the War Manpower condition, see Malcolm S. MacLean to General Frank J. McSherry, September 25, 1942; Walter White to Hon. Paul V. McNutt, October 13, 1942; Lester A. Walton to Franklin D. Roosevelt, October 22, 1942, all in OF 4245, Box 3, FDR Papers; Walter White to Hon. Franklin D. Roosevelt, December 8, 1942; M. H. McIntyre to Walter White, December 14, 1942; Walter White to Hon. Franklin D. Roosevelt, December 18, 1942, all in OF 93, Box 5, FDR Papers; *Chicago Defender,* November 7, 1942, p. 2; Louis Ruchames, *Race, Jobs, and Politics: The Story of the FEPC,* pp. 46–50; John Beecher, "8802 Blues," *New Republic* 108 (February 22, 1943): 250.

25. E. G. Trimble to H. M. Lavender, August 31, 1942, Reel 77, HQ Files, FEPC Records.

26. E. G. Trimble to Lawrence W. Cramer, September 14, 1942, Reel 77, HQ Files, FEPC Records.

27. E. G. Trimble to O. A. Dever, September 12, 1942, Reel 77, HQ Files, FEPC Records.

28. Lawrence W. Cramer to E. G. Trimble, September 2, 1942, Reel 77, HQ Files, FEPC Records.

29. E. G. Trimble to C. R. Kuzell, September 12, 1942, Reel 28, HQ Files, FEPC Records.

30. E. G. Trimble to Lawrence W. Cramer, September 14, 1942, Reel 77, HQ Files, FEPC Records.

31. Wendell A. Phillips to Paul V. McNutt, September 15, 1942, Reel 28 HQ Files, FEPC Records.

32. *Union,* September 14, 1942, p. 18.

33. Lawrence W. Cramer to Ernest G. Trimble, September 19, 1942, Reel 77, HQ Files, FEPC Records.

34. E. G. Trimble to Lawrence W. Cramer, September 21, 1942, Reel 77, HQ Files, FEPC Records.

35. C. R. Kuzell to Dr. E. G. Trimble, September 23, 1942, Reel 28, HQ Files, FEPC Records. See also *Union,* July 13, 1942, p. 12.

36. E. G. Trimble to Horace Moses, September 22, 1942, Reel 77, HQ Files, FEPC Records.

37. A. S. Winther to E. G. Trimble, September 30, 1942; and T. H. O'Brien to E. G. Trimble, October 2, 1942, both in Reel 28, HQ Files, FEPC Records.

38. E. G. Trimble to Lawrence Cramer, September 24, 1942, Reel 77, HQ Files, FEPC Records.

39. Ernest G. Trimble to A. S. Winther, October 8, 1942; and Ernest G. Trimble to T. H. O'Brien, October 8, 1942, both in Reel 28, HQ Files, FEPC Records.

40. Ernest G. Trimble to Sam Morris, October 16, 1942; Ernest G. Trimble to A. S. Winther, October 20, 1942; Ernest G. Trimble to T. H. O'Brien, October 20, 1942, all in Reel 25, HQ Files, FEPC Records.

41. T. H. O'Brien to E. G. Trimble, October 26, 1942, Reel 28; A. S. Winther to

Ernest G. Trimble, October 31, 1942, Reel 25, both in HQ Files, FEPC Records.

42. Ernest G. Trimble to Lawrence W. Cramer, "Discrimination in the Southwest" [n.d.; October 25, 1942], Reel 28, HQ Files, FEPC Records.

43. For examples of the complaints of discrimination that the FEPC continued to receive from Phelps Dodge employees, see D. W. Wallace to E. G. Trimble, September 8, 1942; "Complaint of Rafael Robles," September 11, 1942; "Complaint of Ramon M. Vasquez," September 22, 1942; D. E. Wallace to E. G. Trimble, October 2, 1942; D. E. Wallace and Bruno Ruiz to E. Trimble, October 15, 1942; Joe P. Chavez to E. G. Trimble, October 27, 1942, all in Reel 28, HQ Files, FEPC Records.

44. D. E. Wallace to E. G. Trimble, October 2, 1942; Ernest G. Trimble to Lawrence W. Cramer, "Discrimination in the Southwest" [n.d.; October 25, 1942], both in Reel 28, HQ Files, FEPC Records.

45. C. R. Kuzell to E. G. Trimble, September 23, 1942, Reel 28, HQ Files, FEPC Records.

46. C. R. Kuzell to E. G. Trimble, November 12, 1942, Reel 28, HQ Files, FEPC Records.

47. Lawrence W. Cramer to C. R. Kuzell, November 18, 1942, Reel 28, HQ Files, FEPC Records.

48. D. E. Wallace to E. G. Trimble, October 15, 1942, Reel 28, HQ Files, FEPC Records.

49. J. P. Dyer to Ernest G. Trimble, November 18, 1942; Lawrence W. Cramer to J. P. Dyer, December 5, 1942; J. P. Dyer to Lawrence W. Cramer, December 21, 1942; Lawrence W. Cramer to J. P. Dyer, January 29, 1943; Lawrence W. Cramer to J. P. Dyer, April 3, 1943; J. P. Dyer to Lawrence W. Cramer, April 5, 1943, all in Reel 28, HQ Files, FEPC Records.

50. *Termination Report of the National War Labor Board: Industrial Disputes and Wage Stabilization in Wartime,* vol. 1, p. 150.

51. Stanley V. White to Lawrence W. Cramer, October 23, 1942, Reel 28, HQ Files, FEPC Records.

52. National War Labor Board, "In re Phelps Dodge Corporation [Douglas, Arizona] and International Union of Mine, Mill and Smelter Workers, Local No. 470 (CIO), No. 5, February 5, 1942," *War Labor Reports*: 29–35.

53. National War Labor Board, "In re Phelps Dodge Corporation [Douglas, Arizona] and International Union of Mine, Mill and Smelter Workers, Local No. 470 (CIO), Nos. 5 and 114, June 24, 1942," *War Labor Reports* 2: 62.

54. Stanley V. White to Lawrence W. Cramer, October 23, 1942, Reel 28, HQ Files, FEPC Records.

55. Stanley V. White, "Preliminary Report" [Phelps Dodge Copper Queen Smelter], September 15, 1942, U.S. Conciliation Service, Record Group 280, Box 818, File No. 209-6227, Federal Records Center, Suitland, Maryland (hereafter cited as USCS Records, RG 280).

56. Lawrence W. Cramer to Hon. William H. Davis, November 11, 1942, Reel 28, HQ Files, FEPC Records.

57. William H. Davis to Lawrence W. Cramer, November 15, 1942, Reel 28, HQ Files, FEPC Records.

58. Malcolm S. MacLean to William H. Davis, November 23, 1942, Reel 28, HQ Files, FEPC Records.

59. George W. Taylor to Malcolm S. MacLean, December 30, 1942, Reel 28, HQ Files, FEPC Records.

60. Malcolm S. MacLean to George W. Taylor, January 6, 1943; George W. Taylor to Malcolm S. MacLean, February 8, 1943, both in Reel 28, HQ Files, FEPC Records. As subsequent conflicts over the issue were to demonstrate, the elimination of the offending contract language did not eliminate discriminatory promotion practices at the Douglas smelter.

5. From Bad to Worse

1. John Beecher, "8802 Blues," *New Republic* 108 (February 22, 1943): 248–250; Louis C. Kesselman, *The Social Politics of FEPC,* pp. 15–20; Louis Ruchames, *Race, Jobs, and Politics: The Story of the FEPC,* pp. 46–47; *Chicago Defender,* August 15, 1942, p. 2; Will Maslow, "The Law and Race Relations," *Annals of the American Academy of Political and Social Science* 244 (March 1946): 77–78.

2. Malcolm S. MacLean to Paul V. McNutt, August 14, 1942, Reel 4, HQ Files, FEPC Records.

3. Lawrence W. Cramer to Marvin H. McIntyre, October 29, 1942, OF 93, Box 5, FDR Papers.

4. George M. Harrison to Marvin H. McIntyre, November 17, 1942, OF 93, Box 5, FDR Papers; Herbert Garfinkel, *When Negroes March,* pp. 139–140.

5. MHM [Marvin H. McIntyre] to the President, November 18, 1942, OF 93, Box 5, FDR Papers.

6. A copy of the transcript of McNutt's press conference is in the Records of the Office of the Chairman, War Manpower Commission Records, Record Group 211, National Archives. See also *Chicago Defender,* January 16, 1943, pp. 1–2; ibid., January 23, 1943, pp. 1–2; ibid., January 30, 1943, p. 15; *New York Times,* January 12, 1943, p. 14; Ruchames, *Race, Jobs, and Politics,* pp. 50–51; Beecher, "8802 Blues," p. 248; *Pittsburgh Courier,* January 16, 1943, p. 1.

7. Charles H. Houston to Malcolm S. MacLean, January 16, 1943, OF 4245G, Box 3, FDR Papers.

8. Charles H. Houston to President Franklin D. Roosevelt, January 18, 1943, OF 4245G, Box 3, FDR Papers.

9. Beecher, "8802 Blues," p. 250.

10. Lawrence W. Cramer to Marvin H. McIntyre, January 18, 1943, OF 4245G, Box 10, FDR Papers.

11. Walter White to the President of the United States, January 22, 1943, OF 4245G, Box 3, FDR Papers.

12. Jonathan Daniels to Marvin McIntyre, January 26, 1943, OF 4245G, Box 3, FDR Papers.

13. Francis Biddle, "Memorandum for the President," January 29, 1943, OF 4245G, Box 3, FDR Papers.

14. White House Press Release, February 3, 1943, OF 4905, Box 2, FDR Papers.

15. *Chicago Defender,* February 27, 1943, p. 1; Ruchames, *Race, Jobs, and Politics,* p. 53.

16. "Report of the President's Committee on Fair Employment Practice," May, 1943, p. 83 (marked "confidential"), Reel 8, HQ Files, FEPC Records.

17. Ruchames, *Race, Jobs, and Politics,* p. 54.

18. Lawrence W. Cramer to A. S. Winther, December 12, 1942, Lawrence W. Cramer to T. H. O'Brien, December 12, 1942, both in Reel 28, HQ Files, FEPC Records.

19. E. G. Trimble to Jesus Gutierrez, December 14, 1942, Reel 28, HQ Files, FEPC Records (letters to the other complainants can also be found in Reel 28).

20. See chapter 4.

21. D. E. Wallace to E. G. Trimble, October 15, 1942, Reel 28, HQ Files, FEPC Records.

22. E. G. Trimble to Victor Rose, December 19, 1942; E. G. Trimble to Orville Larson, December 19, 1942, both in Reel 28, HQ Files, FEPC Records.

23. *Union,* October 12, 1942, p. 5; ibid., February 15, 1943, p. 2; ibid., April 12, 1943, p. 3. See also George Knott to E. G. Trimble, March 15, 1943; George Knott to E. G. Trimble, April 12, 1943, both in Reel 28, HQ Files, FEPC Records.

24. *Union,* February 8, 1943, p. 3.

25. A. S. Winther to Lawrence W. Cramer, January 1, 1943, Reel 28, HQ Files, FEPC Records.

26. T. H. O'Brien to Lawrence W. Cramer, December 31, 1942, Reel 28, HQ Files, FEPC Records.

27. Ernest G. Trimble to D. E. Wallace, January 6, 1943, D. E. Wallace to E. G. Trimble, January 21, 1943, both in Reel 28, HQ Files, FEPC Records.

28. Joe P. Chavez [to E. G. Trimble], October 27, 1942, Reel 28, HQ Files, FEPC Records.

29. J. P. Chavez to E. G. Trimble, November 25, 1942, Reel 28, HQ Files, FEPC Records.

30. Ernest G. Trimble to Joseph P. Chavez, December 4, 1942, Reel 28 HQ Files, FEPC Records.

31. *Mining Congress Journal* 28 (September 1942): 23–24; ibid. (October 1942), p. 15; ibid. 29 (February 1943), p. 21; *Engineering and Mining Journal* 143 (September 1942): 42, 77–78; ibid. (October 1942), p. 41; "Regulations on Wartime Control of Manpower," *Monthly Labor Review* 55 (October 1942): 714–717. See also "Manpower Shortages in Western Copper Mines and in Other Western Metal Mines," June 23, 1943, Labor Production Division, War Production Board, p. 8, in Box 2379, NMC Records, NWLB, RG 202.

32. "Metal Mining's Manpower Problem," *Mining Congress Journal* 28 (September 1942): 23.

33. Joe P. Chavez [to E. G. Trimble], January 15, 1943, Reel 28, HQ Files, FEPC Records.

34. E. G. Trimble to Joseph P. Chavez, January 28, 1943, Reel 28, HQ Files, FEPC Records.

35. Daniel R. Donovan, "Report on Complaints of Discrimination against Span-

ish-Americans (Mexicans) by Phelps Dodge Corporation: Morenci-Clifton Area" [n.d.; mid-August 1942], pp. 1–3, Reel 48, HQ Files, FEPC Records.

36. Theodore Provencio to G. C. Davis and E. Wittneau, November 9, 1942; Theodore Provencio to F. D. Roosevelt, November 28, 1942; E. G. Trimble to Theodore Provencio, December 19, 1942; Lawrence W. Cramer to Theodore Provencio; December 22, 1942, all in Reel 28, HQ Files, FEPC Records.

37. Lawrence W. Cramer to Theodore Provencio, January 29, 1943, Reel 28, HQ Files, FEPC Records.

38. Theodore Provencio to President's Committee on Fair Employment Practice, March 16, 1943, Reel 28, HQ Files, FEPC Records. Provencio's claim that Phelps Dodge's discriminatory employment practices remained fully in force at its Morenci operations received independent confirmation from the Office of the Coordinator of Inter-American Affairs. Reporting the results of an investigation of conditions in the area, an OCIAA agent concluded that due to the influence of Phelps Dodge "discrimination has broadened and grown steadily worse in Morenci." See Joseph E. Weckler to Victor Borella, "Discrimination against Spanish-speaking People in Morenci, Arizona," February 25, 1943, RG 229, Box 1717, OCIAA Records.

39. Lawrence W. Cramer to Theodore Provencio, April 7, 1943, Reel 28, HQ Files, FEPC Records.

40. E. G. Trimble to D. E. Wallace, January 30, 1943, Reel 28, HQ Files, FEPC Records.

41. George Knott to E. G. Trimble, April 12, 1943, Reel 28, HQ Files, FEPC Records.

42. H. C. Splawn to E. G. Trimble, April 20, 1943, Reel 28, HQ Files, FEPC Records.

43. Orville Larson to E. G. Trimble, April 24, 1943, Reel 28 HQ Files, FEPC Records.

44. Ernest G. Trimble to H. C. Splawn, May 7, 1943, Reel 28, HQ Files, FEPC Records.

45. C. R. Kuzell to Lawrence W. Cramer, May 18, 1943, Reel 28, HQ Files, FEPC Records.

46. Phelps Dodge Corporation, Copper Queen Branch, Smelter Division, Douglas, Arizona, "Report on Disposition of Complaints Filed against the Company" [n.d.], Reel 28, HQ Files, FEPC Records.

47. Ernest G. Trimble to H. C. Splawn, June 23, 1943, Reel 28, HQ Files, FEPC Records.

48. Verne Curtis to Mrs. Franklin D. Roosevelt, April 28, 1943; Verne Curtis to Mrs. Franklin D. Roosevelt, June 2, 1943, both in Eleanor Roosevelt Papers, Series 100, Franklin D. Roosevelt Library, Hyde Park, New York.

49. David J. Saposs, "Memorandum for the Files," November 30, 1942, RG 229, Box 1717, OCIAA Records.

50. David J. Saposs, "Memorandum for the Files re: Second Inter-Agency Meeting on Problems of Spanish-speaking Peoples Held December 10, 1942," December 11, 1942, RG 229, Box 1717, OCIAA Records.

51. Toward the end of December federal officials had concluded, on the basis of exceedingly scant and dubious evidence, that the problem of discrimination against

Chicanos was easing throughout the whole of the Southwest. See David J. Saposs, "Memorandum for the Files," December 22, 1942, RG 229, Box 1717, OCIAA Records.

52. Charles A. Graham to Lawrence Cramer, January 19, 1943, NMC Records, Box 2379, NWLB, RG 202.

53. *Union,* May 25, 1942, p. 3.

54. Jessica Rhine to Reid Robinson, December 14, 1942, NMC Records, Box 2379, NWLB, RG 202.

55. A confidential report by the War Production Board in June of 1943 also concluded that copper companies in the Southwest continued to discriminate against Chicano workers. See "Manpower Shortages in Western Copper Mines and in Other Western Mines," p. 5; and Clinton S. Golden, "Recommendations on Manpower Problem in Non-Ferrous Metals," June 23, 1943, War Production Board, both in NMC Records, Box 2379, NWLB, RG 202.

56. War Manpower Commission, "Nonferrous Metal Mining Current Situation and Progress in Current Program," June 21, 1943, p. 2, NMC Records, Box 2379, NWLB, RG 202.

57. *Union,* September 13, 1943, p. 21. The *New York Times* reported in July that the U.S. Army was releasing men from military service in order to help relieve manpower shortages in the copper industry. See *New York Times,* July 21, 1943, p. 8. See also *Monthly Labor Review* 57 (November 1943): 972.

6. *Starting Over*

1. MHM [Marvin H. McIntyre] to the President, March 3, 1943, OF 4245G, Box 3, FDR Papers.

2. "Memorandum for the President," March 2, 1943, OF 4245G, Box 3, FDR Papers.

3. James F. Byrnes to the President, March 15, 1943, OF 4245G, Box 3, FDR Papers.

4. Walter White and others to the President, March 23, 1943, OF 4245G, Box 3, FDR Papers.

5. Ibid.; Earl B. Dickerson to the President, April 14, 1943; E. M. W. [General Edwin M. Watson] to Secretary [Marvin] McIntyre, April 30, 1943 [plus attachment]; and MHM [Marvin H. McIntyre] to the President, May 6, 1943, all in OF 4245G, Box 3, FDR Papers.

6. James F. Byrnes to the President, March 15, 1943, OF 4245G, Box 3, FDR Papers.

7. Will W. Alexander to Jonathan Daniels, April 14, 1943, OF 4245G, Box 5, FDR Papers.

8. Francis Biddle to the President, January 29, 1943; James F. Byrnes to the President, March 15, 1943, both in OF 4245G, Box 3, FDR Papers.

9. Franklin D. Roosevelt to Harold Ickes, March 30, 1943; Harold Ickes to the President, April 1, 1943, both in OF 4245G, Box 3, FDR Papers.

10. *Chicago Defender,* April 24, 1943, p. 15; Louis Ruchames, *Race, Jobs, and Politics: The Story of the FEPC,* pp. 54–55.

11. Will Alexander to Jonathan Daniels, April 14, 1943, OF 4245G, Box 5, FDR Papers; Jonathan Daniels to Marvin McIntyre, April 24, 1943; MHM [Marvin H. McIntyre] to the President, May 6, 1943, both in OF 4245G, Box 3, FDR Papers.

12. "The Future of the FEPC," *New Republic* 108 (May 10, 1943): 620–621.

13. Francis Biddle to the President, April 23, 1943, OF 4245G, Box 3, FDR Papers.

14. Jonathan Daniels to Marvin McIntyre, April 24, 1943, OF 4245G, Box 3, FDR Papers.

15. Lawrence W. Cramer to Major General Edwin M. Watson, May 1, 1943, OF 93, Box 5, FDR Papers.

16. MHM [Marvin H. McIntyre] to the President, May 6, 1943, OF 4245G, Box 3, FDR Papers.

17. Franklin D. Roosevelt to Hon. George W. Norris, May 8, 1943, President's Personal File 292, FDR Papers.

18. *New York Times,* May 20, 1943, p. 23.

19. Letters to the president expressing approval of his selection of Father Haas are in President's Personal File 3067 and OF 4245G, Box 4, FDR Papers.

20. Walter White to Honorable Franklin D. Roosevelt, May 18, 1943, OF 4245G, Box 4, FDR Papers.

21. Francis Biddle to the President, May 22, 1943, OF 4245G, Box 4, FDR Papers.

22. Francis Biddle to the President, May 25, 1943, OF 4245G, Box 4, FDR Papers.

23. Harold D. Smith to the President, May 26, 1943, OF 4245G, Box 4, FDR Papers.

24. Committee on Fair Employment Practice, *First Report, July 1943–December 1944,* pp. 11–12, 102; Ruchames, *Race, Jobs, and Politics,* p. 59.

25. MHM [Marvin H. McIntyre] to the President, June 26, 1943, OF 4245G, Box 4, FDR Papers.

26. *Chicago Defender,* July 3, 1943, p. 1; Ruchames, *Race, Jobs, and Politics,* p. 56.

27. Roosevelt's letters of appointment to the members of the new committee can be found in OF 4245G, Box 3, FDR Papers.

28. Francis J. Haas to Marvin H. McIntyre, July 5, 1943, with attached document "To Insure Employment of Minority Group Members," OF 93, Box 5, FDR Papers.

29. Walter White to Honorable Franklin D. Roosevelt, May 18, 1943, OF 4245G, Box 4, FDR Papers.

30. *Minutes of the Meeting of the President's Committee on Fair Employment Practice,* July 13, 1943, Reel 1, HQ Files, FEPC Records; Office of War Information, FEPC, "Advance Release," July 8, 1943, Reel 70, HQ Files, FEPC Records.

31. Francis J. Haas to Hon. Rafael de la Colina, July 6, 1943, Reel 70, HQ Files, FEPC Records. On the employment status of Chicano refinery workers, see Adolfo G. Domínquez, "Memorandum on Racial Discrimination at the Shell Refin-

ing Co., Houston, Texas," April 26, 1943; Adolfo G. Domínquez, "Memorandum on Conference Held Friday May 14th, 1943, at Mexican Consulate in Houston, Texas, Relative to Discrimination of Mexican Workers at Shell Oil and Refining Company," May 15, 1943; Rafael de la Colina to Executive Secretary, FEPC, June 30, 1943; E. G. Trimble to John E. Grossland, July 15, 1943; Marjorie M. Lawson, Summary of Compliance: "Humble Oil and Refining Company, Baytown, Texas," November, 1943, all in Reel 70, HQ Files, FEPC Records.

32. "Summary of Actions Taken by the Committee at Its Meeting in Washington, D.C., July 6 and 7, 1943," July 13, 1943, Reel 1, HQ Files, FEPC Records.

33. Jesus B. Gutierrez [to Ernest G. Trimble], July 23, 1943, Reel 28, HQ Files, FEPC Records. See also Ernest G. Trimble to Jesus Gutierrez, July 2, 1943; Jesus B. Gutierrez to Ernest G. Trimble, July 10, 1943; and Ernest G. Trimble to Jesus Gutierrez, July 14, 1943, all in Reel 28, HQ Files, FEPC Records. The Mine, Mill and Smelter Workers Union also continued to allege that discrimination against Chicano copper workers remained as great a problem as ever in the Southwest. See *Union,* September 13, 1943, p. 21.

34. E. G. Trimble to Jesus B. Gutierrez, September 29, 1943, Reel 28 HQ Files, FEPC Records.

35. Office of War Information, FEPC, "Advance Release," August 10, 1943, Reel 70, HQ Files, FEPC Records. See also Will Maslow to Carlos Castañeda, September 17, 1943; and Malcolm Ross to Carlos Castañeda, November 27, 1943, both in Reel 41, HQ Files, FEPC Records; testimony of Carlos E. Castañeda, in U.S. Congress, Senate, Subcommittee of the Committee on Education and Labor, *Hearings on S. 2048, A Bill to Prohibit Discrimination in Employment Because of Race, Creed, Color, National Origin, or Ancestry,* 78th Cong., 2d sess., p. 206 (hereafter cited as U.S. Senate, *FEPC Hearings*).

36. Marjorie M. Lawson, Summary of Compliance: "Phelps Dodge Corporation," November, 1943, p. 5, Reel 70, HQ Files, FEPC Records.

37. Marjorie M. Lawson, Summary of Compliance: "Conclusions and Recommendations," November, 1943, pp. 1–4, Reel 70, HQ Files, FEPC Records.

38. Marjorie M. Lawson, Summary of Compliance: "Humble Oil and Refining Company," p. 4.

39. Malcolm Ross to Wilfred C. Leland, October 12, 1943, Reel 70, HQ Files, FEPC Records.

40. John E. O'Gara to Malcolm Ross, October 19, 1943, Reel 70, HQ Files, FEPC Records.

41. Marjorie M. Lawson, Summary of Compliance: "Conclusions and Recommendations," p. 4.

42. On Castañeda's background, see Félix D. Almaráz, Jr., "Carlos Eduardo Castañeda, Mexican-American Historian: The Formative Years, 1896–1927," in *The Chicano,* ed. Norris Hundley, Jr., pp. 57–72; and Mario T. García, *Mexican Americans: Leadership, Ideology, and Identity, 1930–1960,* pp. 231–251.

43. Robert C. Williams to Francis J. Haas, September 1, 1943; Ernest G. Trimble to Robert C. Williams, September 4, 1943, both in Reel 28 HQ Files, FEPC Records; Carlos E. Castañeda to Will Maslow, September 20, 1943, Reel 41, HQ Files, FEPC Records.

44. National War Labor Board, "In re Southport Petroleum Company [Texas City, Texas] and Oil Workers' International Union, Local 449 (CIO), Case No. 771 (2898-D), June 5, 1943," *War Labor Reports* 8: 714–721.

45. G. James Fleming to Ernest G. Trimble, June 17, 1943, Reel 41, HQ Files, FEPC Records.

46. On this point, see *Union,* April 12, 1943, pp. 3, 5; ibid., July 7, 1943, p. 3; National War Labor Board, "In re Phelps Dodge Corp. [Morenci, Ariz.] and Clifton-Morenci Metal Trades Council (AFL), Case No. 111-1529-D, September 4, 1943," *War Labor Reports,* vol. 2, pp. 71–75; "Memorandum for the Record: Phelps Dodge Corporation, Morenci, Arizona," May 6, 1943, Records of the U.S. Conciliation Service, Box 1014, File No. 300-6716, Record Group 280, National Archives (hereafter cited as USCS, RG 2780); "Memorandum for the Record: Phelps Dodge Mining Corporation, Douglas, Arizona," September 1, 1943, USCS, Box 117, File No. 301-2625, RG 280.

47. Charles F. Mulford to Harry O. King, Sr., August 21, 1943; H. O. King to Charles F. Mulford, September 1, 1943; and Charles F. Mulford to H. O. King, September 14, 1943, all in box 2379, NMC Records, NWLB, RG 202; Robert C. Williams to Francis J. Haas, September 1, 1943; Ernest G. Trimble to Robert C. Williams, September 4, 1943, both in Reel 28, HQ Files, FEPC Records.

48. Carlos E. Castañeda to Will Maslow, September 20, 1943, Reel 41, HQ Files, FEPC Records.

49. Will Maslow to Carlos E. Castañeda, October 16, 1943, Reel 41, HQ Files, FEPC Records; *Minutes of the Meeting of the President's Committee on Fair Employment Practice,* December 4, 1943, Reel 1, HQ Files, FEPC Records.

50. Region X of the FEPC encompassed the states of Texas, New Mexico, and Louisiana. In December of 1944 Region X was reconstituted to include western Texas, New Mexico, and Arizona, which had originally been a part of Region XII, with headquarters in San Francisco. See Committee on Fair Employment Practice, *First Report: July 1943–December 1944,* appendix 3, pp. 106–107.

51. Malcolm Ross to Carlos Castañeda, November 27, 1943, Reel 41, HQ Files, FEPC Records.

52. Malcolm Ross to Jonathan Daniels, November 4, 1943, OF 4245G, Box 5, FDR Papers.

53. Lawrence Duggan, "Memorandum on Department's Present Attitude toward Hearings in Southwest by Committee on Fair Employment Practices [*sic*]," November 12, 1943, OF 4245G, Box 10, FDR Papers. See also Carey McWilliams, *North from Mexico,* pp. 270–274; Otey M. Scruggs, "Texas and the Bracero Program, 1942–1947," *Pacific Historical Review* 32 (August 1963): 251–264; "No Mexicans Allowed," *Inter-American* 2 (September 1943): 8–9; Peter N. Kirstein, *Anglo over Bracero: A History of the Mexican Worker in the United States from Roosevelt to Nixon,* pp. 53–54.

54. On Messersmith, see Jesse H. Stiller, *George S. Messersmith, Diplomat of Democracy,* especially pp. 146–263.

55. G. S. Messersmith to Philip W. Bonsal, November 18, 1943, OF 4245G, Box 10, FDR Papers.

56. Malcolm Ross, et al., to the President, January 31, 1944, OF 4245G, Box 6, FDR Papers.

57. Malcolm Ross, et al., "Memorandum to the President," January 31, 1944, OF 4245G, Box 6, FDR Papers.

58. Franklin D. Roosevelt to the President's Committee on Fair Employment Practice, February 3, 1944, OF 4245G, Box 6, FDR Papers. Perhaps because he hoped the information would be useful to him in responding to future FEPC claims that circumstances in the Southwest justified forceful action in defense of fair employment practices, Jonathan Daniels asked the Federal Bureau of Investigation for a confidential report on the status of "racial and minority relations" in the mining regions of Arizona. Only two weeks after receiving Daniels's request FBI director J. Edgar Hoover forwarded a report that, remarkably, denied the existence of any significant forms of discrimination against Chicanos in any of the principal mining centers of the state. See J. Edgar Hoover to Jonathan Daniels, March 29, 1944; and Federal Bureau of Investigation, "Re: Racial and Minority Relations, Southeastern Arizona," March 24, 1944, both in OF 4245G, Box 14, FDR Papers.

59. *Minutes of the Meeting of the President's Committee on Fair Employment Practice,* February 11–12, 1944, Reel 1, HQ Files, FEPC Records.

60. Carlos E. Castañeda to Will Maslow, January 26, 1944, Reel 41, HQ Files, FEPC Records.

61. Carlos E. Castañeda to Will Maslow, March 25, 1944, Reel 48, HQ Files, FEPC Records.

62. Will Maslow to Robert E. Brown, Jr., March 28, 1944, Reel 41, HQ Files, FEPC Records.

63. Malcolm Ross, *All Manner of Men,* pp. 240–256; Ruchames, *Race, Jobs, and Politics,* pp. 73–99.

7. Divided Counsel

1. National War Labor Board, "In re Miami Copper Company [Miami, Ariz.], International Smelting and Refining Company [Inspiration, Ariz.], and Inspiration Consolidated Copper Company [Inspiration, Ariz.] and International Union of Mine, Mill and Smelter Workers, Local 586 (CIO), Case Nos. 111-718-D (22-D-41), 111-717-D (22-D-42), and 111-716-D (22-D-43), Feb. 5, 1944," *War Labor Reports* 14: 146–165, 760–765.

The NMC's decision was upheld on appeal by the War Labor Board on September 7, 1944. See National War Labor Board, *War Labor Reports* 18: 591–593. See also *Union,* February 14, 1944, p. 5. An effort by the Mine, Mill and Smelter Workers Union to mount a similar challenge to the allegedly discriminatory wage policies of the Phelps Dodge Corporation failed when the NMC ruled that the issue was not among those properly certified to it for settlement by the U.S. Conciliation Service. See File No. 444-1327, Box 1486, Records of the U.S. Conciliation Service, Record Group 280, National Archives. See also "Memorandum by International Union of Mine, Mill and Smelter Workers, CIO, on Discriminatory Wage Rates in the Southwest," May 4, 1944, Reel 28, HQ Files, FEPC Records; and J. Glenn Donaldson to

George W. Taylor, May 30, 1945, Box 2382, Records of the Nonferrous Metals Commission, National War Labor Board, Record Group 202, National Archives. Also D. H. Dinwoodie, "The Rise of the Mine-Mill Union in Southwestern Copper," in *American Labor in the Southwest,* ed. James C. Foster, pp. 52–55.

2. *Union,* March 13, 1944, p. 11.

3. *Minutes of the Meeting of the President's Committee on Fair Employment Practice,* March 18, 1944, Reel 1, HQ Files, FEPC Records.

4. Carlos E. Castañeda to Will Maslow, April 2, 1944, Reel 19, HQ Files, FEPC Records.

5. Stanley D. Metzger to Will Maslow, April 4, 1944, Reel 19, HQ Files, FEPC Records.

6. Carlos E. Castañeda to Will Maslow, April 2, 1944, Reel 19, HQ Files, FEPC Records.

7. Carlos E. Castañeda to Malcolm Ross, May 4, 1944, Reel 19, HQ Files, FEPC Records.

8. Ibid.; Carlos E. Castañeda to Will Maslow, July 4, 1944, Reel 19, HQ Files, FEPC Records.

9. Carlos E. Castañeda to Malcolm Ross, May 4, 1944, and Carlos E. Castañeda to Will Maslow, July 4, 1944, both in Reel 19, HQ Files, FEPC Records.

10. Carlos E. Castañeda to Will Maslow, April 26, 1944, Reel 19, HQ Files, FEPC Records.

11. Carlos E. Castañeda to Will Maslow, May 16, 1944, Reel 19, HQ Files, FEPC Records.

12. Carlos E. Castañeda to Will Maslow, July 4, 1944, Reel 19, HQ Files, FEPC Records.

13. Carlos E. Castañeda to Will Maslow, May 21, 1944, Reel 19; War Manpower Commission, "Recommendations on the Manpower Problem in the Copper Industry in Arizona," March 25, 1944, Reel 28, both in HQ Files, FEPC Records.

14. Carlos E. Castañeda to Will Maslow, April 25, 1944 (plus attachments), Reel 19; Will Maslow to Leonard M. Brin, April 27, 1944, Reel 41, both in HQ Files, FEPC Records. See also Ruth Landes, "Report on Globe USES for Miami and Inspiration Companies," May 1, 1944, Reel 19, HQ Files, FEPC Records.

15. Carlos E. Castañeda to Will Maslow, July 4, 1944, Reel 19, HQ Files, FEPC Records. See also Carlos E. Castañeda to Will Maslow, May 8, 1944, Reel 19, HQ Files, FEPC Records. The detailed reports filed by Castañeda following each stop on his itinerary can be found in Reel 19. Additional records and correspondence relating to the investigation are in Reel 96, Field Files, FEPC Records.

16. Carlos E. Castañeda to Will Maslow, July 4, 1944, Reel 19, HQ Files, FEPC Records. Despite the reluctance of many Chicano workers to file formal complaints with the committee, Castañeda reported at several of his stops that the anger and discontent fueled by continuing discrimination had led them to threaten walkouts and mass resignations.

17. Carlos E. Castañeda to Will Maslow, July 4, 1944, Reel 19, HQ Files, FEPC Records.

18. Carlos E. Castañeda to Malcolm Ross, May 4, 1944, Reel 19, HQ Files, FEPC Records.

19. Stanley D. Metzger to Clarence M. Mitchell, July 12, 1944, Reel 19, HQ Files, FEPC Records.

20. George M. Johnson to Clarence M. Mitchell, July 22, 1944, Reel 28, HQ Files, FEPC Records.

21. Carlos E. Castañeda to Will Maslow, July 29, 1944, Reel 19, HQ Files, FEPC Records.

22. Testimony of Carlos E. Castañeda, in U.S. Congress, Senate, Subcommittee of the Committee on Education and Labor, *Hearings on S. 2048, A Bill to Prohibit Discrimination in Employment Because of Race, Creed, Color, National Origin, or Ancestry,* 78th Cong., 2d sess., p. 212 (hereafter cited as *FEPC Hearings*).

23. Committee on Fair Employment Practice, *First Report, July 1943–December 1944,* p. 44.

24. Testimony of Carlos E. Castañeda, *FEPC Hearings,* p. 207; Harry L. Kingman, "Report Covering Operations of the President's Committee on Fair Employment Practice, Region XII," September 12, 1944, Reel 77, HQ Files, FEPC Records.

25. Robert E. Brown, Jr., "Annual Report for Los Angeles Area" [n.d.; September 1944], Reel 77, HQ Files, FEPC Records. Arizona was still included in Region XII as of September 1944.

26. Kingman, "Report . . . Region XII," Reel 77, HQ Files, FEPC Records.

27. W. Don Ellinger to Will Maslow, September 23, 1944, Reel 77, HQ Files, FEPC Records.

28. Testimony of Carlos E. Castañeda, *FEPC Hearings,* pp. 205–212. See also Carlos E. Castañeda to John A. Davis, "Annual Report," August 30, 1944, Reel 77, HQ Files, FEPC Records.

29. Carlos E. Castañeda to Will Maslow, September 1, 1944, Reel 19, HQ Files, FEPC Records. Correspondence relating to Castañeda's efforts to negotiate settlements of individual complaints of discrimination can be found in Reel 96, Field Files, FEPC Records.

30. Will Maslow to the Committee, September 7, 1944, Reel 28, HQ Files, FEPC Records.

31. Carlos E. Castañeda to Will Maslow, September 29, 1944, Reel 19, HQ Files, FEPC Records.

32. *Minutes of the Meeting of the President's Committee on Fair Employment Practice,* October 11, 1944, Reel 1, HQ Files, FEPC Records.

33. Frank D. Reeves to Bruce Hunt, October 13, 1944, Reel 28, HQ Files, FEPC Records.

34. Evelyn N. Cooper to George M. Johnson, October 17, 1944, Reel 41, HQ Files, FEPC Records.

35. Long after receiving Cox's opinion the committee continued to explain, and justify, its cautious approach to enforcement as a function of the ambiguous wording of Executive Order 9346. When Harry Kingman, the director of Region XII, complained early in 1945 that "the case by case method of handling discrimination" should "be subordinated to a more significant and comprehensive method" that would allow the committee "to make a lasting rather than a fleeting and insignificant dent on employment discrimination," director of operations Will Maslow rather testily responded, "Everyone agrees with you that if we had a free choice we would

abandon reliance upon the case method. Unfortunately, there are questions of our legal authority to act except on the basis of a complaint." In responding to the same complaint, Theodore Jones, the committee's budget director and chief administrative officer, wrote, "As you probably know, the Committee has always expressed reluctance to proceed on any matter in which it did not have a specific complaint. Several of us have, from time to time, attempted to change the Committee's position in this regard and have proposed that survey type investigations be allowed and that the staff be permitted to improve its cooperative relationships with other government agencies and local groups in civic communities." See Harry L. Kingman to Will Maslow and Theodore Jones, January 18, 1945; Theodore A. Jones to Harry L. Kingman, February 9, 1945; Will Maslow to Harry L. Kingman, February 26, 1945, all in Reel 41, HQ Files, FEPC Records.

36. Carlos E. Castañeda to Will Maslow, October 23, 1944; Carlos E. Castañeda to Robert E. Brown, Jr., October 28, 1944, both in Reel 96, Field Files, FEPC Records.

37. Frank D. Reeves to Bruce Hunt, "Phelps-Dodge Copper Corporation" (Morenci Branch), November 1, 1944, Reel 28; Frank D. Reeves to Bruce Hunt, "Inspiration-Consolidated Copper Company," November 3, 1944, Reel 19, both in HQ Files, FEPC Records; Frank D. Reeves to Bruce Hunt, "American Smelting and Refining Company," November 1, 1944; Frank D. Reeves to Bruce Hunt, "Phelps-Dodge Refining Company," November 7, 1944; Frank D. Reeves to Bruce Hunt, "Kennecott Copper Corporation," November 15, 1944, all in Reel 96, Field Files, FEPC Records.

38. *Minutes of the Meeting of the President's Committee on Fair Employment Practice,* October 11, 1944, Reel 1, HQ Files, FEPC Records.

39. "Re: Southwest Hearings—Excerpts from Bruce Hunt's letter of December 16, 1944," Reel 19, HQ Files, FEPC Records.

40. Carlos E. Castañeda to A. Bruce Hunt, December 20, 1944, Reel 19, HQ Files, FEPC Records.

41. On November 30 the Division of Review and Analysis reported to the director of Region X, which included Texas and New Mexico, that of thirty-seven complaints in his region that had been pending for six months or more as of October 1, 1944, thirty-one—or nearly 84 percent—were against copper companies. See Eugene Davidson to W. Don Ellinger, November 30, 1944, Reel 41, HQ Files, FEPC Records.

42. A. Bruce Hunt to George M. Johnson, January 13, 1945, Reel 19, HQ Files, FEPC Records.

43. Carlos E. Castañeda to Will Maslow, January 2, 1945, Reel 19, HQ Files, FEPC Records.

44. Carlos E. Castañeda to George M. Johnson, January 25, 1945, Reel 19, HQ Files, FEPC Records.

45. Carlos E. Castañeda to Will Maslow, January 23, 1945, Reel 19, HQ Files, FEPC Records.

46. *Minutes of the Meeting of the President's Committee on Fair Employment Practice,* February 12, 1945, Reel 1, HQ Files, FEPC Records.

47. Following a bruising congressional debate during the late spring and early summer of 1945 over the future of the FEPC, a compromise was reached that ex-

tended the committee's life until June 1946, but in so starved and weakened a condition that it existed in little more than name only. On the FEPC's demise, and the ultimately fruitless campaign to reconstitute it on a permanent basis, see Louis Ruchames, *Race, Jobs, and Politics: The Story of the FEPC,* pp. 121–213; Louis C. Kesselman, *The Social Politics of FEPC: A Study in Reform Pressure Movements,* pp. 25–228; Malcolm Ross, *All Manner of Men,* pp. 170–202, 240–263, 287–314; Herbert Garfinkel, *When Negroes March,* pp. 148–185; Will Maslow, "FEPC—A Case Study in Parliamentary Maneuver," *University of Chicago Law Review* 13 (June 1946): 407–444; Frank P. Huddle, "Fair Practice in Employment," *Editorial Research Reports* (January 18, 1946): 33–51; A. Bruce Hunt, "The Proposed Fair Employment Practice Act: Facts and Fallacies," *Virginia Law Review* 32 (December 1945): 1–38; and *Congressional Digest* 24 (June–July 1945): 163–192.

8. Promises to Keep

1. Committee on Fair Employment Practice, *Final Report,* p. 38.
2. Ibid., pp. 82–83. See also G. Raymond Booth to Lawrence I. Hewes, March 15, 1946, Reel 2, HQ Files, FEPC Records.
3. Ross, *All Manner of Men,* p. 25.
4. Ibid., p. 164.
5. Ibid., p. 160.
6. Chicano activists among both the leadership and the membership of the Mine, Mill and Smelter Workers Union in the Southwest did succeed in making the elimination of discriminatory employment practices one of the principal goals of the long strike the union conducted against the country's leading copper companies in 1946. See Mario T. García, *Mexican Americans: Leadership, Ideology, and Identity, 1930–1960,* pp. 190–198.

Works Cited

Acuña, Rodolfo. *Occupied America: The Chicano's Struggle toward Liberation.* San Francisco: Canfield Press, 1972.

Alexander, Will W. "Aliens in War Industries." *Annals of the American Academy of Political and Social Science* 222 (September 1942): 138–143.

Almaráz, Félix D., Jr. "Carlos Eduardo Castañeda, Mexican-American Historian: The Formative Years, 1896–1927." In *The Chicano,* ed. Norris Hundley, Jr., pp. 57–72. Santa Barbara: Clio Books, 1975.

Altus, William D. "The American Mexican: The Survival of a Culture." *Journal of Social Psychology* 29 (May 1949): 211–220.

Anderson, Jervis. *A. Philip Randolph: A Biographical Portrait.* New York: Harcourt Brace Jovanovich, 1972.

Arizona: A State Guide. Federal Writers' Project, Works Projects Administration. Rev. ed. New York: Hastings House Publishers, 1956.

Arizona's Hispanic Perspective, Research Report Prepared by the University of Arizona, May 17–20, 1981.

Barrera, Mario. *Race and Class in the Southwest.* Notre Dame, Ind.: University of Notre Dame Press, 1979.

Beecher, John. "8802 Blues." *New Republic* 108 (February 22, 1943): 248–250.

Bennett, Lerone, Jr. *Confrontation: Black and White.* Baltimore: Penguin, 1966.

Beshoar, Barron B. "Report from the Mountain States." *Common Ground* 4 (Spring 1944): 23–30.

Blum, John M. *V Was for Victory: Politics and American Culture during World War II.* New York: Harcourt Brace Jovanovich, 1976.

Bogardus, Emory S. "Current Problems of Mexican Immigrants." *Sociology and Social Research* 25 (November 1940): 166–174.

Broom, Leonard, and Eshref Shevsky. "Mexicans in the United States: A Problem of Social Differentiation." *Sociology and Social Research* 36 (January–February 1952): 150–158.

Burma, John H. *Spanish-speaking Groups in the United States.* Durham, N.C.: Duke University Press, 1954.

Burnhill, James. "The Mexican People in the Southwest." *Political Affairs* 32 (September 1953): 43–52.

Byrkit, James W. *Forging the Copper Collar: Arizona's Labor-Management War of 1901–1921*. Tucson: University of Arizona Press, 1982.

Camarillo, Albert. *Chicanos in a Changing Society: From Mexican Pueblos to American Barrios in Santa Barbara and Southern California, 1848–1930*. Cambridge: Harvard University Press, 1979.

Carter, Hugh, and Bernice Doster. "Social Characteristics of Aliens from the Southwest Registered for Selective Service during World War II." *Immigration and Naturalization Service Monthly Review* 8 (1951): 88–94.

Clark, Victor S. *Mexican Labor in the United States*. Bureau of Labor, Bulletin No. 78. Washington, D.C.: U.S. Government Printing Office, September, 1908.

Cleland, Robert Glass. *A History of Phelps Dodge, 1934–1950*. New York: Alfred A. Knopf, 1952.

Committee on Fair Employment Practice. *Final Report*. Washington, D.C.: U.S. Government Printing Office, 1947.

———. *First Report, July 1943–December 1944*. Washington, D.C.: U.S. Government Printing Office, 1945.

Congressional Digest 24 (June–July 1945): 163–192.

Corwin, Arthur F. "Early Mexican Labor Migration: A Frontier Sketch, 1848–1900." In *Immigrants—and Immigrants: Perspectives on Mexican Labor Migration to the United States*, ed. Arthur F. Corwin, pp. 25–37. Westport: Greenwood Press, 1978.

Crawford, W. Rex. "The Latin American in Wartime United States." *Annals of the American Academy of Political and Social Science* (September 1942): 123–131.

Dinwoodie, D. H. "The Rise of the Mine-Mill Union in Southwestern Copper." In *American Labor in the Southwest*, ed. James C. Foster, pp. 52–55. Tucson: University of Arizona Press, 1982.

Doyle, Judith Kaaz. "Maury Maverick and Racial Politics in San Antonio, Texas, 1938–1941." *Journal of Southern History* 53 (May 1987): 194–224.

Dubofsky, Melvyn. *We Shall Be All: A History of the Industrial Workers of the World*. Chicago: Quadrangle Books, 1969.

Eulau, Heinz H. F. "Sinarquismo in the United States." *Inter-American* 3 (March 1944): 25–27, 48.

Fitch, John A. "Arizona's Embargo on Strike-Breakers." *Survey* 36 (May 6, 1916): 143–144.

"The Future of the FEPC." *New Republic* 108 (May 10, 1943): 620–621.

Galarza, Ernesto. *Merchants of Labor: The Mexican Bracero Story*. Santa Barbara: McNally and Loftin, Publishers, 1964.

García, Mario T. *Desert Immigrants: The Mexicans of El Paso, 1880–1920*. New Haven: Yale University Press, 1981.

———. *Mexican Americans: Leadership, Ideology, and Identity, 1930–1960*. New Haven: Yale University Press, 1989.

———. "Racial Dualism in the El Paso Labor Market." *Aztlán* 6 (Summer 1975): 197–217.

García, Richard A. "The Making of the Mexican-American Mind, San Antonio, Texas, 1929–1941." Ph.D. dissertation, University of California, Irvine, 1980.

García y Griego, Manuel. *The Importation of Mexican Contract Laborers to the United States, 1942–1964: Antecedents, Operation and Legacy.* Working Papers in U.S.–Mexican Studies, No. 11. San Diego: University of California, Program in United States–Mexican Studies, 1981.

Garfinkel, Herbert. *When Negroes March: The March on Washington Movement in the Organizational Politics for FEPC.* New York: Free Press, 1959.

Gomez-Quiñones, Juan. *Development of the Mexican Working Class North of the Rio Bravo.* Popular Series No. 2. Los Angeles: Chicano Studies Research Center Publications, UCLA, 1982.

Gosnell, Harold F. "Symbols of National Solidarity." *Annals of the American Academy of Political and Social Science* 222 (September 1942): 157–161.

Grattan, Brian F., Arturo Rosales, and Hans DeBano. "A Sample of the Mexican-American Population in 1940." *Historical Methods* 21 (Spring 1988): 80–87.

Grebler, Leo, et al. *The Mexican American People.* New York: Free Press, 1970.

Griffith, Beatrice W. *American Me.* Boston: Houghton Mifflin, 1948.

Griswold del Castillo, Richard. *La Familia: Chicano Families in the Urban Southwest, 1848 to the Present.* Notre Dame, Ind.: University of Notre Dame Press, 1984.

———. *The Los Angeles Barrio, 1850–1890.* Berkeley: University of California Press, 1979.

Guzman, Ralph C. *The Political Socialization of the Mexican American People.* New York: Arno Press, 1976.

Hardin, Frances Anne. "The Role of Presidential Advisors: Roosevelt Aides and the FEPC, 1941–1943." M.S. thesis, School of Industrial and Labor Relations, Cornell University, 1975.

Harris, William H. "A. Philip Randolph as a Charismatic Leader." *Journal of Negro History* 64 (Fall 1979): 301–315.

Huddle, Frank P. "Fair Practice in Employment." *Editorial Research Reports* (January 18, 1946): 33–51.

Hunt, A. Bruce. "The Proposed Fair Employment Practice Act: Facts and Fallacies." *Virginia Law Review* 32 (December 1945): 1–38.

Jensen, Vernon H. *Heritage of Conflict: Labor Relations in the Nonferrous Metals Industry up to 1930.* Ithaca, N.Y.: Cornell University Press, 1950.

———. *Nonferrous Metals Industry Unionism, 1932–1954.* Ithaca, N.Y.: Cornell University, 1954.

Jimenez, Andres. *Political Domination in the Labor Market: Racial Division in the Arizona Copper Industry.* Working Papers Series, No. 103. Berkeley: University of California, Institute for the Study of Social Change, 1977.

Jones, Robert C. *Mexican War Workers in the United States: The Mexico–United States Manpower Recruiting Program and Operation.* Washington, D.C.: Pan American Union, 1945.

Kesselman, Louis C. *The Social Politics of FEPC: A Study in Reform Pressure Movements.* Chapel Hill: University of North Carolina Press, 1948.

Kibbee, Pauline R. *Latin Americans in Texas.* Albuquerque: University of New Mexico Press, 1946.

Kirstein, Peter N. *Anglo over Bracero: A History of the Mexican Worker in the United*

States from Roosevelt to Nixon. San Francisco: R and E Research Associates, 1977.
Kluger, James R. *The Clifton-Morenci Strike: Labor Difficulty in Arizona, 1915–1916*. Tucson: University of Arizona Press, 1970.
Lamb, Ruth S. *Mexican Americans: Sons of the Southwest*. Claremont: Ocelot Press, 1970.
Linquist, John H., and James Fraser. "A Sociological Interpretation of the Bisbee Deportation." *Pacific Historical Review* 38 (November 1968): 401–422.
McDonogh, Edward C. "Status Levels of Mexicans." *Sociology and Social Research* 32 (July–August 1948): 944–953.
McWilliams, Carey. *Brothers under the Skin*. Revised edition. Boston: Little, Brown and Company, 1951.
———. "The Forgotten Mexican." *Common Ground* 3 (Spring 1943): 65–78.
———. *North from Mexico: The Spanish-speaking People of the United States*. New York: J. B. Lippincott, 1949.
Maslow, Will. "FEPC—A Case Study in Parliamentary Maneuver." *University of Chicago Law Review* 13 (June 1946): 407–444.
———. "The Law and Race Relations." *Annals of the American Academy of Political and Social Science* 244 (March 1946): 77–78.
Meier, Matt S., and Feliciano Rivera. *The Chicanos: A History of Mexican Americans*. New York: Hill and Wang, 1972.
"Metal Mining's Manpower Problem." *Mining Congress Journal* 28 (September 1942): 23–24.
Miller, T. H. "Copper in 1941." *Mining Congress Journal* 28 (February 1942): 45–47.
Monroy, Douglas. "An Essay on Understanding the Work Experience of Mexicans in Southern California, 1908–1939." *Aztlán* 12 (Spring 1981): 59–74.
———. "Mexicans in Los Angeles, 1930–1941: An Ethnic Group in Relation to Class Forces." Ph.D. dissertation, University of California, Los Angeles, 1978.
Montejano, David. "A Journey through Mexican Texas, 1900–1930: The Making of a Segregated Society." Ph.D. dissertation, Yale University, 1982.
National Catholic Welfare Council. *The Spanish-speaking of the Southwest and West*. Washington, D.C.: Department of Social Action, 1944.
"No Mexicans Allowed." *Inter-American* 2 (September 1943): 8–9.
Nostrand, Richard L. "'Mexican American' and 'Chicano': Emerging Terms for a People Coming of Age:" In *The Chicano,* ed. Norris Hundley, Jr., pp. 143–160. Santa Barbara: Clio Books, 1975.
Nunn, Guy. *White Shadows*. New York: Reynal and Hitchcock, 1947.
Park, Joseph. "The History of Mexican Labor in Arizona during the Territorial Period." M.A. thesis, University of Arizona, 1961.
Rasmussen, Wayne D. *A History of the Emergency Farm Labor Supply Program, 1943–1947*. Monograph No. 13. Washington, D.C.: U.S. Department of Agriculture, 1951.
"Regulations on Wartime Control of Manpower." *Monthly Labor Review* 55 (October 1942): 714–717.
Reisler, Mark. *By the Sweat of Their Brow: Mexican Immigrant Labor in the United States, 1900–1940*. Westport: Greenwood Press, 1976.
Report on Bisbee Deportations Made by the President's Mediation Commission to Presi-

dent of United States, November 6, 1917. Washington, D.C.: U.S. Government Printing Office, 1918.

Romano, Octavio. "The Anthropology and Sociology of the Mexican-Americans: The Distortion of Mexican-American History." *El Grito* (Fall 1968): 13–26.

Ross, Malcolm. *All Manner of Men*. New York: Reynal and Hitchcock, 1948.

Ruchames, Louis. *Race, Jobs, and Politics: The Story of the FEPC*. New York: Columbia University Press, 1953.

Sanchez, George I. *Forgotten People*. Albuquerque: University of New Mexico Press, 1940.

Schlesinger, Arthur M., Jr. *The Age of Roosevelt: The Politics of Upheaval*. Boston: Houghton Mifflin, 1960.

Scott, Robin F. "The Mexican-American in the Los Angeles Area, 1920–1950: From Acquiescence to Activity." Ph.D. dissertation, University of Southern California, 1971.

Scruggs, Otey M. "The Evolution of the Farm Labor Agreement of 1942." *Agricultural History* 341 (July 1960): 140–149.

———. "Texas and the Bracero Program, 1942–1947." *Pacific Historical Review* 32 (August 1963): 251–264.

Servin, Manuel P. *The Mexican Americans: An Awakening Majority*. Beverly Hills: Glenco Press, 1970.

———. "The Pre–World War II Mexican American: An Interpretation." *California Historical Society Quarterly* 45 (1966): 325–338.

Servin, Manuel P., and Robert L. Spude. "Historical Conditions of Early Mexican Labor in the United States: Arizona—a Neglected Story." *Journal of Mexican American History* 5 (1975): 43–56.

Sheridan, Thomas E. *Los Tucsonenses: The Mexican Community in Tucson, 1854–1941*. Tucson: University of Arizona Press, 1986.

Stiller, Jesse H. *George S. Messersmith, Diplomat of Democracy*. Chapel Hill: University of North Carolina Press, 1987.

Taft, Philip. "The Bisbee Deportation." *Labor History* 13 (Winter 1972): 3–40.

Termination Report of the National War Labor Board: Industrial Disputes and Wage Stabilization in Wartime. Vol. 1. Washington, D.C.: U.S. Government Printing Office, 1946.

Tuck, Ruth D. *Not with the Fist*. New York: Harcourt, Brace, 1946.

U.S. Congress. Senate. Subcommittee of the Committee on Education and Labor. *Hearings on S. 2048, A Bill to Prohibit Discrimination in Employment Because of Race, Creed, Color, National Origin, or Ancestry*. 78th Cong., 2d sess. Washington, D.C.: U.S. Government Printing Office, 1944.

U.S. Department of Commerce. Bureau of the Census. *Sixteenth Census of the United States: 1940, Population*. Vol. 2, part 1. Washington, D.C.: U.S. Government Printing Office, 1943.

White, Walter. *A Man Called White*. New York: Viking Press, 1948.

"Who's Blocking the Labor Supply." *Mining Congress Journal* 28 (October 1942): 15.

Wyllys, Rufus Kay. *Arizona: The History of a Frontier State*. Phoenix: Hobson and Herr, 1950.

Index